DATE DUE

MAY 2 2 1996	
OCT 2 8 1996	
NOV 1 8 1996 DEC 1 9 1996	
DEC 1 1 1996	
MAR 1 8 1997	
DEC 1 2 1997	
MAY 1 1 1998	
DEC 0 8 1998	
DEC 1 8 1998	
DEC 1 5 2000	

GAYLORD   PRINTED IN U.S.A.

The American School

and the Melting Pot

Minority Self-Esteem and Public Education

Natalie Isser and Lita Linzer Schwartz

Wyndham Hall Press

THE AMERICAN SCHOOL AND THE MELTING POT

Minority Self-Esteem and Public Education

Natalie Isser and Lita Linzer Schwartz
The Pennsylvania State University

SECOND EDITION

(First Edition Published in 1985.)

Library of Congress
Catalog Card Number
85-051432

ISBN 0-932269-52-2 (paperback)
ISBN 1-55605-090-9 (clothback)

Printed in the United States

ACKNOWLEDGEMENTS

We are indebted to many individuals who have given us support and assistance as we worked. First and foremost are the administrators and library staff of the Ogontz Campus of Pennsylvania State University. They gave us access to opportunities and materials that have had a significant impact on this book, and without which our research would have been a much more difficult task.

Our appreciation is extended to the Superintendent and other professionals in the Cheltenham Township (Pa.) School District for their courtesies and cooperation; to Mrs. Au, of the Sinclair Library (University of Hawaii), who personally gave us access to the Witz Collection of Historical Textbooks; and to the many helpful staff members at the Beaver College Library, Penimen Library (University of Pennsylvania), Philadelphia Free Library, Library Company of Pennsylvania, New York Public Library, and YIVO Research Center. In addition, Allyn and Bacon, Harper & Row, and Sadlier Publishing Company were kind enough to share texts and teacher editions with us that also reduced the time needed for travel and locating books. We are also most grateful to the late Norman Rockwell for his permission to use his painting, "The Golden Rule," as our frontispiece.

We are extremely fortunate to have Lucy Woodman as a co-worker on this project. She participated in our many discussions and contributed constructive criticisms of the manuscript that were most helpful and welcomed.

Last but not least, we acknowledge the contributions of our families -- Leonard Isser, Frances Kleinman and the late David Kleinman, Dorothy Linzer, and the late Pincus and Fannie Linzer and the late David and Tina Linzer -- for their support and sharing of their experiences.

                              Natalie Isser

                              Lita Linzer Schwartz

Abington, PA

TABLE OF CONTENTS

Current attitudes

PREFACE

This book is the result of that often-quoted aphorism about "The best-laid plans . . ." We began our research into the role of textbooks vis-a-vis Asian and Jewish immigrant children of the 1890-1920 period because of a common curiosity. If much of the philosophical orientation was historical, the practical aspects were clearly related to psychology and education. As we became more engrossed in our research, we thought that it might be instructive and interesting to compare our findings with an examination of the same groups with respect to contemporary textbooks. We soon found, in both time periods, that it was impossible to divorce textbooks from the schools as a whole. Further, one cannot consider "the schools" without considering the teachers. Our original plans went further afield, the outline was continually revised, and we now have a comprehensive study that reflects history, psychology, education, anthropology, law, and other disciplines of the social and behavioral sciences. it is more than a "psycho-history"; it reflects an interdisciplinary scholarly effort that is neither radical nor revisionist. Rather, we believe it to be a realistic appraisal of the situation certain immigrant groups have faced in American schools.

For several reasons, as delineated in the first chapter, we have focused on two major groups in our research. We could as easily, although working from other premises, have stressed other groups. Certainly the framework of our design and the methods of study can be applied to any group of any race, national origin, religious conviction (or lack of it), sex, or age-group. Similarly, in applying the conclusions reached and implementing the recommendations made, extensions can be made to other segments of our culturally pluralistic population. One of our objectives is doing the study was to develop a pattern of research and application that is "exportable." We believe that the objective can be stamped "mission accomplished."

Parts of the research study have been presented at the World Educators Conference on Multicultural Education (Honolulu, 1976), the Mid-Atlantic Region meeting of the Association for Asian Studies (University Park, Pa., 1976), the First Congress on Education of the Canadian School Trustees Association (Toronto, 1978), and the American Educational Research Association (Montreal, 1983). Two papers based on the book have also been published: "Attitudes toward the Jewish minority in public education," JEWISH EDUCATION, 1977, 45, (3), 33-39; and "Forgotten minorities, self-concept, and the schools," THE SOCIAL STUDIES, 1978, 69, 187-190.

CHAPTER ONE

SETTING THE SCENE

Introduction

The United States, like many other countries, is a nation composed of countless minority groups. At present, as a nation, we are concerned with trying to integrate members of these groups as full participants in society through a variety of programs and laws, while simultaneously we are reassessing past attitudes and policies toward minorities. This activity has led to a proliferation of studies about immigration, past and present, and the characteristics of minority groups in general. The complexity of this task is spiraling.

Even the definition of minority status is difficult. Minority status may be seen as an inferior position to one group and may be perceived as an elite position by another group. This variation in perception frequently depends upon the power wielded by the group in question. Thus, minority status can be expressed in terms of socioeconomic status, social aspirations, civil rights, or even as a psychological phenomenon. The study of a community of varying ethnic groups, of different races and religions, requires special scholarly efforts. There is a sharp and pressing need in this type of study for interdisciplinary efforts, employing sociology, political science, history, and psychology, in order to understand more fully the various difficulties and problems of minority groups.[1] Further, there is a need to focus on specific aspects of minority group problems if suggested constructive solutions are to be practical and effective.

In our study, we examined particularly the relationship between the "melting pot" concept and elementary school teachers and textbooks during the period of the great immigration, 1880-1920, to determine the possibility of relating our findings to present problems of "immigrant children" in the public school. Analysis of this relationship is based upon the prevailing events and opinions of the period.

The study focused on elementary texts for two reasons: 1) in the 1890-1920 period, eight grades of education was the total formal schooling for most of the population; and 2) the elementary school years, then, as now, are those when the child is most strongly influenced by course content and teachers. The teachers, of course, were the prime influence in the classroom, but they depended heavily on the texts. The texts included and evaluated were the readers, history, and geography books used through grade eight in the 1890-1920 period. We also examined current elementary textbooks to determine whether there has been a continuation of the values and attitudes prevalent in that period or whether a meaningful change has occurred.

It has been generally assumed that the schools played a significant role in acculturating the immigrants - "melting down" their differences, and that the schools provided the means for the acceptably rapid social mobility of immigrant children. In reality, only a few ethnic groups achieved fairly rapid social and economic advancement in the first and second generations. Most dramatic was the progress of Jews and Asians*, who also happened to be among the least welcomed immigrant groups. These two groups not only suffered from discrimination, but shared a common orientation toward education. Our study, therefore, focused on Jews and Asians, for we found that these groups best exemplified the extreme with respect to prejudice, influence of the schools, and the maintenance of ethnic identity.

The revival of interest in problems of the immigrant masses is evident in the enormous increase in ethnic studies published by scholars and journalists in the past ten years. The civil rights movement of the 1960's gave a sharp impetus to this revival as blacks openly began to seek their own cultural and historical identity. The drive for recognition and awareness, demands for affirmative action, and questioning of American values have all led to a re-examination by other ethnics of their own traditions and heritage. the concept of the "melting pot" itself, which had been widely accepted by social workers and teachers, and widely praised by political orators, has come under fire. The question has been raised whether the United States **ever** achieved its much vaunted "melting pot" status.[2] Greer, using today's values, has been one of the most vocal critics of the school's role in trying to attain that status. He has pointed out that the melting

*Note: We shall group the Chinese and Japanese as "Asians," but remind the reader that there are other national groups that could be included under the same heading.

4

pot was a mythical theory of assimilation, in which it was expected that biological mergers and cultural blending would yield a new and unique entity, the "American." In fact, the prevalent ideology **and** practice in the schools, during and since the great waves of immigration, was the conformity theory of assimilation, in which fragments would surrender their cultural differences in favor of the dominant sociocultural mores and behaviors.[3]

One of the objectives of this study was to examine the textbooks of the period 1890-1920 to see if they had any influence on the creation of the negative attitudes toward minority groups that flourished during "the great immigration" period and erupted in the 1920's. The study also examined the changes in teaching and textbooks in the past three decades with respect to their treatment of minority groups, and consequently, this backward look also questioned whether the "melting pot" theory or philosophy is, or ever was, viable.

History of post-Civil War immigration

The needs of rural mid-nineteenth century America, as the frontiers of the young nation were pushed outward, were largely to maintain the status quo. Class lines were fluid and social distinctions were muted. Respect for learning existed, but schooling itself was a secondary priority on the farm and frontier. Hence only a small number of young people attended schools, and few of these went further than elementary or "common" school. After the Civil War, America began to change, rapidly becoming more industrialized and urban. Social classes were less fluid. New ideas replaced the older rural values. Belief and support was given to the business class and its ethics: a stress on the values of hard work, thrift, frugality, perseverance, and acquisitiveness, qualities preached but not often practiced by business leaders. The growing urban masses adopted these ethics and desired the opportunity to make money and rise socially, if not for themselves, then for their children.

Into this shifting society came great waves of immigrants. Asians came to the West Coast in increasing numbers in the last quarter of the nineteenth century, despite efforts to restrict their numbers. Then, in the 1890-1920 period, additional hundreds of thousands of immigrants came each year to the East Coast. The latter were largely from Southern and Eastern Europe, refugees from pogroms and poverty.

All of the immigrants suffered to some extent upon coming to the United States. They all had grave economic problems. The all sufferred generational conflicts and alienation coupled with both hostility and discrimination from older generations of Americans. Although these experiences were somewhat similar for all the newcomers, the degree of hostility was not the same for all. The adjustments to the new world varied according to the ethos and mores the immigrants brought with them. Those from the Russian Empire, Austria-Hungary, Italy, and the Balkans came burdened with standards of living lower than that in the United States, with very high illiteracy rates, and with dreams of "golden sidewalks." They came from areas of authoritarian rule, with religious backgrounds decidedly different from those of earlier arrivals: orthodox Jews, Roman Catholics, and Greek Catholics.[4]

Far away from the families and stable village communities of their homelands, the adventurers tended to settle among those whose backgrounds seemed similar, where they could develop institutions and associations, and maintain habits and customs (sometimes modified) that bore a resemblance to their European or Asian past. Inevitably, throughout America, small communities of ethnics flourished, providing comfort and security for the newcomers in the harsh realities of the New World.

On both coasts, ethnic neighborhoods exemplified the worst evils of city life. Living conditions, already bad in the 1850's as a consequence of growing industrialization, became worse.

The relationship between the big-city political boss and the immigrant developed as the political organizations helped the poverty-stricken newcomer with his immediate needs: jobs, food, fuel, and assistance with the law. Urban corruption and inefficiency flourished in the cities, until the notorious political "machines," which offended American middle and upper class sensitivities, became a target for reform by the progressive movement.

Progressivism arose in response to the new problems, the new urgencies of an emerging urban industrial-technological civilization in the United States. In politics, it was best heralded and demonstrated by Theodore Roosevelt, Tom Johnson, John Altgeld, Clarence Darrow, Louis Brandeis; and in social work, by Jane Addams, Lillian Wald, and others.

The progressives blamed the immigrants' ills upon the evils of corruption, urbanization, and untrammeled industrialization. They believed in the theory of the "melting pot" and felt the schools should be the avenue of acculturation for the young. They were aware that frequently

6

these children absorbed the worst features of American life, and that if their parents clung to the customs and habits of the past, alienation often resulted. Therefore, the progressives began programs to assist the immigrant: settlement houses, visiting nurse associations, and other service agencies. Others advocated adult education to "Americanize" the parents.[5]

In American education, the need for new approaches was also felt, and was affected by these trends. The progressives wanted to extend "the American dream" to everyone, to provide equality of opportunity for all - in short, to use the schools to improve the lot and life of everyone. To reach this objective, the schools were to include within their purview not merely instruction in reading and quantitative skills, but also training in health, family, and community life and responsibility. Teacher training, limited and inadequate in the nineteenth century, was to be expanded and intensified so that the new ideas engendered by psychology, the humanities, and the social sciences could be applied in the classroom. If teaching was to be directed to new immigrant children, then the learning had to be relevant and meaningful to them. Just as the progressives believed that reform and good government rested on the spreading of democracy (hence their support of direct election of senators, initiative, and referendum), so the educators of the movement passionately supported "democratization" of education: the ideal of educating many more people vocationally as well as culturally.

At the diametric extreme were the opponents of immigration and the Social Darwinists. Stereotypes of generalizations about the newcomers, involving mainly inimical but occasionally positive attitudes, were commonly expressed in the media. The most prevalent of these stereotypes was the erroneous concept that radical movements such as anarchism and socialism were part of the immigrants' culture, especially among Finns and Russian Jews. The reality that the majority of newcomers were conservative or apolitical, and only a small minority were actually radical, did not in any way diminish the popularity of the stereotype. The Japanese were perceived by some as careless, preoccupied, and untrustworthy; by others, as hyper-efficient. The Chinese were "people having a low standard of living," and the heirs of a culture that was uncivilized and barbaric. That this was not so did not matter to the general public, as the press circulated these calumnies widely at the turn of the century.[6]

The wealthy expressed their distaste in the public press, calling the new immigrants "rag-tag, bob-tail cutthroats of Beezlebub, scum and offal of the earth. . . "[7] But the working man imbued with nativist sentiments and prejudiced stereotypes, was even more virulently opposed to the immigrant because he was an economic rival: he was willing to work for less money, and he was systematically used as a strikebreaker. Ethnocentric prejudice and economic fears combined in the latter part of the nineteenth century to help stimulate new groups: The United Order of Deputies, Minute Men of 1886, the American Patriotic League, Loyal Men of America, the American Benefit Association, and others, all of which lumped together immigrants, Catholics, and radicals as the greatest threats to American society. The most significant of the new groups was the American Protective Association, which extended its influence through the Republican Party.[8]

These influences, plus the chauvinism that occurred during World War I, which further heightened American xenophobia, began to produce additional questions about immigrants. Added to the anxieties and doubts ws the development of a concept that was to bear fruit in the 1920's: the popularity of Social Darwinism among the New England intellectual elite. Preaching a pseudo-racist doctrine, they emphasized the superiority of the Anglo-Saxon and Teutonic races. These groups were led by Richmond Mayo-Smith, Nathaniel S. Shaler, Francis A. Walker (president of M.I.T.), Prescott F. Hall, and Henry Cabot Lodge. They divided mankind into biological species, with fixed immutable racial characteristics. Heredity thus fixed inferiority.[9] Madison Grant called for the exclusion of the inferior Alpine, Mediterranean, and Jewish breeds as the only means of preserving America's old Nordic stock. Unless that were done, he declared, "the great race," which alone possessed the qualities to make ". . .soldiers, sailors, adventurers. . .explorers. . .rulers, organizers, aristocrats. . ." would be replaced by ". . .the weak, the broken, and the mentally crippled of all races."[10] Labor opposed immigration as well, but forces other than racism affected its nativist sentiments.

The "Red Scare" of the early 1920's and the fears of immigrant radicalism were best illustrated by the Sacco-Vanzetti case. An outgrowth of these anxieties and prejudices also led to an upsurge in anti-semitism, especially in rural areas. The fantastic growth of the Ku Klux Klan with its anti-Catholicism, racism, and anti-semitism contributed to the anti-immigration agitation.

Prominent among the new arrivals after the Civil War were East European Jews, Chinese, and Japanese immigrants. Although they came for varying reasons, they shared ultimately in discrimination

8

by the majority because of their religious difference on the one hand, and their racial difference on the other. (This is not to say that other groups never suffered form discrimination. However, where earlier Jewish immigrants rarely experienced overt hostility because of their small numbers, and the early Asian immigrants were welcomed because they were needed, the large numbers of the later arrivals were perceived as threatening.) The two million Jews who came after 1880 differed from the earlier European immigrants in several ways. They had been subjected to brutal religious persecution in Czarist Russia and Poland. They had been prevented by law from owning and working the land. They were forced to live in small towns (shtetls), where they engaged in trade or skill occupations such as tailoring and shoe-making. They were, as a result of this peculiar circumstance, job-oriented, skilled, and therefore better able to cope with urban life than most newcomers. Further, they enjoyed a religious belief that stressed the importance of learning and scholarship. Many, indeed, were Hebraic scholars.

Across the country, the Chinese initially had been encouraged to migrate to the West Coast in order to provide cheap labor, especially during the Gold Rush of the late 1840's. Their numbers swelled as they were employed as strikebreakers and "coolie" laborers on the railroad constructions. Most of these laborers intended to amass their savings and then return to China. As long as prosperity kept labor scarce, the Chinese were tolerated, but the depression of 1873 brought racial antipathies to the fore that were expressed bitterly, even violently. Reacting to the demands of West Coast residents, Congress passed the Chinese Exclusion Act of 1882. A few continued to come, finding loopholes in the law, but further violence necessitated the passage of additonal legislation that virtually excluded all Chinese from migrating to the United States, and restricted the civil rights of those who remained. The Chinese found almost all jobs barred to them: mining, railroad labor - all jobs save domestic labor which the shortage of women on the frontier had made available. They opened laundries, which required little capital or skill. Persecuted again, they drifted back to the cities, where they took their laundries and worked long, hard hours. Many moved from this employment to the restaurant business. They preserved their culture and institutions wherever they could. Working incredibly long hours, and being very frugal in their life-style, later, as they brought their families over, they were gradually able to enable their children to gain an education and higher status as the animus against them eased.[11]

As Chinese immigration ceased, a new wave of Asians came to western

9

shores, the Japanese. American prejudice shifted to this group. The Japanese, unlike the Chinese, did not depress wages and were not seen as a threat to labor. They were too successful in small farming, where they were most efficient and diligent. This aroused other feelings of hostility toward them. As these feelings increased among Californians and other westerners, they were expressed in the segregation of a mere one hundred Japanese students in the schools of San Francisco, the passage of laws preventing Japanese from owning land, and attempts to bar Japanese immigrants.[12] Through the press, the prejudices were fomented and spread.

What were the factors that could create such attitudes, opinions, and stereotypes in the United States? Why were magazines, the press, and other opinion-molding forces able to spread bigotry, provincialism, and nativist sentiments? As we answer these questions in the following pages, it will be easier to understand the role played by the schools.

One of the problems of a study of public opinion is to ascertain attitudes and prejudices of the non-articulate, the less educated, "the silent majority." Without polling devices, surveys, or sampling reports, what can the historian discover about public opinion? He has access to the reading material of the public: press, magazines, the novel, and other books. Since these, however, did not express "everyman's" ideas, but those of the articulate majority, one way of analyzing the source of unspoken opinion would be to study the social institutions that shape men's ideas and attitudes: the school, the church, clubs. After the family, the school is primary, and based on our study of the earlier period, we concluded that the textbook was even more significant then than it is today as a means of shaping opinion.

Role of the schools

One of the avenues of advancement, of rising upward, was through the schools, where children could be trained in the skills needed to make their way in business. These goals were enunciated in the reforms that were proposed in the early 1900's by the National Education Association and the American Historical Association. Their aims were to make American education more practical, and more useful to the future work life of the student, rather than to create the cultured and scholarly "gentlemen" characteristic of more traditional educational goals.

However, schools of the time were neither inspiring nor hopeful. Rural schools generally were in bad shape physically. They were ungraded and badly taught by inadequately prepared teachers. Recitations continued for 10 minutes per subject per class, and teacher continued "the same old drill in the same old readers" - using the same textbook used by their parents.[13]

The city schools were not much better. They were faced with constantly increasing numbers in buildings that were poorly lighted, poorly heated, over-crowded, and unsanitary. Classroom numbers were up to 70 or 80, and large numbers of these children were immigrants. Corruption, already a part of the political system, pervaded the establishment. Boards of education were tied to the political establishment. Teaching and administrative posts were bought and sold. Books, school building contracts, and every phase of the schools were subjected to political supervision. Little, if anything, was taught to the prospective teacher about the immigrant child who was her prospective pupil, except "Americanize him!" Little, if anything, was said in the textbooks used in the elementary schools, which provided all the education for most people, about the good in minority groups and the bad in majority groups. Indeed, if the existence of minority groups was noticed in the texts, the references were at best insignificant.

The pedagogical techniques used in the schools enhanced the importance of the textbook as the purveyor of attitudes. Teachers relied on rote memorization. The dominant teaching method of memorization intensified the perceptions so learned. Little attention was paid to the meaning or concepts of the books. Professionalization of the teacher came very slowly. By the end of the nineteenth century, the idea of teacher training had become acceptable, but so little money was spent on education that, in many regions of the country, teaching was still in the hands of inexperienced young girls. Though texts had improved by the twentieth century, earlier ones still in use were poorly written, composed of compilation and plagiarism. The texts, good or bad, dated or modern, were preserved and used through many generations. Despite the attempt of the progressives to revitalize teaching, to improve texts in quality and relevancy, many schools continued to rely on bad books.[14] Teachers themselves often relied upon the text (and its accompanying teacher's manual) for the planning of the entire course, for the day to day lessons, and, in addition, forced pupils to memorize whole pages without explanation.[15]

Only memoirs or reminiscences can tell us of the effect of the teacher or the impact of the school upon the individual, but the one sure route to evaluating prevalent opinion inculcated in the young is via the textbook. These were probably the most widely read and intensively read books by Americans except, perhaps, the Holy Bible. Thus, the ways in which authors chose to present their ideas in their books and the values they chose to emphasize probably had an enormous effect on how Americans judged themselves and how they perceived European and Asian immigrants, institutions, and cultures. Did the textbooks and teaching contribute to the increased anti-semitism? Did texts reflect the racist views of Social Darwinism so popular at the turn of the century. Did the schools contribute to the stereotypes and prejudice? Finally, if this situation was indeed the case, how did the negative attitudes affect the self-concept of Asian and Jewish children? These questions are basic to our study.

Self-concept of the immigrants

If maintenance of the status quo, rather than respect for cultural differences, was the situation in the early part of this century, one can hypothesize about the impact of such practices on the self-concept of the immigrant child. For the Asian child in San Francisco, native-born or not, there was the ignominy of being forced into a separate Oriental school by laws passed in 1870 and 1905 that reflected the then-current view of the Asians as an undesirable minority. The restrictions against them in the California Education Code persisted until 1946! (Legally-enforced segregation is not the same as voluntary separatism established to maintain cultural identity, a point of view espoused by some Asians in the 1970's.) An immediate question that would occur to one of these children would be, "Why can't I go to the school down the street? Am I not good enough?" The inevitable response from most Californians of that time would evoke strongly negative feelings of self-worth.

Lack of sensitivity to cultural mores created similar negative feelings among Jewish children. In 1914, for instance, a spokesman for the Jewish community in Atlanta asked the school board there and the Georgia legislature to excuse pupils absent on the religious holy days; that they cease teaching THE MERCHANT OF VENICE with its prejudicial view of the Jewish usurer; and that the requirement of reading a Bible chapter (King James' version) daily in the schools be dropped.[16] Each of these practices were perceived as a direct insult to the Jewish child, and as an indirect means of teaching prejudice and the detriments of non-conformity.

Another problem raised by critics was that educational practices tended to pit the immigrant child against not only himself, but also

12

against his family and culture. Contempt for the experience and culture of the immigrant parents, as expressed by teachers in their behavior,[17] and the absence of any mention of non-Anglo contributions to the nation's growth,[18] combined to accentuate the negative self-concept of the child. What was "different" was not taught, respected, or even recognized except in terms of inferiority and rejection. According to one critic, "Ethnic 'self-hatred' with its debilitating psychological consequences, family disorganization, and juvenile delinquency, were not unusual results" of the Americanization effort.[19] A principal weapon used to teach this self-hatred was **shame**. The children ". . .were **taught** to be ashamed of their faces, their family names, their parents and grandparents, and the class patterns, histories, and life outlooks."[20] Difference, or diversity, had to be divisive, and divisiveness could not be tolerated.

How, then, did the schools **help** the immigrant and his children achieve upward mobility and Americanization? If schools created negative feelings, self-hate, and alienation, they should also have created havoc with family life, leading to neuroses, crime, delinquency, and family breakdown. Indeed, this is what happened to many. Among the exceptions were the Chinese, the Japanese, and the Jews. Yet these groups suffered more rejection, more disabilities, and were the objects of more intense dislike even through the Depression and World War II, than most other immigrant groups. (Recall, for example, the Japanese incarceration at relocation camps and the rejection of haven-seeking refugees from Hitler's Germany.)

Why, then, were these groups among the exceptions? These immigrants perceived the schools as the agent of opportunity. True, the schools became a rival to the family's authority and the parents' wisdom. True, the language of the schools was English, which differed from that of the ethnic community. And true, very often, the schools criticized outright the cultural patterns and ways of the immigrants. Indeed, the schools were only trying to meet one of the goals of progressive education: to alter the immigrant patterns, to create "good citizens," in short, to create a "melting pot."[21] Despite all this, despite the fact that the schools were the source of unhappiness, disagreement, bewilderment, rebellion, hurt, and conflict for many families, the Jews and the Asians saw the schools as the agent of social mobility, the road to good citizenship, and the route to future achievement for their children.

What, then, were the factors that prevented breakdown or anomie, and enabled these groups to achieve rapid social mobility? The most facile and frequent answer to this enigma was their use of the public schools. Statistics demonstrate that these groups' children rapidly entered the professions and business, and through hard work and diligent application left their ethnic enclaves behind them. Certainly it was not that the teachers and schools were more receptive to their peculiar needs. Few teachers or textbooks treated Jews or Asians favorably or even with sympathy. Indeed, the school systems perpetuated the stereotypes and inflicted prejudices upon the children.

Asians and Jews alike tried to counter these efforts by establishing, and requiring their children to attend, after-school classes in which the cultural history, values, pride, and group language were taught. That this effort was worthwhile can be seen in the comparatively low frequency of Asian and Jewish delinquency rates until very recently. The tactic was not totally successful, however, in eradicating the feelings of shame. The Jews, as the Asians, were passionately devoted to the pursuit of knowledge.

The cohesiveness of these immigrants also helped, apparently. Jews and Asians were very community oriented. They were, despite their varied internal disagreements, united to protect their good name, and also to assist each other. The pogroms in Russia had given a focus to Jewish attempts to aid their co-religionists, resulting in the formation of groups such as the American Jewish Committee and B'nai Brith's Anti-Defamation League to protect Jewish rights and fight prejudice. Wherever they could, Asians similarly organized self-help groups. The East European Jews were religiously observant, but even when ties were loosened with acculturation, the ethnic and religious heritage that stressed charity remained a forceful obligation. They transplanted to the new environment thriving Yiddish culture that had flourished in their European settlements. (Between 1885 and 1915, there were more than 150 Yiddish language papers, theatre groups, lectures, concerts, and coffeehouses to nourish the love of learning.[22]). The schools contributed the needed skills and information to aid this self-help operation; the "push" came from the group itself.

A contemporary view

Too often, the prevalent American optimism has sought simplistic answers to enormously complex social and economic questions. Simply pass the proper legislation, declare a "war on poverty," see that everyone goes to schools, and we will eradicate injustice, prejudice, and create an enduring social and economic equality. A major force in these answers, and one of the most persistent and pervasive beliefs,

14

is that somehow the public school system can and should be the agency to bring about such social change.

Yet, while Americans expect **and** demand that our educational structure be the vanguard of social progress, they also expect and demand that education be responsive to their own peculiar social, economic, and political pressures. As taxpaying parents and as active political participants, they expect the schools to be responsive to their wishes. One has only to review the current conflicts over busing, decentralization, and textbooks in Boston, Philadelphia, New York City, and West Virginia, to realize that social change is a good thing -- somewhere else. Still the assumption of the social progress role of the schools persists. The schools must perform certain "tasks": socialize the young, "Americanize" the immigrant, create middle-class values for the poor. Studies have indicated that schools cannot and do not perform any tasks unless these tasks are part of the community's beliefs and desires.

Public education, therefore, is subject to the desires of the public and reflects public opinion. Prejudice was a part of the American tradition in the nineteenth century, and the schools and textbooks perpetuated notions of racism and bigotry. Gradually, more textbook authors were **trying** to be objective and many were even relatively unbiased; their sins were more frequently those of omission rather than commission.

Despite the inclusion of Haiku poetry, tales of African village life, and central European folk wisdom in today's readers, has the situation changed? Do today's texts continue to emphasize American homogeneity by the omission of the pluralistic nature of American society and the inherent value of cultural diversity? Has the goal of American education, **in practice,** changed from the melting pot theory to one that respects and encourages such diversity within political and economic integration? Do we **now** enhance the different child's self-image?

To find answers to the questions we have raised required explorations into attitudes, philosophy about immigration, self-concept development, and history, as well as examination of the textbooks themselves. Discussion of these significant areas precedes our statement of methodology and subsequent evaluation of more than 750 texts and related materials. Following these chapters, there is a revealing look at contemporary attitudes, events, and laws that underlie the recommendations made in the concluding chapter.

NOTES

1. Discussion in the session of "The Historical Phenomenon of Minorities," XIV International Congress of Historical Sciences, San Francisco, August 25, 1975.

2. Colin Greer, THE GREAT SCHOOL LEGEND, A REVISIONIST INTERPRETATION OF THE AMERICAN SCHOOL SYSTEM (New York: Basic Books, 1972); Colin Greer, ed., THE DIVIDED SOCIETY (New York: Basic Books, 1974).

3. Greer, DIVIDED SOCIETY, p. 87.

4. Edward G. Hartmann, THE MOVEMENT TO AMERICANIZE THE IMMIGRANT (New York: Columbia Univ. Press, 1948), p. 17.

5. C. F. Hartmann.

6. Dennis M. Ogawa, FROM JAPS TO JAPANESE: AN EVOLUTION OF JAPANESE-AMERICAN STEREOTYPES (Berkeley: McCutchan Publishing Corp., 1971), pp. 13-21; Rose Hum Lee, THE CHINESE IN THE UNITED STATES OF AMERICA (Cambridge: Oxford Univ. Press, 1960), pp. 362-363.

7. John Higham, STRANGERS IN THE LAND (New Brunswick: Rutgers Univ. Press, 1955), pp. 166- 172-174.

8. Zane L. Miller, THE URBANIZATION OF MODERN AMERICA (New York: Harcourt, Brace, Jovanovich, 1973), pp. 93-95.

9. Maldwyn A. Jones, AMERICAN IMMIGRATION (Chicago, London: Univ. of Chicago Press, 1960), pp. 237-68.

10. **Ibid.**, p. 269; Madison Grant, THE PASSING OF THE GREAT RACE OR THE RACIAL BASIS OF EUROPEAN HISTORY (New York: Scribner's Sons, 1916).

11. S. W. Kung, THE CHINESE IN AMERICAN LIFE (Seattle: Univ. of Washington Press, 1962), pp. 55-60; H. B. Melendy, THE ORIENTAL AMERICANS (New York: Hippocrene Books, 1972), p. 27; Leonard Dinnerstein and David M. Reimers, ETHNIC AMERICANS, A HISTORY OF IMMIGRATION AND ASSIMILATION (New York: Dodd Mead, 1975), p. 39.

12. Roger Daniels, THE POLITICS OF PREJUDICE (Berkeley: Univ. of California Press, 1962), p. 42; Lee, p. 55.

13. Edgar B. Wesley, N.E.A. THE FIRST HUNDRED YEARS (New York: Harper & Row, 1957), pp. 819-821.

14. R. M. Elson, GUARDIANS OF TRADITION (Lincoln: Univ. of Nebraska Press, 1964), pp. 2-6; John A Nietz, OLD TEXTBOOKS (Pittsburgh: Univ. of Pittsburgh Press, 1961), pp. 268-69.

15. Alfred L. Hall-Quest, THE TEXTBOOK (New York: Macmillan Co., 1920), pp. 2-9.

16. Arnold Shankman, "Atlanta Jewry, 1900-1920," AMERICAN JEWISH ARCHIVES, 25 (November, 1973), 147

17. Jane Addams, "Foreign-born Children in the Primary Grades," N.E.A. Journal of the Proceedings and Addresses of the Thirty-sixth Annual Meeting. Chicago, 1897, pp. 104-112 in MAKERS OF AMERICA (Chicago: Field Publishing, 1971), V, pp. 107-10.

18. David Sue, "A Silent Minority Speaks Out," TODAY'S EDUCATION, 53, No. 2 (1974), 104-06.

19. Milton M. Gordon, ASSIMILATION IN AMERICAN LIFE (New York: Oxford Univ. Press, 1964), p. 138.

20. William Greenbaum, "America in Search of a New Ideal: an Essay on the Rise of Pluralism," HARVARD EDUCATIONAL REVIEW, 54, (1974), 430-31.

21. Oscar Handlin, THE UPROOTED, 2nd ed. (Boston, Toronto,: Little, Brown and Co., 1973), p. 218; Lawrence A. Cremin, THE TRANSFORMATION OF THE SCHOOL (New York: Knopf, 1961), pp. 67-69.

22. Dinnerstein and Reimers, p. 53.

CHAPTER TWO

ATTITUDES AND IMMIGRANTS

With the exception of the American Indian, now called the Native American or AmerIndian, we are all immigrants or descendants of immigrants to this country. One can look back to several waves of immigration and see differing reasons for them -- religious persecution, dreams of enrichment, political exile, adventure. Some groups were welcomed as peers; other accepted only as inferiors to tend to menial tasks. Through much of immigrant history, there was no question that the new arrivals must accommodate to the developing American pattern of life as adapted from the dominant British heritage. With the advent of the massive immigration in the 1890-1920 period, however, diverse views arose. One philosophy became paramount for several decades, the amalgamation theory, only to be replaced in the past decade by a new ethnicity. The nature of these differing philosophies and attitudes, the ways in which they were transmitted through the press and the schools, and the measurement of the resulting attitudes in different generations are the themes of this chapter.

Varying viewpoints

We may characterize the philosophies toward immigrants of an earlier day as favoring assimilation or amalgamation. American attitudes concerning immigrants varied on how the new arrivals, particularly those of minority groups, should adjust to American society. There were those who felt America had evolved into a genuinely distinct culture which was based on an Anglo-Saxon tradition and heritage. Logically it followed that the newcomer must accept that prevailing culture and abandon his own language, customs, heritage, in favor of adopting completely the dominant life-style in the United States. That is, the immigrant must become assimilated. To those who held this point of view, the United States was a homogeneous society to which all must adjust, becoming indistinguishable from the whole. This notion was sustained and supported by the then fasionable racist

18

theories which characterized the "first" migration (Northern Europeans such as the English, Scotch, German, Scandinavian, and Irish) as racially superior, and the "second" migration, from 1880 on, of Southern and Eastern Europeans as inferior and perhaps even undesirable.[1] Many social agencies and some of the schools readily adopted this point of view and actually promoted it in their work.

The desire for homogeneity expressed in so many quarters and by so many groups was accentuated during World War I by the patriotic ardor that stridently emphasized the need for national unity. the cry was for "Americanization," which came to mean the denial of ethnicity and of cultural differences. It denigrated the cultural heritage of the immigrant, and was psychologically inimical to the personality of the immigrant, widening differences between himself and his children. "Americanization" was also marked by the desire to ensure conformity. Social workers, school principals, and teachers were nervous about coping with those they did not understand or wish to understand. Hence, in general, they exhibited disdain for the language and ideology of other groups and disregarded the feelings of their charges; their insistence was on total conformity. These attitudes and behaviors affected the self-concept and self-esteem of the immigrant child.

The practice of enforcing "Americanization" so prevalent in many American institutions, and the contempt and disdain expressed so openly by many Americans toward to the immigrant and his culture, had long-term ramifications. As already indicated, the teachers and social workers tended to create more problems than they knew, both socially and psychologically. They tore asunder respect for the community, for parents, denigrated the ethnic background, and in general, created alienation and self-doubt. Even among the immigrants who were themselves caught in the struggle to earn a livelihood and who were disturbed by the process of acculturation, these demands for conformity tended to lead to the destruction, or at least the weakening, of marital relationships, as well as creating social anomie. Delinquency, materialism, and alcoholism were frequently the fruits of the policy of destroying traditional family and community relationships. However, the lesser impact of these pressures toward acculturation and the resulting feelings of alienation on the Asians and Jews specifically is a central theme of the next chapter.

Despite the continual stress to indoctrinate the immigrant with the concepts of citizenship and conformity, however, force was not used to achieve these aims. Foreign language newspapers were not suppressed. There were never any mass internments or massive deportations during the first World War or even during the Red Scare of the 1920's. The one exception was the Japanese internment during World War II.[2] Indeed, there had been many groups, beginning in William Penn's time, who attempted to secure the rights of ethnic minorities. Penn himself sought to protect Indians and immigrants; Franklin, Rush, and a variety of Abolitionist groups worked on behalf of Indians and blacks; and the Moravians valiantly worked for the benefit of the Indians. Concern for the rights of the few and the different is not a twentieth century phenomenon.

The Progressives were more sympathetic than most people at the turn of the century to the immigrant and believed passionately in the immigrants becoming more assimilated; they were not as obsessed with racial theories or the belief in the superiority of Anglo-Saxon civilization. They conceived of the "Melting Pot" idea, a new philosophy of "Americanization," but a less cruel approach. This theory advocated the disappearance of the different cultures and styles within the newly created meld of a unique American gestalt. The melting pot advocates wished, therefore, to force the immigrant to become severed from his cultural heritage and linguistic past, but they did not insist that the Anglo-Saxon culture was superior. A new American culture created from a medley of races and cultures would produce a more democratic and tolerant civilization. The most eloquent expression of this hope was expressed by Israel Zangwill in his play, THE MELTING POT: "America is God's crucible, the great melting pot where all the races of Europe are melting and reforming! The real American has not yet arrived. He is in the crucible. I tell you, he will be the fusion of all races, perhaps the coming superman. . . ."[3] This was the vision of amalgamation.

Many of the Progressives -- Jane Addams, Frances Keller, immigrants such as Steiner and Ravage -- who were sympathetic, warm, and often of inestimable help to the immigrant, nevertheless conceived of no program that recognized the **intrinsic worth** and significance of traditional ethnic values. Amalgamation differed from "Americanization" only in degree. The teachers and social workers imbued with this theory wanted to avoid hurting the immigrant, and wanted to preserve his self-esteem. The problem of broken families, and the consequent social disasters, were to be avoided by keeping the children loyal to their community. Instead of working through the children, the parents would be indoctrinated and taught American ways. The process of acculturation needed to be gradual to avoid anomie; consideration was to be maintained for the language, customs, and social environment of the students, and thus **gradually** create Americans. The Progressives stressed the individual's unique character- istics. Therefore, progressive educators were more sympathetic and more sensitive to the immigrant child and his problems. They saw the final enrichment of American traditions through the contribu- tions of many diverse individuals to the fulfillment of a new and richer environment. But the melting pot still meant that group identity was negated, that ethnicity was invalid. Complete absorption would be the final result. It would mean the end of separate schools, commun- ity life, and cultural institutions that had flourished in the United States.

The concept of cultural pluralism differed from that of homogeneity and was a minority viewpoint. The vision of stable ethnic institutions and culture within the larger society was very new. Even more radical was the concept that government and society respect, perpetuate, or at the least, not hinder their development or continuity. While supporting the notion of English as a common language, and that there should be common governmental rules, regulations, and social goals, the holders of this minority view felt that ethnic distinctions should be be eradicated; rather the aesthetic, cultural, and religious inheritances of each group should be encouraged. The afternoon or evening language schools served the purpose of maintaining and transmitting the ethnic cultures and values. This theory of cultural pluralism, as expressed by Horace M. Kallen,[4] claimed that the United States was a federation of diverse nationalities and that it was neither possible nor even advantageous that they should abandon their identity. The political system and the English language would be esteemed by all, and all groups would cooperate and seek the best for the general welfare of the nation as a whole.

Higham has pointed out that even today, these conflicting views create "another American dilemma." In his analysis, he states:

> While making success a species of disloyalty, assimilation lays a stigma of failure on those who keep the ancestral ways. The assimilationist's assurance that individuals need only an opportunity to prove their worth had led innumerable under-achieving ethnics into an emotional cul-de-sac. They must conclude either that they are indeed unworthy or that the proffered opportunity was fraudulent. The result is either self-hatred or alienation from society. It can frequently be both.

The liabilities of a pluralistic ethic are hardly less severe. Whereas assimilation penalizes the less ambitious and successful groups and individuals, pluralism circumscribes the more autonomous and adventurous. To young people fired by curiosity and equipped with a cosmopolitan education, the ethnic community can be intensely stultifying. . . While assimilation sacrifices the group for the sake of individual, pluralism would put the individual at the mercy of the group.[5]

None of these theories were applicable to the Asian immigrants. Legislation had been passed that made the Chinese and Japanese "ineligible for naturalization." This law included also those from Korea, Burma, Malaya, Polynesia, and Tahiti. Obviously, these people suffered double handicaps. They were not thought suitable or fit to become naturalized citizens and at the same time, they were perceived as being incapable of assimilation. And what of their children? They were citizens by birth, but beset by racism as well as the problems of acculturation. They could never be perceived wholly as either Asians or Americans.

Students interviewed in California in the 1920's sadly related some of their conflicts. One girl complained: ". . .In ancestry and in physical appearance we are Japanese, while in birth, in education, in ideals and in ways of thinking we are American. Nevertheless, the older Japanese will not accept us into their group because, as they see us, we are too independent, too pert, and too self-confident, and the Americans bar us from their group because we retain the yellow skin and the flat nose of the Oriental . . ."[6] Another student replied to the questions in the same way: "In language, in customs, in everything, I was American. But America wouldn't have me. She wouldn't recognize me in high school, she put the picture of those of my race at the tail end of the yearbook."[7] These youngsters remained in limbo straddling diverse cultures, never fully accepted by either one.

The new ethnicity

Time and circumstances have altered all these diverse conceptions. The notion of cultural pluralism has developed a new meaning today. The image of the melting pot has proved in the end, for many, to be illusory. Whether sought by the immigrant, or by the pressures of society, or by the necessity of earning a living in the United States, initial acculturation took place rapidly. Members of the second generation frequently rejected their background and their cultural heritage with feelings of hostility compounded of guilt and repressed anger.

Their children, however, the third generaton, had not encountered the emotional upheavals engendered by the outside environment. The grandchildren spoke English and they were completely American. They were not consumed with the mixed feelings of their parents. However, their grandparents' customs and language have now acquired charm and quaintness. Furthermore, in recent years the mobility, the constant changes, and the breakdown of the value systems that had been reinforced earlier by the extended family and stable institutions, have caused many to begin the search for their own identity and beliefs in their heritages. Cultural identification became more vital when it was stimulated by the Civil Rights movement of the 1960's. Ethnicity has changed character, however, from the early days of the great immigrations. The ethnic "ghettos" have been largely dissipated, the old lingual and traditional ways are no longer extant or even viable, except for the new migrants who have not yet begun the process of acculturation.[8]

What, then, do we mean by ethnicity or cultural diversity? We define it as meaning that within our society there are many different social groups, each of which shares its own values or life-styles, most often derived from a common place in Europe or Asia (or elsewhere). These groups share a common language, a common experience in the United States, and sometimes a common religion. From the crucible of their historical conflicts in this country, the group members have developed, partly based on the traditions of their "old country," and partly based on American customs, attitudes concerning marriage, childrearing, and education. Institutions have been maintained within these communities that provided the milieu in which individual members socialized, communicated, courted, and influenced each other. To the outsider, certain dances, foods, wedding customs, and slang words connoted ethnicity, but these were only surface manifestations of the community life from which they had emerged. The ethnic groups no longer resemble the inhabitants of the old country ghettos or even the cultural environments of Europe or Asia. The third generation Jew or Asian has become far removed from his forebears, but still maintains a tenuous relationship with them.

The ethnic culture that has emerged today is uniquely American, based on the group's experiences in this country, created in the meld of native customs mingled with the different heritages from the same land. In the United States, the Chinese, principally from Canton province, lived together and developed a mix of common Chinese practices and American customs to produce the modern Chinese-American ethnic group. The same type of development occurred with the Jews:

German, Roumanian, Lithuanian, Polish, Ukranian, and Russian. In their communities, they quarreled, they differed, but in the space of three generations, the internal differences and the American experience produced a Jewish community with a new identity and purpose. thus, the immigrants who were once distant members of identifiable ethnic groups merged that identity into a new one, and in doing so changed the character of their community while retaining some separate and distinct characteristics. The neighborhoods had disappeared, but the institutions based on this peculiar history have emerged to create a new ethnic identity. As one historian noted:

A candid recognition that the melting pot did not work, that we remain a congeries of peoples, that there are many American ways of life rather than one, might help us to discard our notion of ourselves as a "chosen people," and to affirm our common humanity with the rest of mankind.[9]

The media

The problem of immigration had begun to engage public attention in the press very early in our history. No immigrant group was either welcomed or treated with toleration. All peoples that differed from the majority were viewed and treated in a belligerent manner by the majority of Americans. We have only to recall the virulent anti-Catholic sentiments reflected in the Know-Nothing Party and the anti-Irish riots of pre-Civil War days. If Americans had difficulty in adjusting to the waves of Scandanavians, Germans, and Irish because they were "different" -- how much greater was their antagonism to the "new" migrants: Asians and those from Southeastern Europe. The frontier had closed; the mature industrial economy no longer needed immigrants. They had worked for lower wages, a source of bitterness to established labor. Even if they rose too rapidly economically through hard work, thrift, and educational efforts, they presented a threat to the established social status quo (particularly the Jews and the Japanese).[10]

Coincident with economic and social rivalries came new racist doctrines that reinforced the already prevailing antipathies to the new immigrants. Both the scholarly and the popular newspapers and magazines became obsessed with topics relating to a very long bitter debate over unrestricted immigration. The arguments ranged from pseudo-scientific racism to genuine concern for the economic and social integration of the newcomers to the most blatant, prejudiced polemics.

Said some, the United States had too many immigrants who could not be satisfactorily absorbed. These newcomers settled in the most congested areas of the cities and thereby created new difficulties. The "new" immigrants did not assimilate or they adjusted too slowly.

> There is great danger in the evolution of the human species, for the development of a people who should keep and draw all other races up to a higher plane of living. The duty of the United States is not to herself alone, but to all the world. The problem of immigration is but a part of the great conservation movement. It has to do with the conservation of the American people, and all that it stands for.[11]

Another writer asserted that the Jews were not a pure race because they had been absorbed by the peoples among whom they lived. They were also city dwellers and had become a better race physically because of their long struggle for survival. However, residence in New York City might weaken the race because of bad living conditions and the sweat shops.[12] The new immigrants contributed to crime, poverty, and lowered political standards claimed some scholars. Even though many immigrants desired to educate their children and so adjust to the American environment, problems had become too massive. Another author wrote: "We are trustees of our civilization and institutions with a duty to the future, and as trustees in the stocks of population in which we invest should be limited by the principle of a careful selection of immigrants."[13] The Jew, said another, despite his "long residence in Europe, is still, as he always had been, an Asiatic race, while the Syrians, Chinese, Japanese, and Hindus are still more removed from the civilization of Northern Europe and America." He continued, "Intermarriage with these groups will one day mongrelize our race" - and our Western states felt the same way about Asians for both racial and economic reasons.[14] Newspapers echoed these sentiments. The Philadelphia LEDGER of December 6, 1892, declared that immigration should be restricted, thus preventing those who were "injurious and undesirable and whose physical, moral or mental condition is at variance with good American citizenship."[15] The New York HERALD was harsher in its assessment: "We are overwhelmed, submerged and almost drowned out by a great flood-tide of European riff-raff, the refuse of every nation on the continent, paupers, criminals, beggars, and the muddy residuum of foreign civilizations. . . ."[16] The West coast press, though little affected by the tide of these immigrants, also were unsympathetic. THE DENVER REPUBLICAN (December 2, 1892) claimed that immigrants in steerage were the poorer peasants who were filthy, and ignorant of sanitation. Those from Russia in particular were carriers of cholera.[17] THE PORTLAND OREGONIAN (November 28, 1892) suggested that the Chinese exclusion laws serve as an example to Congress. Time had proved the efficiency of the act by preventing the entry of the Chinese. Once such an act passed it would be difficult to once more open the doors freely to newcomers.[18]

Writers frequently noted that the Jew was different from the other immigrants. They observed that the Jew was concerned with education, that he worked hard, that he was thrifty. In fact, it was his upward mobility that soon gave rise to an overt social discrimination and a rising chorus of anti-semitic stereotypes. The Jews departed from the "ghettos" as soon as they financially were able to do so; they sent their children to college. Gradually discrimination appeared quite openly. They were shut out of clubs, many summer resorts, and private schools. Quotas were established at some colleges; they were excluded from fraternities and faculties. Restrictive covenants were common in housing areas, and job opportunities were scarce in much of the business world.[19] These anti-semitic feelings were often reflected in both the press and the media.

THE NEW YORK TRIBUNE published the following:

> Numerous complaints have been made in regard to the Hebrew immigrants who lounge about the Battery Park obstructing the walks and sitting on the chairs. Their filthy condition has caused many of the people who are accustomed to go to the park to seek a little recreation and fresh air to give up this practice. The immigrants also greatly annoy the persons who cross the park to take the boats to Coney Island, Staten Island and Brooklyn. The police have had many battles with these newcomers, who seem determined to have their own way.[20]

Prejudices were also fanned by the caricatures that were popular on the dramatic and vaudeville stage that emphasized the distinct physical features, clothing, forms of expression, and intonations commonly ascribed to Jews. Above all, these prejudices stressed the Jews' constant concern with money.[21] Jews were accused of being too clannish, and clinging to their ethnic folkways -- yet they aroused hostility when they assimilated too rapidly.[22]

> Their habits are quite incompatible with American standards of life. The persistence of unsanitary conditions for which they are responsible forms a permanent menace to the health of the

community. One of the notorious abuses tending directly to a vital reduction in the standard of wages and of existence was the sweating system introduced by the Jews.[23]

Gradually European images began to infiltrate propaganda, the specter of the Jewish banking houses that introduced the myth of the international wealthy Jews. A not uncommon view was that "The Jews were a parasitical race, who producing nothing, fasten on the produce of land and labor and live on it, choking the breath of life out of commerce and industry as sure as the creeper throttles the tree that upholds it."[24] These feelings were complicated by the fact that the developing dislike of the city fastened upon the Jew, the symbol of the urbanite and the businessman.

Henry Ford, in the DEARBORN INDEPENDENT, expressed his negative sentiments most stridently. the elitist writings of Madison Grant and others began to penetrate to the masses in popular magazines. In 1922, the SATURDAY EVENING POST printed a series of articles by Kenneth Roberts preaching Nordic supremacy.[25] These ideas were expanded and reinforced by the publication of the Army's wartime psychological test results that purported to show that Southern and Eastern European background soldiers had markedly lower I.Q. scores than those from the northern parts of Europe. A State Department paper, that was later incorporated in the House Committee's report and later served as a basis for the Immigration Act of 1921, described the immigrants from the Russian city of Tiflis in these terms:

> The great bulk of emigrants to the U.S. from this district are highly undesirable as material for future American citizens. . . Their physical and moral courage is greatly depleted, as well as their physical constitutions. The bulk of them have been habituated either to lawlessness or to the exercise of violence in the name of the law for so long that if not actually impregnated with Bolshevism they are good material for Bolshevik propaganda.

> Our restrictions on immigration should be so rigid that it would be impossible for most of these people to enter the United States. Reference is made especially to Armenians, Jews, Persians, and Russians of the ordinary classes, all of which have been so driven hither and thither since 1914 that they cannot be regarded as desirable population for any country. . .[26]

Another report claimed, "The great mass of aliens passing through Rotterdam at the present time are Russian Poles or Polish Jews of the usual ghetto type. Most of them are frankly getting out of Poland to avoid war conditions. They are filthy, un-American, and often dangerous in their habits."[27]

The results of this publicity, constant agitation, and propaganda led to the passage of very strong and restrictive immigration laws in 1924.

In spite of the majority of opinions that seemed to give approbation to the above viewpoints, Progressives blamed most of the difficulties of the immigrants upon the evils of the industrial system and desired that ameliorative legislation and social and economic measures be taken to alleviate the sufferings in the slums, and above all, that the public schools, evening schools, adult education, and community associations partake in a massive compaign of education to Americanize the immigrant.

Education will solve every problem of our national life, even that of assimilating our foreign element. The ameliorating effects of general education would be evident in a decade in every manifestation of social life. . . The nation has a right to demand intelligence and virture of every citizen and to obtain these by force if necessary. Compulsory education we must have as a safeguard for our institutions.[28]

A number of writers felt the problem of the immigrants would be solved if they were widely dispersed throughout the countryside, preventing the formation of ghettos with their "unhealthy and unsanitary conditions."[29]

The Asian immigrants had **no** defenders at all. The Chinese had been welcomed at first as a source of cheap and much needed labor, but as the demand lessened for their services, they became despised as the root of all the problems that enveloped California during the 1870's and 1880's.[30] The major complaints were economic -the Chinese worked for lower wages and enjoyed a lower standard of living. They were accused of being dishonest and unreliable, of indulging in opium smoking, gambling, and prostitution, and finally their racial characteristics made assimilation impossible.

We have won this glorious land inch by inch from the red man in vain; we have beaten back the legion of George III for nothing; we have suppressed rebellion and maintained the integrity of our country for no good purpose whatsoever, if we are not to surrender it to a horde of Chinese, simply because they are so degraded that they can live on almost nothing, and underbid our own flesh and blood in the labor market. The people of California cannot endure it.[31]

The Chinese were faced with discriminatory tax laws; they were not allowed to testify in court, nor could they hope to become citizens. They were attacked, robbed, and lynched, and rarely were their complaints heard or justice done. Discrimination and prejudice were fanned by Denis Kearney, and labor was abetted and reinforced by the press and public officials who responded to popular feelings. "The Chinese are so many vampires sucking the life blood out of any portion in which they remain," said the MONTANA POST. The Missoula and Cedar Creek PIONEER declared that the Chinaman "clings to his idolatry and heathenism with the tenacity of life . . . lives on refuse . . .devotes his sister to the basest lusts of humanity and makes her an unsexed prostitute to disseminate disease and death among the devotees of base passions."[32] The western press in general expressed the belief that the Chinese were mysterious, with different racial characteristics that made them incapable of relinquishing old customs and habits that prevented them from progressing or assimilating, and these sentiments were echoed by the eastern papers. The NEW YORK TIMES (March 6, 1882) claimed: "I do not see how any thoughtful lover of his country can countenance this Mongolian invasion, involving as it does the subversion of our civilization."[33] Eventually public clamor caused Congress to pass legislation restricting the entry of Chinese laborers for ten years in 1882. This was renewed in 1902, and a new bill was later passed which excluded Chinese laborers permanently. And again the media (for the most part) supported the exclusion laws. "The American form of government is unsuitable to handle the Chinese criminal classes. . ."[34] Senator Boies Penrose (of Pennsylvania) declared that demagogery had nothing to do with the debate: "Economic principles are involved which are of the highest order of importance and affect not only the prosperity of the individual, but the welfare of the state."[35] An eminent scholar, Edward A. Ross, wrote in a prestigious journal, ". . .members of a great race and culture like the Chinese show no disposition even when scattered sparsely among us to assimilate to us or to adopt our standards."[36]

As Chinese immigration ceased, a new wave of Asians came to the Western shores. Feelings of hostility were transferred to this new group. The emergence of Japan as a great power also exacerbated the prejudices. Feelings toward the Japanese were colored by these twin stereotypes until World War II. Homer Lea was the best known and the most eloquent writer on this theme. He felt that the Anglo-Saxon race was the most qualified to rule the world. Our mission was threatened by the Japanese. In 1909, he published a book entitled THE VALOR OF IGNORANCE in which he predicted the Japanese conquest and occupation of the West Coast. This feat would be aided by the constant stream of immigration that would have weakened the American race.[37] This idea was echoed by another scholar who in most serious tones argued that the Japanese could not assimilate or become citizens because their racial inheritance and religion prevented it. The Japanese, he proclaimed, worship the Mikado and that is a factor that is a "permanent and insurmountable barrier between them and that real American citizenship. . . They cannot be transmuted into good American citizens."[38]

Most of the opposition to the Japanese was expressed in a series of emotionally charged articles in the San Francisco CHRONICLE in February, 1905. The Japanese were accused of being criminals, a menace to American women, and of course, all were spies.[39] The PACIFIC RURAL PRESS in 1906 claimed that the "Japanese are careless, preoccupied and untrustworthy."[40] These articles were the start of a campaign to reduce the privileges of the Japanese. They were denied citizenship, barred from migrating to the United States. Japanese anger, that finally led to the Gentlemen's Agreement, did not find sympathy or respect in the United States.[41] In 1920, in a hearing before the Senate Committe on Immigration and Naturalization, Senator Phelan declared that the "Japanese are an immoral people . . .(who will steer) California toward mongrelization and degeneracy." Another California lawmaker described the Japanese as "bandy-legged, bugaboos, miserable, craven simian, degenerated, rotten little devils."[42] At the same time, Wallace Irwin's novel SEED OF THE SUN was popularized in serial form in the SATURDAY EVENING POST. The plot warned that the Japanese were buying land on the West Coast as part of a conspiracy to aid the Mikado in his bid to rule the world.[43] Attitudes and feelings were created in this nation that led to the passage of discriminatory laws against the Japanese; restrictions that were perfectly acceptable to both the media and the public.

Public attitudes

The press did, indeed, play an important role in the shaping of the attitudes of much of the population. Attitudes, whether positive or negative, are learned in a variety of settings and in a variety of ways. The receptivity of the public to what they read or heard had developed earlier, however. There had to be a nourishing soil in which anti-Asian and anti-semitic attitudes could grow and flourish. The soil came from the home, and a little later, from the school.

Earliest, and probably most persistent, are those attitudes acquired as a result of the child observing and assimilating parental behavior. Indeed,

> . . .group stereotypes and prejudices may be viewed as part of the taken-for-granted, socially approved stock of knowledge that the individual acquires through the process of socialization. . . .as socially transmitted knowledge about the place of different groups in the social structure, as well as about the alleged stereotypical traits of different groups.[44]

A second source of attitudes is the school, through its teachers, textbooks, and time available for instruction. There is debate today about whether the school can overcome "undesirable" attitudes learned in the home, but there is not doubt that the school itself does influence attitudes. In a four-year study of suburban elementary schools near New York, Niel and Kiester found that, among suburban parents, the school was perceived as second only to the family as an institution shaping the child's feelings toward other people.[45]

It has long been the mission of the schools to influence attitudes and behaviors so as to transmit the national heritage to each generation. In so doing, it has reflected an ideal society (according to the elitists), e.g., the melting pot, and the practices of the real, if less than ideal, society that pays the educational bills. Thus, the equality of man was taught in segregated schools by teachers who were white and middle-class-oriented, using textbooks that stressed the virtues only of the United States and the faults and occasional virtures of other countries, depending upon which ones they were.

As Lasker wrote in 1929,

> . . .without ever coming in personal contact with a Chinese, a child would be likely to be influenced toward that race in very different ways in California and in Boston; his attitudes toward "foreigners" as such would be likely to change considerably between an early childhood in a small hill town of Tennessee and later childhood in Jersey City.[46]

Further,

Without a word or gesture, the adult world can and does impress him with the inferiority of this or that racial group, when it carefully excludes it from those common undertakings or the use of those common services which all other people share, regardless of their age, sex, or social standing.[47]

In the case of Asians, this was perhaps more explicit because of the Exclusion laws that affected their immigration, citizenship, rights to own property, and segregated education (in California). In the case of the Jews, there was an official and

. . . all but universal agreement that Jews, like other immigrants, should be accorded those benefits of legal equality that are contingent upon citizenship. . . . The Jews were to be allowed, even required, to become Americans -- but at arm's length. And in this policy there was a paradox that gentile America has never been quite able to resolve: Jews were steadily criticized for being too clannish, yet if once they moved onto the avenues leading toward assimilation, they found many barriers on their path.[48]

The exclusions were considered subtle -- college admission quotas, property deed exclusions, occasionally a too visible sign that read "No dogs or Jews allowed" at a hotel or private club.

There is no question that the schools effectively conveyed attitudes toward those who did not quite fit the mold of "an American" in the early twentieth century, and even later. Bogardus cited the role of the textbook in this practice as particularly invidious.

Textbooks skillfully written often depict the favorable traits of the given nation and its peoples without mentioning the worst practices. Concomitantly, they may emphasize the less worthy features of other reaces to the neglect of the best traits. Coupled with such texts there may be "injunctions" issued to the teachers "to teach the textbooks only" and to raise no "troublesome questions" in the minds of pupils. In this way systematic education may distort parts of the truth at the expense of other parts and promulgate dangerously inaccurate racial attitudes.[49]

Lasker, too, points out that

. . . teachers will use historical textbooks, knowing them to be prejudiced or false on a given point, thinking that later reading will correct whatever false impression may be obtained now. But later reading does not always have this corrective power. It may, of course, substitute a new for an old notion, but the emotional response to an early, gripping situation does not get eradicated except with difficulty.[50]

Lest it be thought that this view is typical only of the earlier twentieth century, consider the finding of Lambert and Klineberg in the 1960's:

In general, television, movies, and to a lesser extent parents, constitute the major sources of information about foreign peoples for the 6-year-old American children. For the 10-year-olds, television and movies are still important, but **school-connected sources such as courses and textbooks begin to be cited** while parents become negligible as sources. At the 14-year-old level, **school-connected sources are predominant**, along with books, magazines, and other mass media. Personal contact with other peoples is a minor factor.[51] (italics added)

Attitude surveys

That the "school-connected sources" did their job well is seen in the reports of attitude surveys taken in the 1920's and early 1930's with adult subjects educated in the 1890-1920 period in American schools. The consistent view of Jews and Asians is negative. Although the surveys were conducted in different sections of the country, Katz and Braly found that racial attitudes varied more by socioeconomic class than by region, with one exception noted (students at New York University in Guilford's study).[52]

The Bogardus Social Distance Scale, a measure often used in these surveys, asks respondents to indicate the degree of closeness to which they would admit persons of varying national/ethnic/religious origins. The categories included are: (1) close kinship, marriage; (2) club, personal chum; (3) neighbors; (4) employment in my occupation; (5) U.S. citizenship; (6) visitor only to U.S.; and (7) exclude. In today's era of sophisticated sampling and testing techniques, this Scale and the ensuing studies would be considered naive at best. Indeed, most attitude studies are still suspect because of the ease with which respondents can falsify their answers. However, the consistency of response trends warrants the inclusion of these data as indicative of their time.

In 1928, Bogardus reported on the reactions of 1725 Americans to 40 different "races." The sample included 178 Jews, 18 Japanese, and 14 Chinese among its 30 groups of native-born Americans. Those in the sample had a high school or college education and were mainly younger middle-class adults. An excerpt from Bogardus' report indicates the reactions to five of these groups.

Table 1. Reactions on a Social Distance Scale
Toward Five Groups By Percentage[53]

	(1)	(2)	(3)	(4)	(5)	(6)	(7)
English	93.7	96.7	97.3	95.4	95.9	1.7	0
Jews, German	7.8	2.1	25.5	39.8	53.5	25.3	13.8
Jews, Russian	6.1	18.0	15.7	30.1	45.3	22.7	13.4
Japanese	2.3	12.1	13.0	27.3	29.3	38.8	2.5
Chinese	1.1	11.8	15.9	27.0	27.3	45.2	22.4

With the benefit of hindsight, we can explain the differences between the two groups of Jews and the two groups of Asians. In the case of Jews, those from Germany had migrated earlier to the United States than those from Russia. They were more acculturated and thus less visible than the later arrivals. In the case of the Asians, the Chinese had been the source of more economic competition and for a longer period in much greater numbers than the Japanese. Since Bogardus' study was done on the West Coast, the prejudice against the Chinese extant there appears to be reflected in his findings. Further, Bogardus specifically cites the courteous behavior of Japanese children, but not Chinese, as a reason for favorable teacher response to this group.[54]

Two other large studies reported by Katz and Braly have similar findings. Thurstone found in Chicago in 1928 that Jews, Japanese, and Chinese were far down on the list of 21 groups ranked in order of ethnic preference. Guilford, in 1931, surveyed 1100 students at seven scattered colleges and universities and again found the same pattern, except for students at New York University, where 71 percent of the subjects in Guilford's sample were of Jewish parentage.[55] In Katz and Braly's own study of group preferences among Princeton undergraduates (N=60), the Japanese, Jews, and Chinese were ranked

6th, 7th, and 8th respectively in a list of 10 groups, followed only by Turks and Negroes. They concluded that racial prejudice is ". . . a generalized set of stereotypes of a high degree of consistency which includes emotional response to race names, a belief in typical characteristics associated with race names, and an evaluation of such typical traits."[56]

If these were the views of educated middle-class adults, one can only assume that the laboring class of the period held even more negative attitudes. It was apparent in the 1930's and 1940's, furthermore, that these attitudes had changed very little, for there was no public outcry to open our doors to the Jews fleeing Hitler or the Chinese fleeing the Japanese or the Communists. It is also apparent from our survey of texts in the years between the 1890-1920 period and the early 1980's that there was little demand for changes in their content as a means of attempting to alter attitudes.

Two informal surveys of college-age students, one in the mid-1960's and the other in the mid-1970's, used Bogardus Scale-type questionnaires. In the first instance, 100 student nurses were asked to rate 20 groups that included representatives of Europe, the Middle East, Africa, Asia, and Australia. Of these, the groups most relevant to the present study were ranked as follows: 7th - Jews; 9th - Samoans; 11th - Japanese; 15th - Javanese; 16th - Chinese Nationalists; and 20th - Chinese Communists. Others in the first ten preferred groups were all of Western European origin. Certainly the sampling distribution of this survey differed from the earlier ones. However, since one of the degrees of social distance was directly related in this survey to nursing care, one wonders how much progress had been made between 1920 and 1965 in improving attitudes among cultural groups.

In the second survey, the list of groups was slightly modified and the number increased to 25 groups, including the long-deceased Sumerians. There were 190 subjects in the sample, all college students, although some did not rank all groups. The results reflected a sample with a substantial number of Jewish students who were, in turn, reflecting reactions to the anti-Zionist United Naitons resolution passed two months earlier. The Lebanese were ranked 23.4 (tied with Congolese). Other rankings relevant to this study were: 5 Jews; 14.5 - Japanese (tied with Mexicans); 17 - Chinese (undifferentiated); 20 - Samoans. Israelis were 12th among 20 in 1965; they were 8th among 25 a decade later. Again, the others preferred among the first ten groups were Europeans.

The differences between the two more recent surveys appear to be more a function of sample composition than any expansion of knowledge or change in attitude. Indeed, on the 1976 survey, several subjects commented that they knew nothing about the Armenian, Bolivian, Congolese, Ghanian, Lebanese, Samoan, Sumerian, and Watusi groups. Not only does this reveal a deplorable lack of awareness or knowledge of other peoples, but the rankings in ignorance reveal the continuing existence of significant amounts of prejudice - of emotional response to race or group names. Further, despite a marked increase in textbook and public attention to blacks, beginning in the mid-1960's, even this group improved in rank only moderately from 14th out of 20 in 1965 to 13th out of 25 in 1976, even with an increase in the number of black subjects in the later sample. One can only conclude that to achieve substantial changes in attitude, or reductions in prejudice, more is required than black or yellow faces in texts, or legislation and legally-proclaimed observances.

NOTES

1. Isaac B. Berkson, THEORIES OF AMERICANIZATION, A CRITICAL STUDY (New York: Teachers College Press, Columbia Univ., 1920), pp. 55-56; John Higham, STRANGERS IN THE LAND (New Brunswick: Rutgers Univ. Press, 1955), p. 20.

2. Higham, p. 247

3. Zangwill, Israel's drama "The Melting Pot" (1909) cited in Emory S. Bogardus, "Cultural Pluralism and Acculturation," SOCIOLOGY AND SOCIAL RESEARCH, 34 (November, December, 1949), 125.

4. Horace Kallen, "Democracy Versus the Melting Pot," NATION, 100 (May, 1915), 219-20.

5. John Higham, "Integration Versus Pluralism: Another American Dilemma," CENTER MAGAZINE, 7, No. 4 (July, August, 1974), 67-73.

6. William C. Smith, THE SECOND GENERATION ORIENTAL IN AMERICA (Honolulu: R & E Research Associates, 1927), p. 5.

7. Ibid., p. 22.

8. Marcus L. Hansen, "The Third Generation in America," COMMENTARY, 14 (November, 1952), 492-500; Bernard Lazerwitz and Louis Rawitz, "The Three-Generation Hypothesis," AMERICAN JOURNAL OF SOCIOLOGY, 69 (March, 1964), 529-38; Vladimir Nahirny and Joshua A. Fishman, "American Immigrant Groups: Ethnic Identification and the Problems of Generations," THE SOCIOLOGICAL REVIEW, 13 (November, 1965), 311-365; John J. Appel, "Hansen's Third-Generation 'Law' and the Origins of the American Jewish Historical Society," JEWISH SOCIAL STUDIES, 23 (January, 1961), 3-20.

9. Rudolph J. Vecoli, "Ethnicity" a Neglected Dimension of American History," in Herbert J. Bass, ed., THE STATE OF AMERICAN HISTORY (Chicago: Quadrangle Books, 1970), p. 84.

10. John Higham, "Another Look at Nativism," CATHOLIC HISTORICAL REVIEW, 44 (July, 1958), 147-158; Oscar Handlin, ed., IMMIGRATION AS A FACTOR IN AMERICAN HISTORY (Englewood Cliffs: Prentice-Hall, 1959), 3-4; c.f. Burton L.Hendrick, "The Jewish Invasion of America," MCCLURE'S MAGAZINE, 40 (March, 1913), 125-28.

11. Henry P. Fairchild, "Immigration Differences," YALE REVIEW, 19 (May, 1910), 79-97; c.f. Henry Cabot Lodge, "Efforts to Restrict Undesirable immigration," CENTURY, 67 (January, 1904), 466-69; Frederic A. Ogg, "American Immigration at High Tide," WORLD'S WORK, 14 (May, 1907), 8879-86.

12. Albert Allemann, "Immigration and the Future American Race," POPULAR SCIENCE MONTHLY, 75 (December, 1909), 586-96; c.f. W.Z. Ripley, "Race Progress and Immigration," ANNALS OF THE ACADEMY OF POLITICAL AND SOCIAL SCIENCES, 34 (July, 1909), 130-38; John E. Watkins, "Curbing the Flood of Immigrants," TECHNICAL WORLD, (July, 1907), 499-505.

13. Prescott F. Hall, "Selection of Immigration," ANNALS OF THE ACADEMY OF POLITICAL AND SOCIAL SCIENCES, 24 (1904), 183-84; c. f. Edward T. Devine, "Immigration as a Relief Problem" SURVEY, 12 (February 6, 1904), 129-33; Francis A. Walker, "Immigration," YALE REVIEW, 1 (August, 1892), 125-45.

14. Prescott F. Hall, "The Future of American Ideals," NORTH AMERICAN REVIEW, 195 (January, 1912), 94-102.

15. Philadelphia LEDGER, December 6, 1892, cited in "Immigration," PUBLIC OPINION, 14 (December 10, 1892), 221-22.

16. New York HERALD, December 5, 1892, cited in **Ibid.**

17. DENVER REPUBLICAN, December 2, 1892, cited in **Ibid.**

18. PORTLAND OREGONIAN, November 28, 1892, cited in **Ibid.**

19. Charles S. Bernheimer, "Prejudice Against Jews in the United States," INDEPENDENT, 60 (November 12, 1908), 1105-08.

20. John Higham, STRANGER, p. 67.

21. Oscar Handlin, "American Views of the Jews at the Opening of the Twentieth Century," PUBLICATIONS AMERICAN JEWISH HISTORICAL SOCIETY, 40 (1951), 325-26.

22. Herbert A. Gibbons, "The Jewish Problem," CENTURY MAG-AZINE, 102 (September, 1921), 790.

23. Philip E. Sherman, "Immigration from Abroad into Massachu-setts," NEW ENGLAND MAGAZINE, 29 (February, 1904), 675-76; c.f. John Dewitt Warner, "The Sweating Systems in New York City," HARPER'S WEEKLY, 29 (February 9, 1895), 135-36 in Oscar Handlin, IMMIGRATION, pp. 64-66.

24. "Russian Jews and Gentiles from a Russian Point of View," CENTURY, 23 (1881-1882), 919.

25. Maldwyn A. Jones, AMERICAN IMMIGRATION (Chicago, London: Univ. of Chicago Press, 1960), p. 276.

26. J. Campbell Bruce, THE GOLDEN DOOR: THE IRONY OF OUR IMMIGRATION POLICY (New York: Random House, 1954), p. 35.

27. **Ibid.**

28. John T. Buchanan, "How to Assimilate the Foreign Element in our Population," FORUM, 32 (1902), 691; c.f. "Our Responsi-bility for Immigrants after Landing," SURVEY, 24 (April 9, 1910), 74-77; G. N. Abdian, "The Future American, the Ultimate Man," IMMIGRATION, 1 (November, 1909), 20-22; Irving E. Wood, "Immigration and American Ideals," IMMIGRATION, 2 (June, 1910), 57-60.

29. Frank P. Sargent, "Problems of Immigration," ANNALS OF THE ACADEMY OF POLITICAL AND SOCIAL SCIENCES, 24 (1904), 157;
"Selecting Immigrants," INDEPENDENT, 67 (August 5, 1909), 318-19; c.f. W. S. Rossiter, "Common Sense View of the Immigration Problem," NORTH AMERICAN REVIEW, 188 (September, 1908), 360-71; John R. Commons, "Amalgamation and Assimilation," CHAUTAUQUAN, 39 (May, 1904), 217-27.

30. The best accounts of the Chinese on the West Coast are Mary R. Coolidge, CHINESE IMMIGRATION (1909, rpt Arno Press, 1969); for an excellent interpretation of American attitudes toward the Chinese see Stuart C. Miller, THE UNWELCOME IMMIGRANT (Berkeley: Univ. of California Press, 1969).

31. MARIN JOURNAL, April 13, 1876, cited in Elmer C. Sandmeyer, THE ANTI-CHINESE MOVEMENT IN CALIFORNIA (Urbana; Univ. of Illinois Press, 1939), p. 38.

32. Larry D. Quinn, "Chink, Chink, Chinaman," PACIFIC NORTH-WEST QUARTERLY, 57, no. 2 (April, 1967), 83, 86.

33. Miller, UNWELCOME IMMIGRANT, pp. 191-92.

34. J. E. Bennett, "Chinese Tong War in San Francisco," HARPER'S WEEKLY, 64 (1900), 947.

35. Boies Penrose, "Chinese Exclusion and the Problem of Immigration," INDEPENDENT, 54 (January 2, 1902), 12-15; c.f. Alvan F. Sanborn, "The New Immigration to America," INDEPENDENT 54 (November 13, 1902).

36. Edward A. Ross, "The Cause of Race Superiority," ANNALS OF THE AMERICAN ACADEMY OF POLITICAL AND SOCIAL SCIENCES, 8 (July, 1901), 79.

37. John Higham, STRANGER, p. 172; c.f. Clare Booth, "Ever Hear of Homer Lea," SATURDAY EVENING POST, 214 (March 7, March 14, 1942), pp. 12-13, 69-72; 27, 39-42; Homer Lea, THE VALOR OF IGNORANCE (New York: Harper & Brothers, 1942).

38. V. S. McClatchy, "Japanese in the Melting Pot: Can They Assimilate and Make Good Citizens?" ANNALS OF THE AMERICAN ACADEMY OF POLITICAL AND SOCIAL SCIENCES, 93 (January, 1921), 30-31; for a contrary point of view see Sidney L. Gulick, THE AMERICAN JAPANESE PROBLEM (New York: Charles Scribner's Sons, 1914).

39. Oscar Handlin, IMMIGRATION, p. 171; Roger Daniels, THE POLITICS OF PREJUDICE, (Berkeley: Univ. of California Press, 1962), p. 26; Raymond L. Buell, "The Development of the Anti-Japanese Agitation in the United States," POLITICAL SCIENCE QUARTERLY, 37 (December, 1922), 616-17.

40. Dennis Ogawa, FROM JAPS TO JAPANESE: AN EVOLUTION OF JAPANESE-AMERICAN STEREOTYPES (Berkeley: McCutchan Publishing Corp., 1971), pp. 12-13.

41. Jerome A. Hart, "The Japanese in California," WORLD'S WORK, (March, 1907), 8691.

42. Ogawa, FROM JAPS TO JAPANESE, pp. 12-13.

43. **Ibid.**, p. 13; Wallace Irwin, SEED OF THE SUN (New York: George H. Doran Company, 1921).

44. William M. Newman, AMERICAN PLURALISM: A STUDY OF MINORITY GROUPS AND SOCIAL THEORY (New York: Harper & Row, 1973), pp. 197-98.

45. Alice Miel and Edwin Kiester, Jr., THE SHORT-CHANGED CHILDREN OF SUBURBIA (New York: American Jewish Committee, 1967).

46. Bruno Lasker, RACE ATTITUDES IN CHILDREN (1929, rpt. New York: Greenwood Printing, 1968), p. 44.

47. **Ibid.**, p. 116.

48. Irving Howe, WORLD OF OUR FATHERS (New York: Harcourt, Brace, Jovanovich, 1976), p. 409.

49. Emory Bogardus, IMMIGRATION AND RACE ATTITUDES (Boston: D.C. Heath, 1928), pp. 245-46.

50. Lasker, RACE ATTITUDES, pp. 163-164.

51. Wallace E. Lambert and Otto Klineberg, CHILDREN'S VIEW OF FOREIGN PEOPLES (New York: Appleton-Century Crofts, 1967), p. 35.

52. D. Katz and K. W. Braly, "Racial Prejudices and Racial Stereotypes," JOURNAL OF ABNORMAL AND SOCIAL PSYCHOLOGY, 28 (1933), 175-193.

53. Bogardus, IMMIGRATION, p. 25

54. **Ibid.**, p. 203.

55. Katz and Braly, pp. 176-77.

56. **Ibid.**, pp. 191-92.

CHAPTER THREE

ACCULTURATION AND ALIENATION

The concept of the melting pot ideally synthesized the best character-istics of all the immigrant groups into a new gestalt -- the "American." Such an amalgamation, at least on a physiological basis, is being approached today in Hawaii, where generations of intermar-riage among the Chinese, Hawaiians, Japanese, Polynesians, Portuguese, and other groups are leading to a "Golden Man," an harmonious blend of many racial and cultural strains. In practice on the mainland, however, the melting pot really meant, as we have already noted, assimilation or conformity to the majority. Many individuals did indeed assimilate, in behavior and sometimes in beliefs as well. For some Jews, traditional religion was discarded as they converted to Unitarianism or the Ethical Culture movement in an attempt to remove their most obvious difference from the majority. For some of them, the conversion "took" and has persisted to the present generation of their family, which may know vaguely that once the family was Jewish, but feel that that has nothing to do with them. For others, the conversion was strictly for business and/or social reasons, but within themselves they held on to some of the traditions, making these converts modern day versions of the Marranos. Among the Japanese and Chinese in America, there are Sunday services at Buddhist temples, although such services are alien to that religion. It is an attempt to demonstrate their similarity to other Americans, although they recognize that they cannot quite fully assimilate because physically they can never be "white."

In both amalgamation and assimilation, therefore, we see concurrent and often antagonistic forces at work. There is an effort to become acculturated, to behave "in Rome as the Romans do." In so doing, alienation from the ethnic heritage occurs. The result is often confused identity. Even today, when the melting pot ideal is being abandoned in favor of one of cultural pluralism, confusion is aroused as the individ-ual tries to decide whether he views himself as ____-American or an American-___. Which is he first? Which second? Is it possible to be both ethnic and American? The roots of the answers to those questions lie in the individual's self-concept. That image reflects years of development and socialization, but it is already present when the child enters school.

In this chapter, we move from the family and group to the early efforts at acculturation with the ensuing identity crisis. The acculturation "push" was aimed at the adults sometimes even more strongly than at the children. The self-concept is examined with references to Asians and Jews, both in theoretical terms and from an experiential point of view as seen in memoirs of group members. That alienation often resulted as an outcome of these efforts and crises, either from the cultural group or the larger society, is seen in the behaviors of the second and third generations.

The groups in question

Strange as it may seem, there were a number of similarities among some Asian and Jewish families, and between them and the middle-class oriented value systems to which they had come. "Father knew best," Mother "ruled but did not reign," and children were to be "seen but not heard" in the years when immigration was at its peak. Each of these groups held authority and education in high esteem. In memoirs, school experience is rarely mentioned by immigrants. When it is, the comment may reflect wonder at the availability of free education for all, as education was denied to many in both Europe and Asia. It is apparent, however, from the limited references, that while Jews and Asians were in their enclaves in this country, schools, teachers, texts, and peers counted for far less than the family in terms of influence on the immigrant child and his self-concept, perhaps because the non-family factors were so irrelevant to the children's experiences. The Chinese, Japanese, and Jewish communities alike tried to keep their children close to their heritage through cultural or religion-centered classes in the afternoons after public school classes closed. They shared a tradition of books and learning as well as an orientation toward the future. These efforts, attitudes, and values were not characteristic of all other immigrant groups.

The traditional Chinese family was a very complete, tightly knit social and economic unit as much as it was an emotional entity. It was an example of the extended family model in which the generations interact in all matters, and together provide for the needs of the individual. (Note: This family style is practiced even today in India and other Asian countries.) The elders were revered both in life and death, exercising considerable power over their descendants. The practice of the extended family gradually evolved into the principle that not only did everyone share in the prosperity and the glory of the family, but they also shared in any disgrace, dishonor, and poverty.

Very often, several generations in the male line lived together in the same dwelling. A daughter once married became an integral part of the husband's family, and except for occasional visits, severed almost all connections with her own relatives. Her position was subordinated to the needs and wishes of her husband's family, and her main function was to bear sons to provide for the future of the family. Under these circumstances, the woman did not need nor was she supposed to be educated.

Children's functions were to obey and to work. They were to care for, respect, and sacrifice for their parents. Little affection was displayed by the parents, and absolute obedience was demanded by the adults. Emotional displays of anger, annoyance, distress, were to be avoided and were even forbidden. Ritual forms were developed to disguise these feelings in order to smooth relationships between the various generations, enabling the family to function efficiently and with a minimum of friction.

The emphasis in Chinese culture was obedience to familial authority, ritual observance, and adherence to social codes. Individualism, the free play of emotions, the notions of love, independence, and self-fulfillment were absent in Chinese culture. Parental authority was supreme and included the right to interfere in and direct children's destinies, including marriage arrangements. The father was also responsible for his children's good behavior or their delinquency. Thus if a teacher complained or sent a note to the father about a child's behavior in school, the father would appear the next day to apologize for **his** failure to raise his child properly. This responsibility not only is found in the immediate family, but is also shared by the extended family. As one informant put it, "As you walk around the streets of Chinatown you have a hundred cousins watching you."[1]

Chinese methods of childrearing were also different from Occidental patterns. The baby might be loved, fondled, and cherished, fed when hungry, and permitted enormous latitudes. But as the child matured, the mother withdrew all verbal and physical affection. She attempted to guide her children toward emotional independence and to this end, she insisted that the youngsters emulate adults. She did not confide

45

in or communicate with her offspring, but instead demanded total unquestioning obedience and obtained it by her willingness to administer corporal punishment freely. The father was even stricter and more remote. The end result of such training was that Chinese children were generally better behaved, more obedient, and more self-reliant than their non-Chinese peers.[2] On the other hand, these children had enormous adjustments to make in their early encounters with Occidental customs in the schools and other institutions. Conflicts were intensified because the contrast between the two cultures was so great in some areas. These conflicts became especially bitter in the adolescent years, as the students were torn between the traditional obedience of the Chinese and the individualism of the Americans. The rise of discrimination in these teen years was also apparent, as one youth recalled:

> We have never lived in Chinatown, but have always lived in an American neighborhood. I have always had a number of American friends. I mingled with all the children quite freely, but when I was about twelve years old they began to turn from me and I felt this keenly. Up to that time I never realized that I was in any way different, but then I began to think about it. . . . In high school I did not enter into the different activities because I felt that I was not wanted and I was quite sensitive.[3]

Some memories of the contrasts experienced were related by Jade Snow Wong in her recollections of school. She had been accidentally hurt when a bat hit her hand. The child cried, the teacher came immediately, held the child and rubbed her sore hand.

> It was a very strange feeling to be held to a grown-up foreign lady's bosom. She could not remember when Mama had held her to give comfort. . . In fact, when she was hurt either inside or outside, it was much better not to let Mama or Daddy know at all, because they might criticize her for getting into such a situation in the first place.. . . She found it wonderful comfort to be embraced by her teacher. . ..[4]

"It pleased my father no end to know that I like to go to American school. He informed Mother proudly that it denoted a scholarly spirit well-becoming a Chinese. . . ." The children loved their teacher, herself a daughter of Irish immigrants.

> Coming from immigrant homes where parents were too preoccupied to devote much time to their children, we transferred our youthful

affections to this one person who had both the time and the disposition to mother us. We showered upon our white-haired teacher
the blind, wholehearted loyalty of the young. Our studies we
readily absorbed, not because we particularly liked them so much
as because it was "she" who taught us. Thus, with the three
R's, games, stories, a weekly bath which she personally administer-
ed in the school's bathroom -- two pupils at a time -- and
her love, she whom we staunchly enshrined in our hearts, laid
the rudimentary but firm foundation of our personal brand of
American culture.[5]

The Japanese family was very similar to the Chinese in discipline,
hierarchical subordination, and the servile position of the woman.
Family loyalty and solidarity were equally as important, and large
families were the rule. Japanese relationships, however, tended to
remain non-verbal, supporting the Westerners' perception of the inscrut-
ability of the group. Very little discussion took place between parents
and children, and in fact, was actively discouraged by the parents.
Their culture emphasized shame and dishonor in the group as the
most forceful methods of punishment. First generation Japanese
children were accused by their teachers of being "shame-faced, retiring,
afraid of putting themselves forward." They did not verbalize or
volunteer in class.[6] Like the Chinese children, they attended Japanese
language schools at the behest of their parents. Japanese children
were anxious to be accepted in American schools and many resisted,
regarding themselves as Americans. As they grew older and met
with resistance and discrimination, they began to attempt to learn
more of their cultural heritage. The second generation remained
suspended between the two cultures. "We live a dual life," complained
one youngster. "We are criticized by our parents for speaking an
imperfect Japanese; we are also criticized by the Americans. . .[for
being different.]"[7] Such was the dilemma of the children through
the third generation. This dilemma frequently resulted in neurotic
conflicts even as the children internalized their parents' values.

Japanese acculturation was aided by a value system that was compat-
ible with that of American middle-class culture. The Issei, or immigrant generation, who were their 50's when studied in mid-century,
were found to

> . . .place a high value on the attainment of such long-range goals
> as higher education, professional success, and the building of
> a spotless reputation in the community. These goals the Issei
> have passed on to their children, and the Issei willingly help the

Nisei to attain them because it is the unquestioned expectation of the Issei that their children will in turn fulfill their obligations to their parents.[8]

The Nisei, however, who were in conflict over fulfilling their obligations to their parents, compensated for the anxiety aroused by their feelings of guilt by either becoming passive rather than striving, or not considering their individual success valid unless their achievement also benefited the community and society.[9] A more recent study among Japanese of three generations in Seattle, using an Ethnic Identity Questionnaire, found ". . .a considerable residue of ethnic identity in the third generation Sansei and considerable acculturation of the Issei."[10]

The Filipino-Americans, who regard themselves more as Malays than Orientals, present a contrast to the Chinese and Japanese. They share the characteristics of extended family, demands for responsibility and obedience, and shaming as punishment with the other groups, but not the drive for success or learning. Acceptance of and/or resignation to low achievement has been attributed to their long historical role as colonials.[11] As a result, even those with a quality education but whose qualifications are not recognized in the United States, are quite passive in their acceptance of discrimination. This behavior may go back also to the schooldays when ". . .spankings give way to ridicule and any boldness is looked on as bad. All this leads, in the school, to a striving for adequacy as opposed to excellence."[12]

The conflicts have not disappeared for Asian families even in recent years. Korean children, often only one or two in a school, suffered their isolation in silence because of their inability to speak English and their culturally-ingrained passivity.[13] Vietnamese refugees who arrived in this country in 1975 experienced the same anxiety and feelings of ambivalence about the Americanization of their children. They were pleased that their children learned English so quickly, but feared that the Vietnamese heritage would be lost, particularly among the younger children. Few materials are available for language instruction, but the parents attempt to teach their children Vietnamese culture, customs, and history during their free hours together. They, like their predecessors, are tying to bridge the gap between traditional discipline and the much freer behavior of American-raised children.[14]

The newly arrived Jewish immigrants in the great immigration period had similarly encountered the problems of a strange land, huge cities, new language, and, above all, the need to earn a living in the new and harsh environment. Some men came alone, as the Asians had, although with the intention of making a new life here rather than returning to the native land with full pockets. The purpose of immigration for the Eastern European Jews was not primarily or solely economic. Hope had driven them across the ocean, especially hope for their children. That hope centered not just on attaining social mobility, but also in achieving the twin aspirations of worshipping freely, which was difficult in Russia and Poland, and of sending their children to public school, an opportunity denied them in Roumania and Russia.

Many of the adult Jewish immigrants were anxious to achieve an education for themselves, and by their own efforts set an example for their children. Adult education classes were full, and stories of sacrifice for learning were not uncommon. One man, born in the Ukraine, came to the United States in 1913 with the equivalent of a junior high school education. Upon his arrival he sought work in the garment industry and attended classes at night. "I wanted to study. . . .I went to preparatory school. You had to pay. But there you could go much faster. . ." Others also followed his path, but often were forced to stop because of illness or financial exigencies. Another man emigrated with his family from Galicia (Austrian Poland) because he was ambitious. "He came with the idea to put us all on our feet. . .I was eight when we came." The family responded to the parents' drives: the oldest boy became a doctor, the younger sister a school teacher, and another boy, a social worker. All the children attended college.[15] Reminiscences are full of such stories. One man related that as a boy of fourteen, he was immediately employed in a sweat shop. Despite the long hours and the difficulty of his working day, he also attended night school. "College education was the goal of hundred of immigrants toiling by day for a living and preparing at night, Chautauqua fashion - each for himself."[16]

The adult Jewish immigrants were Orthodox Jews, very religiously observant and traditional in viewpoint. They spoke Yiddish, and insisted that their children, especially the boys, learn Hebrew and observe the customary religious practices. They came from the village, the Shtetl, which had been separated from the Russian and Polish communities, and where the traditions remained medieval in style and custom. Therefore, the parents were faced with enormous problems of acculturation. They had to learn a new language and many were forced to discard customs very important to them quickly, though reluctantly.

Adding to their misery and discomfort was the fact that their children, young and impressionable, were able to acquire the new ways much more quickly than they, even without the added authority of the schools. Like children everywhere, in many eras, much was learned quickly on the streets. The public schools added to the estrangement of the children as the young learned new concepts, the new language, new ways that sometimes led to rejection of the old, scorn or embarrassment at their parents' habits, and sometimes the development of an emotional-social distance that led to either alienation or a generation gap between the two groups. Despite these inner conflicts, children absorbed the parents' aspirations for upward mobility. These problems could not have been avoided because differences between the two cultures were simply too great -- just as it was in the case of the Asian immigrants. Pain and disappointments were inevitable, but they were exacerbated by the prevailing philosophy and attitudes of Americans at the turn of the century, which also dominated the schools. Americanization or assimilation was the demand of a large number of intellectuals, social workers, and perhaps, the "silent majority" of citizens.

Rapid acculturation and assimilation of the European immigrants was the goal of intensive adult education programs tnat flourished through the first four decades of this century. The immigrants flocked to the night classes, anxious to become "Americans," concerned at the growing gap with their children. The Educational Alliance in New York, the evening school in Rochester (N.Y.), the programs across the country, taught English, civics, American History, and "citizenship" in an attempt to reduce cultural differences as rapidly as possible. Aims of a program in Massachusetts, for example, were announced:

> . . . to be chiefly to make English a common medium of speech, to establish better relationships between all Americans, to preserve the best contributions brought from the Old World, and unite them with the best ideals of the New, to prepare aliens for citizens, and to make a united people, loyal to the United States, with one language and one country.[17]

The English language tests and exercises often stressed the virtues of cleanliness as a means of attaining two goals at the cost of one lesson. During this period, it was not uncommon to find the American-born first-grader and the parent or grandparent aiding each other in the struggle to learn to read.

Many of the teachers, at least in the New York schools, approached their pupils with disdain, determined to impress upon them their own standards. These teachers derogated the cultural backgrounds of their charges, lessening the children's respect for their parents. The gulf was widened by the curriculum itself. A large part of the school program was devoted to the teaching of "good" English, cleanliness, and health habits. Constant sermons were delivered about the need for clean nails, brushing teeth, clean hair ribbons, polished shoes, shining scrubbed faces, and neat clothing. Yet the physical reality for these children prevented this outcome; most tenements did not have running water. Many mothers were harried doing piece work to sustain their families; bathing and keeping children clean was almost impossible.[18]

The pain and disappointments mentioned above were compounded by the ambivalent reception accorded the new immigrants by the Jews of an earlier arrival period and a different (German) background. Many German Jews did not view their east European confreres with favor. They looked upon them as filthy, backward, uneducated, and above all, an embarrassment. They were also afraid that the influx of these immigrants might weaken their acquired prestige and status in the community -- a position that was still precarious and that had been achieved only after a long struggle. In the South, where German Jews had behaved and been perceived more as Southerners than as Jews, the threat presented by the newcomers was keenly felt. Since the early 1800's, the former had blended into the populations of Atlanta, Charleston, Savannah, Durham, and New Orleans; held political office; fought for the Confederacy; and attained social status in their communities. Here came their co-religionists who ". . .wore skullcaps in public, spoke in an embarrassing language called Yiddish, lived on the poor side of town, and trucked with the Negroes as customers."[19] The latter-day arrivals were not welcomed warmly.

A report of 1889 to the united Jewish Charities of Rochester complained: ". . .The Jews have earned an enviable reputation in the United States, but this has been undermined by the influx of thousands who are not ripe for the enjoyment of liberty and equal rights."[20] Louis Marshall chided his fellows for what he considered was their disdain of the new immigrants, and felt both the Yiddish press and education would be the means of Americanizing the East European Jews.[21]

The German Jews did provide help to the newcomers and community support. Much of the assistance was predicated on the desire to inculcate their values, and to push the new groups in the direction of Americanization and assimilation. An enormous social and economic gulf sharply, and even bitterly, divided the two groups, which existed into the 1920's and later, but gradually disappeared as the newcomers began to prosper, intermarry with the German Jews, and assimilate with them. Common crises such as anti-semitism, World War II, and the establishment of the State of Israel finally united the Jewish community.

The National Council of Jewish Women, in these years, tried to teach immigrant children the fundamentals of reform Judaism, and "manners, cleanliness, plain sewing, darning, and patching." Reform Jews (essentially the German Jews) felt their brand of religious education could also add to the Americanization attempts.[22] Most of these efforts were vigorously opposed by the immigrants, who were anxious to maintain the older and more austere religious traditions of orthodoxy. Jewish settlement workers also pushed for assimilation, the most notable organization being the Educational Alliance in New York City that was organized for the specific purpose of "humanizing" the immigrant. The Alliance, financed by German Jews, ignored the true aspirations and cultural contributions of the East European Jews while it offered them valuable assistance in learning English, civics, Home Economics, manual trades, and recreational pursuits. No recognition was ever made, nor encouragement given, to the flourishing institutions that had developed around the interests of the "Russian intelligentsia" -- the Yiddish press, theatre, and literature. Even when it came to religious practices, they tried to educate the young in the reform manner, ignoring the orthodox practices of the parents.[23] The Alliance reflected the philosophies of the older German Jews who scorned their Russian co-religionists and who blithely disregarded and rejected their entire vital cultural contribution both to the Jewish tradition and the enrichment of American life in general.

The fears of the German Jews were not altogether unfounded. Where the nineteenth century had been typified by an absence of blatant hostility toward them,

> Perhaps the most important thing to be said about the period between 1910 and 1920 is that a climate of intolerance toward Jews had developed in the nation. Manifested in patterns of social discrimination and sustained by an upsurge in anti-Semitic propaganda, anti-Semitism now figured prominently in American life. Jews, whether German or Russian, middle-class or lower-class, were lumped together with other aliens who were threatening Anglo-Saxon supremacy.[24]

It is evident that the Asians and the Jews of the great immigration period, alike in their middle-class values though different in their heritages, found an uneasy welcome in their new land. There were fewer attempts to acculturate and amalgamate the Asians because of their racial difference from the majority; there were stronger attempts to assimilate the East European Jews into a less traditional "Americanized" life-style. Both groups were beset by an unbelievable emphasis on cleanliness, whether in the schoolhouse bath or the English texts. The immigrants were pressured and prodded into becoming "Americans" while they were being punished by guilt feelings about rejecting their culture and families. With reference to the Jews, however, it has been asserted that they ". . .were able to obtain through accommodation what other immigrant groups managed only through assimilation."[25]

If one looks at the picture of these groups today, in terms of the discrimination they experienced, and the degree to which they have retained their identity and/or accommodated to the larger social structure, the image is changed from the early years of this century, as can be seen in Table 2. Some of this change is the effect of the younger generations being born and raised in this country; some results are from changes in social attitudes; and some has had to come from education.

Table 2. Contemporary View of

Four Minority Groups in America Society[26]

GROUP	DISCRIMINATION	DEGREE OF CULTURAL PLURALISM	DEGREE OF STRUCTURAL PLURALISM
Jewish-Americans	Subtle, likely to increase in crisis periods; some ascription by descent	Variable, depending on generation	High
Japanese-Americans	Rapidly declining	Disappearing with the Sansei	Moderate
Chinese-Americans	Declining	Considerable	Moderate, generational
Hawaii's non-Caucasian Americans	Apparently in process of complete assimilation		

Alienation through education

Consider, if you will, some surprisingly disparate views of the role of education vis-a-vis the immigrant child:

Jane Addams, in speaking of the teacher's role in 1897:

> Her outlook is national and not racial; and she fails, therefore, not only in knowledge of but also in respect for the child and his parents. She quite honestly estimates the child upon an American basis. The contempt for the experiences and languages of their parents which foreign children sometimes exhibit, and which is most damaging to their moral as well as intellectual life, is doubtless due in part to the overestimation which the school places upon speaking and reading in English. This cutting into family loyalty takes away one of the most conspicuous and valuable traits of the . . . child.[27]

From another point of view two decades later, Americanization

> . . . is the beneficent multiple influence of the day school teacher, exerted throughout the day to furnish ideals in habits to our pupils, that insures the transformation of the alien home and the foreign neighborhood. The children in our schools are the treasure-bearers to the foreign home, of that language equipment, that generous enthusiasm for institutional life, and those habits of orderly living, which constitute the essence of democracy.[28]

A third writer, a sociologist, pointed out in 1933 that:

> Too often the Americanization of the school has resulted in social disorganization because the teacher has not understood the cultural history and characteristics of the different national groups. This situation in the school is only a part of a larger situation, a failure to realize that adjustments made by immigrants in the United States must be in terms of their past experiences and that many of their cultural traits must be preserved for a time to prevent social disorganization. The same criticism can be made about schools maintained by immigrants. The teachers do not understand the social order in the United States well enough to prepare the pupils for a normal adjustment in American life; instead they try to insulate them from American culture. . . .The second generation can be assimilated and its first contact with American life is through the school.[29]

Or, in 1959:

> If there is one practical lesson to be derived from the present status of the American melting pot, it is that we should be extremely circumspect in our immigration policies. . . . Biologically, there already are present here so many human types that further additions can hardly enhance the genetic end product. . .[30]

And finally, in 1974, Margaret Mead:

> If each child is to have a sense of its uniqueness - that he or she is **somebody** - it must be somebody in the eyes of those who are trusted or admired, somebody in the eyes of its parents. And how can that be if the parents are denigrated, because of color, race, class, caste or occupation?. . .
>
> One thing we owe all children is a situation where they can think their own parents are beautiful, without having to denigrate the way other children's parents look. . . .[31]

The opprobria of "slant-eyes," "Wop," and "kike" have no place in the classroom. Yet, even without name-calling, Jade Snow Wong recalls that in fourth grade, she ". . . had begun to compare American ways with those of her mother and father, and the comparison made her uncomfortable."[32]

Each of these points of view expresses a philosophy that was or is strong enough to permeate classroom walls and textbook covers. When the masses of immigrants came in the 1890-1920 period, the conflicts between the staunch "Americanizers" and the "Progressives" were developing in intensity. Today, the same basic conflict exists between the heredity partisans on the one hand and the civil rights advocates and environmentalists on the other. In one community, the conflict evokes criticism of multicultural texts; in another, criticism of the "lily-white" editions. Whichever group has the upper hand in a school district essentially dictates the philosophy that shapes the curriculum and selects the textbooks.

In the early years of this century, the public schools, their books, and their presentation of the course of study were either hostile, indifferent, or insensitive to the notion of pluralism, and actively promoted the immigrant children's rapid acculturation. New York City provides an example of this policy. The **majority** of its school pupils in the period immediately preceding World War I were either foreign born or children of immigrants. Jewish children alone provided 40% of the general school population.[33] Yet a very small proportion of teachers or principals were Jewish.[34] The lack of sensitivity on the part of some non-Jewish teachers rankled even years later, as Michael Gold showed, in 1930, in writing of one of his early teachers:

> I knew no English when handed to you. I was a little savage and lover of the street. I slept in my underwear, I was lousy, maybe. To sit on a bench made me restless, my body hated coffins. But Teacher! O Teacher for little slaves, O ruptured American virgin of fifty-five, you should not have called me "LITTLE KIKE."[35]

Not every teacher on the Lower East Side was so brutal. On the other hand, although we know that there were a large number of loving and sympathetic teachers and principals, the official policy was obdurate and quite explicit on this point. The Superintendent of the New York public schools claimed:

> Americanization is a spiritual thing difficult of determination in mere language. Broadly speaking, we mean by it an appreciation of the institutions of this country, absolute forgetfulness of all obligations or connections with other countries because of descent or birth.[36]

This attitude was further expressed as prevailing policy in other educational circles, and became firmly embodied in educational theory in the teachers' colleges and normal schools, thus becoming part of the teachers' acceptable goals. One of the most prominent and prestigious educators said:

> These southern and eastern Europeans are of a very different type from the North Europeans who preceded them. Illiterate, docile, lacking in self-reliance and initiative, and not possessing the Anglo-Teutonic conceptions of law, order and government, their coming has served to dilute tremendously our national stock, and to corrupt our civic life. . . Everywhere these people tend to settle in groups or settlements, and to set up here their national manners, customs, and observances. Our task is to break up their groups or settlements, to assimilate and amalgamate these people as a part of our American race, and to implant in their children, so far as can be done, the Anglo-Saxon conception of righteous law and order and popular government, and to awaken

in them reverence for our democratic institutions and for those things in our national life which we as a people hold to be of abiding worth.[37]

To the new immigrant Mary Antin, acculturation meant surrender of her religious values. Her adjustment was lauded, and regarded with such esteem that her memoirs became a minor classic of their time. Indeed, the chapters on her school experiences were collected into a small volume and used as a supplementary reading book in the public schools.[38] Devout orthodox Jews often found themselves involved in conflict between these schools that often preached Christian values, the Missionary Societies that sought to convert their children, and the problems of generational adjustment to the new land. For the orthodox Jew, the conversion of a child into Christianity, as with Mary Antin, or intermarriage outside the faith, was tantamount to the death of the child. The father said the funeral prayers (kaddish) and sat "shiva" (mourning ceremonies) for his lost young one.

Too often, parents could not battle or counter these influences, and to add to their misery, they themselves, though longing to keep their children devout and loyal to their heritage, had ambivalent attitudes toward the public schools. Many immigrant parents wanted their children to achieve upward mobility, and further education provided the means: better jobs, better neighborhoods, and higher incomes. Thus they were torn, they wished the children to remain loyal to religious values based on the past, but at the same time, they wished them to venture beyond the ghetto and adopt a more modern lifestyle. And when their children proceeded to do the latter at a dizzying pace, the result was frequently alienation, social distance, and worse, insensitivity that led to the lack of communication between generations to which we have already alluded. Under the best of circumstances, the immigrant experience brought as much heartache as fulfillment.[39]

For children, too, schools posed problems: How far and how much Americanization? Did it mean total rejection of their parents, of their language, and even their religion? Children who assimilated too quickly also suffered heartbreak in the estrangement from their parents and their own identity.[40] Psychological effects often included lack of self-esteem, shame of one's traditions, and the burdens of guilt for the rejection of parents and abandonment of their past. Both contemporary and earlier novelists, such as Abraham Cahan and Philip Roth (CRY IT SLEEP), have treated these emotions of estrangement, anger, anomie, and self-hate. Schools did not produce **all** of this damage, but as a reflection of the attitudes of the larger society, they contributed much to the emotional disturbances.

Difficulties for the children in the schools were also aggravated by the economic circumstances of their families. For the Asians and the Jews, the struggle for livelihood was all encompassing and hard. Children were often needed to help provide for the family's daily needs, on the truck farm of the West Coast, in the Chinese family laundries, in the sweatshops of the Lower East Side, selling newspapers, or running errands. Despite the long hours and the hard work, the children went to school in large numbers, and more important, stayed in school. When a girl of fourteen wrote to the editor of the Jewish DAILY FORWARD in 1907 that she felt guilty at costing her parents money by continuing in school, the editor responded that ". . .she should obey her parents and further her education, because in that way she will be able to give them greater satisfaction than if she went out to work."[41] The editor, who served as the "Ann Landers" of the time, commented further:

> The hunger for education was very great among the East Side Jews from Eastern Europe. Immigrant mothers who couldn't speak English went to the library and held up the fingers of their hand to indicate the number of children they had. They then would get a card, give it to each of their children, and say, "Go, learn, read."[42]

The facilities of the night schools, and the free universities were especially frequented by the Jewish youth and young adults.

> . . .The public schools are filled with little Jews; the night schools of the East Side are practically used by no other race. City College, New York University, and Columbia University are graduating Russian Jews in numbers increasing rapidly. . . Altogether there is an excitement and an enthusiastic energy for acquiring knowledge which is an interesting analogy to the hopefulness and acquisitive desire of the early Renaissance.[43]

However,

> No matter how strong the Jewish penchant for education, no matter how deeply it was rooted in Jewish religion and culture, it would have mattered little if room had not existed in the colleges. It was fortuitous that the tide of Jewish immigration

from Eastern Europe coincided with a period of unprecedented expansion in American higher education.[44]

The Chinese, too, held education in high esteem. This respect was a part of Chinese tradition and custom, and Chinese parents possessed a high regard for teachers and felt their children's education a matter of great pride. Therefore, a large majority pursued this goal. In many cases, parents were willing to sacrifice comfort and money to assure their children's education.[45] The Japanese shared these drives with the Chinese and the Jews. Studies of Japanese children indicated high scholastic achievement in the high schools, and upward occupational aspirations that resulted in an unusually high proportion of Japanese young people attending secondary schools and colleges.[46]

All of these groups created their own traditional schools that attempted to preserve their particular culture and language. These schools often used the older traditional teaching methods of rote memorization and strict discipline. They were often hated and scorned by the children, forced to attend them in the hours after public school classes. Many others had mixed attitudes toward these schools. The classes should have widened the gap of distrust and anger between the old ways and the new American cultural standards. That they contributed to alienation is undeniable; they often provided a focus for further rebellion, particularly because they were often tedious, difficult, and sometimes archaic in their methods and attitudes. On the other hand, the very maintenance of the cheder and the Asian language schools **reinforced** the traditional respect for learning in all three cultures. Secondly, teachers in these schools did speak the language of the children's homes, making communication with the parents and appreciation of the children's home conditions easier. Some of these teachers, especially if they were second generation, were able to understand the students' educational and vocational goals, and occasionally were even able to bridge the chasm between the conflicting cultures. They also performed another function, that of reinforcing the traditional values of the immigrant community. The children were constantly inculcated with precepts of duty, respect for their elders, honesty, hard work, and esteem for education.[47] In addition, these schools provided a familiar haven where immigrant children could retreat to the familiar and traditional while attempting to cross into the American culture, and thus could ease the painful and often rebellious feelings that they had.[48] The schools became a source of comfort as they provided a safety valve for anger and rebellious feelings.

All three cultures had differing child rearing practices; all three differed in their outlooks; but all three cultures' children were generally well behaved in school, and juvenile delinquency was either unknown or rare within these groups. The reasons for this conformity and mildness differed, but the children were similar in their behavior.

Strong family loyalties, strong community institutions, and great respect and admiration for education and educators are therefore seen as common to all three cultures. This meant that the Jewish child developing in an environment stressing individualism, and the Asian child thriving in a society emphasizing cooperation, brought to the school the same attitudes necessary for successful learning. They were essentially obedient and civil; they were anxious to learn and intellectually curious. All three groups of children came from societies that saw education and hard work as the necessary tools for upward economic and occupational mobility. Furthermore, the home, the day-school, and the community constantly reinforced these attributes.

For these children, alienated, confused, even unhappy in the process of acculturation, the public school was an agency that their parents and community supported, despite all the misgivings. The public school provided, despite its insensitivity to the pupil's cultural diversity, an avenue through which they were able to achieve. They achieved because their native cultures provided the environment that supported the values of the public school system, inadequacies and all. And the public schools, in turn, brought the American dream to these students, even as it often brought unhappiness.

As we have said earlier, both the Asian and Jewish communities suffered many more disabilities , prejudices, and discriminatory actions from the American people than did other immigrant groups, although these others, too, had faced hostile nativist sentiments at times.

Prejudices were reflected in different ways. The attack on the Asian children's self-esteem was based on racism as well as on differing cultural values. Jewish children, not as readily identifiable, faced hostility to their religion as well as to their culture. They faced a daily struggle with the Protestant oriented school systems that ignored their sensibilities. Even in ghetto schools where the school population was 90% Jewish, the children were subjected to daily Bible reading from the New Testament as well as the Old, the daily recitation of the Lord's Prayer, Christian hymns, and the celebration of the Christian holidays whose religious content was stressed. There is no doubt that these practices upset the Jewish immigrant children. Interviews with adults of the second and third generation about their school experiences indicated dismay with the religious activities. Many of those interviewed were not from devout families, but their recollections all sounded the note of either embarrassment or discomfort. One woman recalled suffering anxiety when asked to read a passage from the New Testament in an eighth grade assembly. Another girl of orthodox persuasion recalled her guilt feelings when participating in the Christmas Chorales. Others interviewed agreed that, although they sang the Christmas carols with great gusto, they never could repeat the words "Jesus Christ." Christmas and Easter were focal points of the elementary school timetable even in the 1940's (and still are), maintaining the inner conflict of the Jewish child. Evans recalls that when the class began to work on its Nativity replica, he would ". . .always try to shift around and work on the animals or the stable walls so I wouldn't have to get involved with any of the real holy stuff."[49] If these memories of the more secular school environment of the thirties and forties are still painful years later, it was even more poignant and difficult for the immigrant child straddling diverse cultures.

The Jewish leadership was aware of the problem and began to protest the inclusion of religious materials in the public school systems, sometimes with the support of the Roman Catholics who resented the use of Protestant religious devotions. For example, Cardinal Gibbons of Baltimore joined rabbis in their opposition to Bible reading in the schools ". . .as it gives the teacher the opportunity to make such selections and comments as may offend the religious beliefs of the scholars. It is an entering wedge that might lead to great abuse."[50] They opposed these practices on the philosophical basis of the separation of Church and State. Attempts were made to eradicate religion from the schools in Tamaqua, Pa., Philadelphia, Baltimore, Atlanta, Binghamton, N.Y., St. Paul, Cincinnati, and Chicago. Again in Baltimore, Jews took issue with the school board on the singing of Christian hymns in public schools. When the school board disagreed, Jews threatened to withdraw their children from the schools. Under a compromise, the hymns were still sung, but children were no longer "compelled" to sing them.[51] What victories were won were always short-lived, because the Protestant clergy bitterly protested any change in the religious practices. The Jews persisted in their vigilant attempts to maintain the separation principles, but their exertions were not fully successful until the Supreme Court decisions of 1963.[52] The final decision of the Court is still being challenged, however, as recent events in New Hampshire have shown, where local boards have attempted to reinstate the Lord's Prayer and Bible reading in the classroom.

The Jewish community efforts did convince the New York school board, however, and in 1908, anything that smacked of "a sectarian or religious character" was barred from the school Christmas celebrations. Just before Christmas, the teachers decided to exclude all carols that made reference to Christ, and the board's policy was seemingly enforced. Many objected strenuously to the Jewish efforts to remove religious teaching. They claimed that if the schools became totally secular, then

> Ought Jewish children not be compelled to work on Yom Kippur and Rosh Hoshannah, and the other times and seasons when they are now excused? And ought not the Jewish teachers to be forced to do the same? A little more logic and a little less bigotry would seem to be in order among our semitic population.[53]

Jews in other cities were seeking the same goals achieved in New York. Wherever action was initiated, it caused enormous controversy, arousing anger among many of the Protestant clergy. In every instance it was difficult for them to realize the psychological problems the religious exercises could and did create for many Jewish children. Rabbi Silverman, in 1908, expressed the Jewish position then that is still relevant today. ". . .Jews do not regard Christmas celebrations of themselves as essentially Christian, and would have no hesitancy in taking part in them if the celebrations were shorn of their distinctly Christian tone. . ."[54] In fact, the caroling continued well into the 1940's in many schools, both inside and outside of New York. Even in recent years, when the carols are often part of a seasonal, interfaith program, a Christian tone has been maintained. A Japanese-American teacher wrote: "The overflow crowd in the multi-purpose room of our elementary school in California was hushed one December afternoon of 1972 as the music of the **universally loved** 'Silent Night' came from the voices of 120 third-grade children." -- in Japanese.[55] (Italics added) The implication is clearly an equality between "universal" and Christian, for even Mrs. Tshkamoto's Buddhist and Shinto, but non-Christian countrymen might not be included among the "universal lovers" of that carol.

If the traditional teaching goals in the nineteenth century had been to inculcate Christian values, little change occurred in many educational circles at the beginning of the twentieth century, and even today, in many urban as well as rural areas. One Jewish college student in 1976 recalls vividly an incident in second grade in a Philadephia school. A Protestant classmate drew a picture of a devil, and said to him, "That's you! You're a devil because you're a Jew!" While educators were united in an avowal of the sanctity of the separation principle, and believed that **sectarian** religious values should not be imparted in the public schools, they continued to believe passionately that American education's function was to prepare children for living in a democracy founded on **Christian** principles. These groups were then, and still are, oblivious to the feelings of the various nonChristians -- Jews, Moslems, buddhists, atheists, and others -- who also attend the public schools.[56]

Many intellectuals, as well as leading churchmen, felt that the spirit of Christianity was among the precious possessions of our civilization, and that these precepts must be taught, but not formally. "It is undesire-able and impossible to introduce explicit and formal instruction in religion into the public school."[57] But Christian principles, claimed many, should be introduced into the daily program with affecting sectarian sensitivities. Thus, they explained, the course of instruction should contain lessons stressing moral principles and civic responsibility. Christian religious holidays were to be observed and taught according to their religious teachings. That was one of the reasons for the continued popularity of **McGuffey's Readers,** and the continued inclusion of Bible stories in the collections of other readers, as well as the observance of religious festivals.

For Asian children, their racial "visibility" made them more vulnerable to cruel prejudice than was experienced by the Jewish students. That kind of injustice was best exemplified by the San Francisco School Board incident. Irritation and anger over the Japanese immigration had been expressed on the West Coast by bitter anti-Asian sentiments. Particular vehemence was written into articles in the San Francisco CHRONICLE and a series of bitter mob incidents punctuated dramati-cally the prejudice felt by the populace in California. Finally, on October 11, 1906, the San Francisco School Board passed a special resolution that stated: The Board of Education

. . .is determined to effect the establishment of separate schools for Chinese and Japanese pupils not only . . .to relieve the conges-tion at present prevailing in our schools, but also . . .that our children should not be placed in any position where their youthful impressions may be affected by associations with pupils of the Mongolian race.[58]

It took intervention by President Theodore Roosevelt to reduce the diplomatic furor that ensued.

The self-concept

The self-concept is that inner image held by an individual in which he perceives himself as good or bad, worthy of attention and approval or unworthy, accepted by others or unacceptable, competent or incompetent, well or ill, ethnic or assimilated, and so on. Although the self-concept often resides at an unconscious level, it influences the individual's behavior nevertheless. We know today much more about the self-concept and its role in a person's life, and about self-fulfilling prophecies and their effects on student achievement, than we knew half a century ago. During the period of the great immigration, little attention was paid to either concept except by scattered individual teachers. Certainly teacher editions of texts offered few words of guidance in these directions. Even today, relatively few teacher editions of readers exhibit much sensitivity to self-concept.

How does the self-concept develop? Initially, it arises as a reflection of the ways in which significant persons in the environment (parents, siblings, other adults) respond to the infant's cries, needs, and efforts to perform in motor, social, and language areas of development. As the infant matures, the behaviors of others toward him continue to convey the message of his acceptability and desirability as a human being, or the opposite of these. For most pre-school children, their significance to others in the family is a positive force (with due exceptions for cultural differences, resentments at having another child to feed to care for in an already strained situation, and similar conditions). The ways in which others affect this feeling of significance are many, and may vary from outright denunciation to "benign neglect," on the negative side, to "tender loving care" and over-indulgence on the positive side.

As part of the socialization process, the child becomes aware of the groups to which he belongs, and their members in turn contribute to his developing self-concept.

> For both "minority" and "majority" group children, group membership may be the source of values and goals, of deep satisfactions and dissatisfactions, of feelings of security or insecurity. When membership in a group is experienced as a source of punishment or ridicule, the child may develop negative or ambivalent feelings toward his own group.[59]

64

In so doing, he also develops these feelings toward himself.

Gestures, unconscious facial expressions, physical contact and physical distance are all non-verbal behaviors that communicate feelings and attitudes of one person toward another. There are, however, varying interpretations of the same non-verbal behaviors according to cultural background. Avoidance of eye contact, for example, is perceived as hostile, defensive, or guilt-expressive behavior in many Western cultures, while it is an expression of respect in several Eastern cultures. When this behavior is misinterpreted, the potential for damage to the self-concept increases. This potential exists, and is particularly potent, wherever teachers and students, in the prolonged proximity of the school day, have cultural differences and perhaps mutual cultural ignorance.

It is at the time of entrance to the larger environment, that is, the school, that the child finds even more influences brought to bear on his emerging self-concept. That which is unique to himself, his name, may provide the first point of conflict.

> Among males it was common, in the 1920's and 1930's, for Isadores to become Irvings, Irvings to become Irwins, Irwins to become Erwins, Sidneys became Sydneys, and Morris underwent Gallicization to Maurice. These fandangoes in nomenclature are but a brief sampling of a larger body of transformations that began in Europe, long ago, in the efforts Jews made to become assimilated, to break out of the ghetto, to evade discriminatory reactions to stereotyped semitic names.[60]

A modern case in point is a Chinese college student (in 1975) who, on her arrival at an urban American school at age 11, was told to choose an "American name as her Chinese name was "too difficult to remember or pronounce." Similarly, in a television documentary, "How's school, Enrique?" the boy is called "Henry" consistently by the school personnel. Thus, worth or acceptability to the larger society, acculturation if you will, immediately hinges on denying an essential aspect of one's significance to one's family, one's culture, and oneself -- the ultimate alienation. This type of incident gives credence to the statement that,

> Despite our politico-philosophic statements about the beauty of diversity and the contributions of all Americans, a major concern of the schools for the past 100 years has been to eliminate differences. We, that is the schools, were a major instrument

in "Americanizing" our people. . . .[61]

The impact on the minority group student of his confrontation with the bureaucracy of the school systems, discriminations, condescension, and low teacher expectations is reflected in negative self-concept, passivity, withdrawal, and in many cases, eventual high dropout (or "push-out") rates.

Students who are not immune to the blandishment and pressures of the school find themselves torn between what the schools demand of them and what their parents expect. Some students become unsure which language to speak, developing a stammer or an overly restrained manner of speech. . . Caught between two cultures, the child may be without roots and culture, having rejected one without being accepted by the other.[62]

This rootlessness was particularly evident in the pre-war Nisei generation, who saw themselves as neither Japanese nor totally American, and more than a generation later with American-born Chinese youth (t'u sheng) who similarly were unsure of their identity.[63] They were both subject to discrimination for which, as children, they blamed their own inadequacies or flaws. The consequent damage to the self-concept persisted even when they became aware that prejudice and discrimination occurred because of their readily identifiable group membership rather than their personal characteristics.

Discrimination can thwart the personality development of children and can impair their characterological development. It adds an additional burden to those critically stressful circumstances with which every young child must cope -- a burden which disastrously results in self-concepts of lowered self-esteem. It impairs affective states and processes, reduces cognitive functioning...[64]

Despite the negative potential of this discrimination, the majority of these children did not drop out of school because of family pressure and support.

Another aspect of significance to others is related to the respect accorded one's cultural heritage in the classroom. During the great immigration period, and indeed almost up to the present day, the Jewish child who was absent for religious holy days, even Rosh Hashonah and Yom Kippur, was subject to penalties and was not excused for having missed a test or other classroom exercise. Interviews with people who were victims of such discrimination in their school

66

days sixty years ago reveal that the memory of shame, non-acceptance, and being "different" at that time is still painful. On their return from a religious observance, they faced the criticism of their teachers and the taunts of their peers. The practice of religious discrimination in this regard had changed in contemporary school systems where there is a relatively high percentage of Jewish students and teachers, so that schools may be closed for those two holy days.

Also tied to the development of the self-concept, according to Cooper-smith, are competence, virtue ("doing the right thing"), and power. Half a century ago, and even today, virtue in this sense means doing things the "American way" for most people, conforming to some major group. Dress, speech, and personal habits of the immigrant child were openly criticized in the classroom as being "unAmerican." As the child moved toward conformity in his search for approbation, shame for his own lack of virtue and, even more, at his parents' lack of virtue, diminished his self-concept and attacked his cultural identity. Acceptance, or being part of the group, is , according to many psychologists and sociologists, ". . .the most significant variable in providing the child with feelings of belonging, which in turn have such great significance for his aspirations, his social expectations, his values and allegiances and his beliefs as to what he may do or become."[66] Minckley, writing in 1917 of the effects of a high school education on the children of immigrants in Frontenac, Kansas, pointed out that for these children "The love for home and father and mother becomes less and less until commencement day draws near,. . . they are a little ashamed of father and mother in their ordinary dress at commencement."[67] Yet it is the family, the ethnic association, the religious affiliation, that provide the sense of identity and security, via a structured system of values and relationships, that are needed for a positive self-concept and strivings for success.[68] Culture shock occurred when the new American child left the sanctuary of the ethnic ghetto, as the rural Kansas teenager did to attend high school, the environment that provided the continuity with his native heritage.

For Asians at the turn of the century in San Francisco, such culture shock did not occur until their entrance to the junior high school, for they were subject to segregation in the "Oriental School" through the early 1900's. The parents

> . . .urged their children to prepare themselves for mental or professional occupations (except in the case of those whose pessimism about employment discrimination against Chinese made them feel this was impractical). . . . Beneath their enthusiasm

67

for education and advancement, however, Chinatown's parents could not repress a sense of anxiety about their children's entrance into outside society and the possible erosion of values which prevailed at home.[69]

Even today, the most important grouping in society for the Chinese is the family and its extended kinships.

The Chinese has been taught since childhood to seek harmony in that group. It was the human beings in that particular type of group who satisfied the Chinese individual's need for success, comfort, affection, sympathy, help, exhilaration, and approbation.[70]

For the Jews, too, these supportive acts came from the family and the Jewish community's social agencies, not from the school. The sense of identity and the growth of a positive self-concept were nourished in these groups, but the power to withstand the assault of culture shock varied among individuals.

In modern-day Hawaii, where there is more of a melting pot than has ever been true on the mainland, this very strong sense of family and culture has been a source of sustenance and has resulted in the Japanese and Chinese having ". . .fewer problems in adapting to the dominant 'white' culture, perhaps because, in doing so they have managed to maintain their own traditions and, at the same time, add some of the flavor of their customs to the overall culture."[71]

The role of competence as it affects the self-concept has also followed diverse paths. Until the emergence of ethnic pride as a virtue in the past decade, there was often a conflict between the desire to demonstrate competence and the discrimination practiced against the competent if they happened to be Asian or Jewish. Among the Jews particularly, there was great interest in intellectual efforts. The second generation, in fact, had such eagerness to learn and to progress that they ". . . invaded American colleges and universities in numbers sufficient to alarm some college administrators."[72] Admissions quotas were commonplace as a result in the years between World Wars. In those earlier years, academic prizes were often withheld from members of both of these groups because of prejudicial community pressures. Indeed, there was conflict within the family as well, for along with parental urgings to learn, there were admonitions not to "stand out," or in contemporary terms to learn but keep a "low profile." This is exemplified by a third generation member, recalling his school years in the 1940's and 1950's:

> . . .Mister Jew wants to make good grades, not the best grades because that will be resented, but good enough grades, and make them effortlessly so that he will not let down the expectations of parents and friends and girls who expect him to be smarter...
>
> To excel, to do better, to make it big and strive for the very top, had alway been a part of our family chemistry. My father stressed leadership by example, that Jews had to be twice as good to achieve half as much.[73]

There is still an undercurrent of resistance when too many honors are awarded to Asians or Jews (or blacks) in some schools, and sometimes quite conscious administrative efforts to award prizes in terms of proportions of ethnic groups in the community or student population. Tsukamoto recalls one of her high school teachers crying because Tsukamoto had written a fine essay for a competition, worthy of being among the finalists, which could not be accepted because her parents were not native born.[74] Despite the competence that may be achieved, therefore, self-concept may not be enhanced because of its non-acceptance by the larger community.

Similarly, the sense of power, the fourth factor in the development of self-esteem, was and is interpreted differently for the majority and the minorities. Where the ability to acquire and manipulate has been praised for the majority, it has been condemned for the Asians and Jews. It has been seen as evidence substantiating the negative attitudes toward these groups expressed, as we have seen, by the "Know-Nothings," legislators, community leaders, and the press. Power in the hands of minorities has been perceived as Machiavellian, characteristic of their "sneakiness" and craftiness. Since this is the attitude of the community, the school, which reflects the community, similarly criticizes and handicaps efforts at leadership by children from minority groups.

Another aspect of power is the feeling of having some control over one's destiny. Those who feel free to move in any direction without undue hindrance have this power, and it enhances their view of self. Those who do not feel free in this way, who believe themselves to some degree to be at the mercy of the majority's whims, have their self-concept diminished. Asians and Jews alike have experienced the latter situation. It is apparent in the schoolyard where the single

Chinese child is not chosen as a partner or teammate, and in the class-room where the Vietnamese child sits without comprehension or assistance. The leader of an East Coast Chinese community speaks of his son in such a situation:

> My son was in trouble for a little while. He didn't want to be Chinese. People teased him. They called him Ching Ching China-man. When he walked down the street they'd bully him, saying, "You know Kung Fu? If you don't, give me 50¢." ...when he started school -- he's 12 now -- he was the only Chinese and the only non-Catholic. At first I took him to school he was so afraid of standing on the corner alone.

The father continued, explaining that his son is now effectively bilingual and is respected for his ability.

> I warn him anytime people stop him, if he gets excited, they will make more fun of him. Ignore it, there's nothing to fight. Now they want him to join the soccer team, the football team. They like him. Now they forget he's Chinese...[75]

In 1971, it was noted that:

> Our typical middle-class teachers are Americans who feel ade-quately powerful about themselves and their abilities. The minor-ity children, the culturally different who are in our schools, feel strangely helpless in the presence of the powerful authority figure of the teacher, demanding conformity to the tenets of his value system. Our public schools, then, instead of motivating and encouraging students from poverty or other subcultures, success-fully inhibit them. Only in recent years has the awareness appeared that permits the use of the phrase, "the school push-out" in lieu of the phrase "the school drop-out." What different connota-tions these two have...[76]

In an overall view, then, it can be seen that the school has tended to negate those very sources of positive self-concept so strongly nurtured in the home and cultural group. The absence of sensitivity to cultural differences, the physical and psychological distance main-tained between teacher and students, the negative reinforcement of competence and leadership, all have been destructive to the develop-ment of a positive self-concept. Added to these are the absence, with rare exceptions, of any mention of Asian or Jewish heritages, contributions to the larger society, or problems of being different, in the curriculum or texts of the first eight grades. Even if such references were made in the texts, few teachers have been prepared to elaborate on them because the teachers, more often than not, have known little about the Jews and even less about the Asians (members of those groups excepted, of course).

One would expect as a result, strong negative feelings of self-concept among children of these groups, and related poor scholastic achievement. Contemporary studies of the correlation between self-concept and achievement do indeed demonstrate such results among groups of "different" or "disadvantaged" children. (Note: Such studies have generally focused on low-income and/or black children.) This has not generally been the case, however, with Chinese, Japanese, and Jewish children. The strong sense of belonging, or ethnic identity, combined with each group's emphasis on the value of learning, has tended to reduce the negative influence of the school situation on these children's self-concept and achievement. They have not conformed to the research picture of minority children who ". . .make little or no effort to learn because of their negative self-concept and the belief that they can never achieve anything, no matter how hard they try."[77]

It would be unrealistic to attempt to analyze the contemporary scene without an understanding of its roots in the nineteenth century. Within the present school atmosphere one can detect lingering traces of past practice, for attitudes and feelings about different groups are based on past learning experiences.

NOTES

1. R. T. Sollenberger, "Chinese-American Child-rearing Practices and Juvenile Delinquency," JOURNAL OF SOCIAL PSYCHOLOGY, 74 (1968), 13-17.

2. B. L. Sung, MOUNTAIN OF GOLD: THE STORY OF THE CHINESE IN AMERICA (New York: Macmillan, 1967), p. 17; Francis Chang, "An Accommodation Program for Second Generation Chinese," SOCIOLOGY AND SOCIAL RESEARCH, 19 (July, August, 1934), 541-553; William C. Allen, "Americanization in Some of Our Public Schools," SCHOOL AND SOCIETY, 22 (October 3, 1925), 422-425; Nora Sherry, "Social Attitudes of Chinese Immigrants," JOURNAL OF APPLIED SOCIOLOGY, 7, No. 6 (July, August, 1923), 325-333.

3. J. Masuoka and C. S. Johnson, ORIENTALS AND THEIR CULTURAL BACKGROUND (Nashville: Fisk Univ. Social Science Institute: Social Science Source Documents, No. 4, 1946), pp. 40-41.

4. Jade Snow Wong, FIFTH CHINESE DAUGHTER (New York: Harper and Brothers, 1945), pp. 20-21.

5. Pardee Lowe, FATHER AND GLORIOUS DESCENDANT (Boston: Little, Brown and Co., 1943), pp. 130-32.

6. Bradford Smith, AMERICANS FROM JAPAN (New York: J. B. Lippincott, 1948), p. 119.

7. William C. Smith, THE SECOND GENERATION ORIENTAL IN AMERICA (Honolulu: R and E Research Associates, 1927), pp. 8,12.

8. W. A. Caudill, "Japanese-American Personality and Acculturation," GENETIC PSYCHOLOGY MONOGRAPHS, 45 (1952), 65.

9. **Ibid.**, pp. 51-52.

10. M. Masuda, G. H. Matsumoto, and G. M. Meredith, "Ethnic Identity in Three Generations of Japanese-Americans," JOURNAL OF SOCIAL PSYCHOLOGY, 81 (1970), 207.

11. F. Cordova, "The Filipino-American, There's Always an Identity Crisis," In S. Sue and N. N. Wagner, eds., ASIAN-AMERICANS: PSYCHOLOGICAL PERSPECTIVES (Palo Alto: Science and Behavior Books, 1973), pp. 136-139.

12. D. F. Duff and R. J. Arthur, "Between Two Worlds: Filipinos in the United States Navy," In Sue and Wagner, eds., **op cit.**, p. 207.

13. M. Hahn and F. Dobb, "Lost in the System: Korean School Children in San Francisco," INTEGRATED EDUCATION, 13, No. 4 (1975), pp 14-16.

14. PHILADELPHIA INQUIRER, March 22, 1976.

15. MSS (interviews), New York: YIVO Research Institute for Jewish Studies.

16. Phillips Davis, "The Story of an Immigrant's Experience," CHAUTAUQUA, 48 (September, 1907), 106; c.f. M.E. Ravage, AN AMERICAN IN THE MAKING: THE LIFE STORY OF AN IMMIGRANT (New York: Harper and Row, 1917).

17. "The Americanization Movement," SCHOOL AND SOCIETY, 9 (January 11, 1919), 52-53.

18. Selma Berrol, "The Schools of New York in Transition, 1898-1914," URBAN REVIEW, 1 (December, 1966), 15-17; Lillian D. Wald, THE HOUSE ON HENRY STREET (New York: Henry Holt and Co., 1915), p. 109.

19. Eli N. Evans, THE PROVINCIALS (New York: Atheneum, 1973), p. 277.

20. Morton Rosenstock, LOUIS MARSHALL, DEFENDER OF JEWISH RIGHTS (Detroit: Wayne State Univ. Press, 1965), p. 16.

21. **Ibid.**, p. 47.

22. Oscar Handlin, ADVENTURE IN FREEDOM: THREE HUNDRED YEARS OF JEWISH LIFE IN AMERICA (New York: McGraw-Hill, 1954), p. 157.

23. MSS, YIVO: Boris D. Bogen, BORN A JEW (New York: Macmillan, 1930), pp. 57-58.

24. Stephen Steinberg, THE ACADEMIC MELTING POT (New York: McGraw-Hill, 1974), p. 9.

25. E. I. Bender and G. Kagiwada, "Hansen's Law of Third Generation Return and the Study of American Religious Ethnic Groups," PHYLON, 29 (1968), 363.

26. Adapted from Charles F. Marden and gladys Meyer, MINORITIES IN AMERICAN SOCIETY, 3rd ed., (New York: American Book Co., 1968), p. 461.

27. Jane Addams, "Foreign-born Children in the Primary Grades," JOURNAL OF PROCEEDINGS AND ADDRESSES OF THE THIRTY SIXTH ANNUAL MEETING (Chicago: National Educational Association, 1897), pp. 108-109.

28. William L. Ettinger, "Americanization," SCHOOL AND SOCIETY, 9 (1919), 130.

29. Lawrence L. Brown, IMMIGRATION: CULTURAL CONFLICT AND SOCIAL ADJUSTMENTS (New York: Longmans, Green, and Co., 1933), p. 241.

30. J. M. Radzinski, "The American Melting Pot: Its Meaning to Us," AMERICAN JOURNAL OF PSYCHIATRY, 115 (1959), 885.

31. Margaret Mead, "Uniqueness and Universality," CHILDHOOD EDUCATION, 51 (1974), 60.

32. Wong, op. cit., p. 21.

33. Isaac B. Berkson, THEORIES OF AMERICANIZATION, A CRITICAL STUDY (New York: Teachers College Press, Columbia Unvi., 1920), p. 59.

34. "Christmas without Christ," CURRENT LITERATURE, 44, No. 1 (January, 1908), 62-63; Sandra Berrol, "Schools," p. 15; Diane Ravitch, THE GREAT SCHOOL WARS (New York: Basic Books, 1974), pp. 168-69, 177.

35. Michael Gold, JEWS WITHOUT MONEY (New York: Liveright Publishing Corp., 1930), p. 37.

36. New York EVENING POST, August 8, 1918, cited in Berkson, p. 59.

37. Ellwood P. Cubberly, CHANGING CONCEPTIONS IN EDUCATION (New York: Houghton Mifflin Co., 1909), p. 9.

38. Mary Antin, AT SCHOOL IN THE PROMISED LAND (New York: Houghton Mifflin Co., Riverside Literature Series, 1911).

39. Harry Roskolenko, "America, the Thief," Thomas C. Wheeler, ed., THE IMMIGRANT EXPERIENCE (Baltimore: Penguin Books, 1971), 151-78.

40. E. G. Stern, MY MOTHER AND I (New York: Macmillan, 1917); B. Schreieke, ALIEN AMERICANS, A STUDY OF RACE RELATIONS (New York: Viking Press, 1936), pp. 18-19; Miriam Blaustein, ed., MEMOIRS OF DAVID BLAUSTEIN, EDUCATOR AND COMMUNAL WORKER (New York: McBride, Nast and Co., 1913), pp. 60-62; Lowe, p. 158.

41. Isaac Metzker, ed., A BINTEL BRIEF: 60 YEARS OF LETTERS FROM THE LOWER EAST SIDE TO THE JEWISH DAILY FORWARD (Garden City: Doubleday, 1971), p. 66.

42. Ibid., p. 66

43. Hutchins Hapgood, THE SPIRIT OF THE GHETTO (1902, rpt. Cambridge: Belknap Press, 1967), pp. 35-37; c. f. AMERICAN JEWISH YEARBOOK (New York: American Jewish Committee, 1918-19), pp. 383-86.

44. Steinberg, op. cit., p. 11; c.f. AMERICAN JEWISH YEARBOOKS.

45. Sollenberger, "Chinese-American Child-rearing," pp. 20-21; Chang, "An Accommodation Program," pp. 541-53.

46. Audrey James Schwartz, "The Culturally Advantaged: a Study of Japanese-American Pupils," SOCIOLOGY AND SOCIAL RESEARCH, 55 (1971), 341-53.

47. B. Hosokawa, NISEI -- THE QUIET AMERICAN (New York: William Morrow and Co., 1969), p. 174.

48. Hapgood, **op. cit.**, pp. 24-25; Bradford Smith, AMERICANS FROM JAPAN, pp. 116-117.

49. Eli N. Evans, THE PROVINCIALS, p. 130.

50. William Rosenau, "Cardinal Gibbons and his Attitudes toward Jewish Problems," PROCEEDINGS OF THE AMERICAN JEWISH HISTORICAL SOCIETY, 31 (1928), 222.

51. Baltimore SUN, December 19, 1913, cited in Isaac M. Fien, THE MAKING OF AN AMERICAN JEWISH COMMUNITY (Philadephia: Jewish Publication Society, 1971), p. 204.

52. AMERICAN JEWISH YEARBOOK (1909-1910), pp. 56-57; (1908-1909), pp. 192-95; (1914-1915), pp. 290-93; (1911-1912), p. 271; (1915-1916), p. 281.

53. "Christ in the Public Schools," BOOKMAN, 26 (January, 1908), 467.

54. "Christmas without Christ," pp. 62-63.

55. Mary Tsukamoto, "An American with a Japanese Face," CHILDREN AND INTERCULTURAL EDUCATION, Part I (Washington: Association for Childhood Education International, 1974).

56. Raymond L. Buell, "The Development of the Anti-Japanese Agitation in the United States," POLITICAL SCIENCE QUARTERLY, 37 (December, 1922), 622-623.

57. Paul H. Hanus, "School Instruction in Religion: Part I," EDUCATION, 27, No. 1 (September, 1906), 10-17; Paul H. Hanus, "School Instruction in Religion: Part II," EDUCATION, 27, No. 2 (October, 1906), 73-84; c.f. Will Herberg, "Religion and Education in America," RELIGIOUS PERSPECTIVES IN AMERICAN CULTURE (Princeton: Princeton Univ. Press, 1961), II, 11-51.

58. Buell, **op. cit.,** pp. 605-38.

59. Helen G. Trager and Marian R. Yarrow, THEY LEARN WHAT THEY LIVE (New York: Harper and Bros., 1952), p. 116.

60. Leo Rosten, THE JOYS OF YIDDISH (New York: McGraw-Hill, 1968), p. 214.

61. J. A. Ether, "Cultural Pluralism and Self-identity," EDUCATIONAL LEADERSHIP, 27 (1969), 233.

62. Tyll van Geel, "Law, Politics, and the Right to be Taught English," SCHOOL REVIEW 83 (1975), 250; c.f. Nancy Boze, "Ethnic Literature: Replacing Old Stereotypes with Positive Concepts," CLEARING HOUSE, 44, No. 9 (1970), 527-28.

63. Carl Wittke, WE WHO BUILT AMERICA (Cleveland: Press of Western Reserve Univ., 1939), p. 471; A. H. Yee, "Myopic Perceptions and Textbooks: Chinese Americans' Search for Identity," JOURNAL OF SOCIAL ISSUES, 29 (1973), 99.

64. J. H. Douglas, "Mental Health Aspects of the Effects of Discrimination upon Children," YOUNG CHILDREN, 22 (1967), 298-99.

65. Stanley Coopersmith, THE ANTECEDENTS OF SELF-ESTEEM (San Francisco: W. H. Freeman, 1967).

66. Douglas, **op. cit.,** p. 299.

67. L. S. Minckley, AMERICANIZATION THROUGH EDUCATION (No publisher, 1917), p. 71.

68. Timothy Smith, "Immigrant Social Aspirations and American Education, 1880-1930," AMERICAN QUARTERLY, 21 (Fall, 1964), p. 536.

69. Victor G. Nee and Brett D. Nee, LONGTIME CALIFORN': A DOCUMENTARY STUDY OF AN AMERICAN CHINATOWN (New York: Pantheon Books, 1973). p. 151.

70. Francis L. K. Hsu, THE CHALLENGE OF THE AMERICAN DREAM: THE CHINESE IN THE UNITED STATES (Belmont: Wadsworth Publishing Co., 1971), pp. 26-27.

71. Esther C. Jenkins, "Multi-ethnic Literature: Promise and Problems," ELEMENTARY ENGLISH, 50, No. 5 (1973), 693.

72. Wittke, **op. cit.**, p. 335; c.f. Steinberg, ACADEMIC MELTING POT, Chap. 1.

73. Eli Evans, **op. cit.**, pp. 162-163.

74. Tsukamoto, **op. cit.**

75. PHILADELPHIA INQUIRER, March 28, 1976.

76. S. Charnofsky, EDUCATING THE POWERLESS (Belmont: Wadsworth Publishing Co., 1971), p. 60.

77. Lita L. Schwartz, EDUCATIONAL PSYCHOLOGY: FOCUS ON THE LEARNER, 2nd ed. (Boston: Holbrook Press, 1977), p. 97.

CHAPTER FOUR

THE SCHOOLS - THEIR TEXTS AND TEACHERS

In order to assess realistically the roles of the textbooks and teachers in American schools following the 1890-1920 period, it was necessary to review briefly the shifting traditions and philosophies underlying pre-twentieth century public education. Examination of past educational curricula helped to determine what textbooks and materials needed to be reviewed and evaluated, what methods would best illustrate and measure the treatment of Asians and Jews in the teaching materials of the past, and gave direction for a parallel study of whether and/or how contemporary educational textbooks and techniques have changed.

Historical background

The settlement of the colonies was closely associated with religious sects, and therefore the first schools were frequently church-sponsored schools, taught by virtuous ladies or by Protestant divines. Literacy in the service of religion was, indeed, the prime reason for the community-supported schools mandated by the Ould Deluder Act of 1647 in the Massachusetts Bay Colony. The purpose of literacy, then, was to enable each of the colonists to read the Bible for himself (and thus evade the Ould Deluder - Satan). With some modification in other colonies, this philosophy continued to be dominant through the eighteenth century and into the nineteenth century. As a result, a tradition existed in which educators considered it their duty not only to train the young to read and write, but also to instill in them proper moral attitudes and wholesome civic feelings. Horace Mann, "father of the common school," strongly urged nineteenth century businessmen to support common school education as a means of investing in the future citizens of the young nation -- to assure that American youth **would** be literate, moral, and civic-minded or patriotic. There was as much emphasis on the proper development of the child's "character" as on his intellectual growth during this

79

era. Prior to the Civil War, the stress in education was "to impress
. . .youthful minds with a prejudice in favor of the the existing order
of things."[1]   Another   authority   succinctly   described   the schools'
role this way:

> No part of the teacher's work requires more watchfulness and
> more painstaking, than that of shaping the child's moral character.
> . . . In lessons on animals, trees, and all the works of nature,
> opportunities should be constantly improved to show the wisdom,
> power, and goodness of the Creator, and to inculcate the rever-
> ence that is due to Him, and a sense of dependence upon Him.[2]

Curriculum in the elementary or common schools at the time of
the Revolution consisted of reading, writing, and arithmetic, all
taught with religious overtones. By 1826, grammar and geography
were added.[3] The geographies frequently contained more than just
physical facts. For example, some included related historical facts
or evaluative descriptions of the peoples of various countries. Although isolated histories of the United States began to appear by
1830, it was not considered a required or necessary separate discipline
until after the Civil War. Historical narratives were arranged so
that patriotic concepts could be introduced into the classroom. Hero
stories, political facts, and military history were given prominent
positions in many textbooks.[4] One author stated his goals as follows:

> The chief purpose of the instruction in history is to inspire the
> young with a broad, sound, generous patriotism and to train
> them for the right discharge, in due time, of the duties of citizen-
> ship. . . pupils should know our political institutions as the source
> of freedom, stability, and the Power of the Nation.[5]

The rapid increase of the American population in the nineteenth
century led to the beginning of public school systems in various
states, starting with Massachusetts in 1827. As the century advanced,
more children not only attended school, but they remained in school
for more years. However, pedagogical techniques were inadequate
in the early American school system. Teachers were often poorly
paid young girls, barely through the equivalent of the modern secondary school, and untrained in the art of teaching.[6] As a result, the
textbook assumed great importance in the teaching process and
its influence was undeniably significant. Rote memorization was
the prevalent method of learning; little attention was paid to the
meaning of what was studied or the concepts underlying the facts
presented. On the whole, pre-Civil War textbooks were poorly written

-- plagiarism was commonplace; some books were nothing more than a compilation of articles and literary selections; and most school districts were parsimonious to the extreme so that textbooks were used until they were worn out.

Why look at textbooks?

The undeniable importance of the role of the textbook provided its own reason for study. The content of the text necessarily reflected the author's values. If the teacher adhered closely to the organization of the text (as, indeed, most did), the author's scope, accuracy and emphases must have deeply influenced the teaching of that material.

Since the teachers themselves were badly educated, they were largely dependent upon teaching material selected by various school officials. As one contemporary professional report by a prominent educational leader in the 1890's complained, "professional weakness of the American teacher is the greatest sore spot of the American schools." He noted that the majority of schools still depended upon drill, rote memorization and the textbook. Progressives had advocated the use of teaching skills to stimulate, to understand, and to make the student happy. He characterized one class in St. Louis:

> During several recitation periods, each of which is from twenty to twenty-five minutes in duration, the children are obliged to stand on the line, perfectly motionless, their bodies erect, their knees and feet together, the tips of their shoes touching the edge of a board in the floor. The slightest movement on the part of a child attracts the attention of the teacher. . .

Attempts to introduce progressive techniques in the Philadelphia schools failed because the teachers were untrained and were unable to grasp the needed skills from the various courses of study -- "consequently it was followed by them in form rather than in spirit; it led to chaotic conditions in the classroom."[7]

In the school, therefore, the textbook became one of the most significant factors in creating lasting values, attitudes, and stereotypes. In addition, schoolbooks became, by the end of the century, the one force used throughout the country that promoted national bonds and provided for a more uniform education.[8] Geographies and histories quite clearly contained the precepts and values of American culture. They revealed to a high degree the American's attitude about his own country and its relationship with other nations and cultures. Apparently, "the American" regarded other peoples suspiciously, and considered them less virtuous than himself. What was so astonishing about these books was the continued prevalence of their ideas although the nation itself had few firmly established institutions and traditions and was undergoing vast changes very rapidly.[9]

It has been indicated that elementary school books were the one source of information held in common by those who attended public school in the 1890-1920 period. Fortunately or unfortunately, this is still true to some extent. Because of this significant role, educators consider it an important responsibility to review elementary texts periodically and to evaluate their contents. A statement published by the American Council on Education in 1949 reflects some of the uncontrollable variables in such reviews, whether they occurred in 1915, 1945, or 1975.

> The influence of the textbook and other aids to instruction varies from pupil to pupil, from teacher to teacher, from school to school. The way a text is used may reduce or increase the power of its printed pages on the minds and attitudes of the pupil. . . A teacher may use a prejudiced book as a bad example or may suffer its prejudice to go unquestioned. Or even more elusively, a book which ignores a social injustice, may be supplemented by a wise teacher, while the insensitive or hurried teacher may follow the book's example and fail to seize an opportunity for the development in pupils of a measure of social sensitivity.[10]

Common measureable aspects of value systems are the attitudes of the community and the resulting standards they use to decide upon the adoption of textbooks. In comparing public attitudes on this score in 1913 and 1976, there were many that had persisted through this changing period, to be sure, but many new ones were also evident, including some positive regard for minorities. As we saw in our surveys, the social distance between "Americans" and other national groups has shrunk. Note that in the standards established for the adoption of textbooks used in Cincinnati, Ohio, in 1913, **not one line, not one statement** indicated concern about the treatment of minority groups, nor was there any interest evidenced for the feelings of minority or immigrant children in that particular city.[11] We could not undertake the examination of all the criteria that various agencies used in the selection of textbooks for adoption; they would have been virtually impossible to locate after half a century. Although we read several articles dealing with selection criteria, we found that we had to rely primarily upon the textbooks themselves to gain insights concerning the attitudes and standards of the community.

We attempted to ascertain through an analysis of textbooks how their authors handled human relations, with our stress on the treatment of the Asian and the Jew. The earlier dates selected - 1890-1920 - were chosen because these were the years of the great waves of immigration to the United States, especially from Eastern and Southern Europe. In the follow-up study of the textbooks in the period 1950-1976, we sought evidence of changes after 50 years, and the direction and strength of these changes.

The organization, illustrations, content, and objectives of the books were examined. We divided the texts into three major groups in the early period: readers, geographies, and histories; the histories were further differentiated as World or United States history. In the later period, readers and social studies were the two groups under consideration. Some of the textbooks were published in series, and many were edited and reedited frequently. Whenever possible, we included the entire series, and if it was feasible, we compared the various editions and noted significant changes, if any. In addition to the textbooks, we have included teachers' manuals and annotated teacher texts, as well as curriculum guides.

Table 3. Texts and

Teachers' Materials Examined

	Texts	Teachers' Manuals
1880-1920	303	49
1950-1972	239	10
1973-1982	76	20
Total	618	79

Teachers' editions contain the complete student text **plus** guidelines for teaching, interpreting, and/or enriching the text content. In earlier years, when control of the classroom teacher was more rigid than it is today, the teacher was to follow these guidelines without deviation. If the guideline instructed the teacher to stress the "Christian virtue" underlying a passage, she did so with no apparent concern for the non-Christians present. For example, even if she was aware of the inventiveness of the Chinese hundreds of years ago, she could not combat a description of "heathen, barbarian Chinese coolies" with her own knowledge. Since we are aware of both the teacher guidelines and the pressures on the teacher to abide by them, we have included them in our study. The results are enlightening.

The evaluation of the teachers themselves was based in part on the requirements for becoming a teacher at that time, and in part from published reports. We were able to infer from the then contemporary publications the level of preparation of teachers during the great immigration period. Even in terms of today's teachers, in very few instances are they required to take any pre-service courses in cultural pluralism or ethnic studies.

Two techniques of studying texts were used. One was the standard descriptive, generalized method of historical narrative. Impressionistic history can fulfill the function of describing the kinds of disparaging stereotypes, positive and negative illustrations, and in general, give the reader the flavor, the feeling, the verbal essence of the books. This was the most important form of analysis for the readers, which varied so much in content, purpose, and selectivity from each other. The other technique was more objective in nature, using frequency counts and percentages (graphically depicted where appropriate), in order to analyze the texts for Asian and Jewish content.

The type of material and the variables to be measured were characterized as follows: How is the text organized? What are the teaching purposes of the author(s)? Are there illustrations? How many? What kind? How accurate are the data presented? Are any minorities mentioned in the text material? If so, which ones, and in what ways? Are the problems, or the factor, of immigration mentioned at all? If it is, how is it handled? Are immigrants regarded favorably, neutrally, or unfavorably? Are Jews or Asians mentioned? How is the story of Christianity handled in World Culture books? Is there any mention of non-western cultures in these texts? How are the immigration laws and their restrictions treated in American History texts? Are the laws even mentioned? Is there a discrepancy between the treatment of immigrants and restrictive legislation?

In geographies, how are the cities described? Are the new immigrants, Asians and Jews, mentioned in relation to the growth of the cities? How do world geographies analyze China and Japan? Are the impressions adequate, accurate, and objective? How do the texts treat foreign relations with China and Japan, if at all? Did changing foreign policy affect the treatment of Asians in the texts? Do the authors mention the growth of relations between the United States and Japan? Do they include Chinese and Japanese reactions to our exclusionary restrictive legislation against Asians?

Are there any texts written expressly for the Southern or Western regions of the United States? Do they differ markedly from other regions in their viewpoints? In what ways do the annotated teacher texts differ from the students' texts? Do they show any sensitivity to minority problems? Do the curriculum guides specify texts and/or teaching techniques? Do they recommend supplementary materials, books, pictures? Do these guides show interest in group relationships? If so, what are their suggestions for teaching materials?

The specific criteria on our checklist as we examined texts were:

A. Text itself

    1. Number of references to Asians and Jews

        a. % positive
        b. % neutral (e.g., informative, definition, fact)

        c. % negative

        d. none

    2. Illustrations - % Asians and clearly Jewish (e.g., rabbi)

    3. Location of references to Asians and Jews

        a. time - ancient, medieval, more recent past, contemporary

        b. place - abroad, U.S.

    4. Subject matter content

        a. Immigrant history

        b. Asians/Jews in American life

        c. Biographies of Asians or Jews (identified as such)

    d. Religious references (Christian, Buddhist, Shinto, Jewish)

    e. Culture conflict - Asians, Jews, immigrants generally, others

    f. World history - persecution, holocaust, genocide, refugees

B. Teacher's editions

  1. Guidance on values clarifications, concepts, objectives

  2. Sensitivity directed to minorities in general

  3. Sensitivity directed to cultural differences - family, social-class, appearance, language, customs

  4. Suggested activities designed to promote sensitivity of the students to cultural pluralism and its positive values

C. Methods texts

  1. Reflection of Progressive movement (i.e., child-centered)

  2. Sensitivity directed to minorities, cultural differences

  3. Guidelines on preparation of supplementary materials

In looking at teacher editions and methods manuals, we were not examining the **methods** of teaching reading or history or geography. Rather we were concerned with the attitudes to be conveyed to students, and with whether or not questions and activities were suggested to the teacher to support story contents.

The answers to our many questions have not, of course, satisfied all queries or revealed the total picture of prejudice of the past, but the results illustrated how the problems of prejudice and stereotypes were handled then, not only by textbooks, but by the teaching profession. Histories and geographies, as well as the readers, revealed the changes occurring in American education, and reflected the transformation of American goals and values in a new industrial society.

Before we could evaluate the treatment of Jews and Asians in the period of immigration, however, we had to ascertain what these books contained prior to 1890.

Early texts of the 19th century

Readers. Readers in prebellum schools consisted of literary selections from varied sources: fragments chosen from the classics, such as Cicero, Livy, Moliere, Shakespeare, and "Poor Richard." There were no introductions or explanations of the pieces selected. Indeed, there was apparently no unity or purpose -- it was generally just a random collection. By the 1830's, these excerpts were replaced by choices which sought to convey specific lessons: "Selections should inculcate moral consciousness. The child's rules of life, his springs of action in times which test his integrity or try his virtue, are in many instances traceable in his school readers."[12] The essays and stories conveyed truths about death, moral probity, the wonders of nature, patriotism, nobility, duty, and courage.[13]

The McGuffey reader made its first appearance in 1836 and was read generation after generation. The truths stressed, however, reflected the prevailing Protestant ethics and the values of an Anglo-Saxon culture. These readers were frequently revised and were used widely throughout the nation during the nineteenth century and into the 1920's. Indeed, as many as a quarter of a million copies of McGuffey's READERS have been sold **since** 1920.* This, in spite of the fact that our population had changed radically from the agricultural society of the nineteenth century, and we had developed into a highly urban culture. Between 1870 and 1920, about thirteen million copies circulated through various school districts. Many prominent Americans recalled these books fondly -- among them, Henry Ford, Senator Beveridge, William McKinley, Lew Wallace, James Whitcomb Riley, Mark Twain, Rutherford Hayes, and Robert LaFollette.[14]

McGuffey's books reflected the attitudes of rural, small town America. Although they did not differ from all the other readers used in the 1850's and 1860's, they were far more popular. Why their tremendous appeal? The firms that published the readers used an attractive format. Their salesmen and the techniques they employed were

---

*The current "back-to-basics" movement in some school districts resulted in plans to reissue the Readers, according to an article in the HONOLULU STAR-BULLETIN AND ADVERTISER (July 11, 1976). They are currently in use in several school districts.

both aggressive and clever. They were particularly shrewd in their handling of the school districts' personnel. In addition, the readers obviously reflected the philosophic tenets and ideals of the times.[15] McGuffey's texts stressed as the basic moral guide the following: the Ten Commandments, the Sermon on the Mount, and parables of the New Testament. Any other codes of behavior, or any other ideas were superfluous. Stories included in his readers were meant to teach students the need and the obligation to adhere to these necessary social virtues -- accuracy, honesty, obedience, kindness, respect, pity, punctuality, justice, and reverence.[16] By 1895, these readers were being slowly pushed aside by other compilations, but they were never totally abandoned.[17]

So impressive were the moral truths to be assimilated by the young that even a collection of mythology stories by the English author, Charles Kingsley, (1853 ed.), contained an introduction that purported to illustrate that Greek myths illuminated Christian truths.

> God sent down philosophy to the Greeks from heaven as he sent down the Gospel to the Jews. For Jesus Christ, remember, is the light who lights every man who comes into the world. And no one can think a right thought or feeling, or understand the real truth of anything in earth and heaven, unless good Lord Jesus teaches him by his spirit, which gives man understanding.

> But these Greeks, as St. Paul told them, forgot what God had taught them and though they were God's offspring, worshipped idols of wood and stone, and sunk at last into sin and shame, and then of course into cowardice and slavery, till they perished out of that beautiful land which God had given them for so many years.[18]

Teachers' manuals were very important in the use of readers. Annotated guides were frequently used to help the teacher implement the analysis for the chosen poems and stories. A collection that on first observation seemed harmless and unbiased was often filled with instructions for the teacher on how to make the stories reveal the proper Christian moral lessons and truths.

Readers began to change at the end of the nineteenth century, not so much in content as in purpose, as the compilers moved from preaching moral lessons to teaching reading and appreciation of literature. One of our objectives was to assay this change in readers and their objectives as related to the influence of the Progressive Movement in education.

Geographies. Early geographies generally had poor illustrations and badly printed maps. They were often just lists of facts about each country or region. The books offered little analysis or even any kind of organization. Early ones occasionally included some historical facts about the United States. In general, the quality was not very good. The earliest geography, which was probably the best, was the Jedidiah Morse text that contained many illustrations, and was used for several generations.

The most notable geography of the nineteenth century was Olney's INTRODUCTION TO GEOGRAPHY AND PRACTICAL SYSTEM OF MODERN GEOGRAPHY. Printed first in 1829, it was reissued and reedited until, by 1841, it had reached its thirty-fourth edition. The notable ground-breaker in maps and text writing was Arnold Guyot, whose work influenced the writing of the most popular texts of the latter half of the century. The geographies closest to Guyot were the ones by Matthew Fontaine Maury. They first appeared in 1868, and later in 1873 and 1888. Revisions of his geographies appeared as late as 1931. Another of the more popular series of texts that continued to appear late into the century were those by Samuel Augustus Mitchell. They first appeared in 1839 and 1840. Even after his death in 1868, his wife and children continued to publish a series of these books using the name S. Augustus Mitchell, and the volumes continued to sell.[19] Durability, if not quality, seemed to have been characteristic of these geographies.

In many of these early geographies, the religious references to the Jews tended to be denigrating. Judaism was viewed as superior to paganism, but definitely inferior to Christianity. The fact that Christianity had Judaic teachings at its roots, or even that Christ was a Jew, was rarely mentioned. Characterizations of Jews were generally unflattering. When mentioned, they were described as traders and peddlers, and were considered greedy, crafty, and often unscrupulous. The success of the Jews in business or their intellectual achievements were often cited as evidence of their greed, cheating, and misuse of power. In discussing Poland, one geography stated, ". . .almost all of the trade of the country (Poland) is in their hands!" In these early texts, the Jew was identified by religion and frequently called Hebrew rather than Jew. The American child was warned that, although Jews might be unpleasant as a cultural and religious group, it was his Christian duty to be tolerant.[20]

The view of the Chinese in these early geographies was equally derogatory and untrue. Asia, declared various authors, was important in mankind's history because man was created there, but since Christianity was not the religion of Asia, that continent was in decline. "Human nature languishes and degenerates into its worst stages, amidst the bounty of Heaven and in every region of its highest and holiest manifestations." The earliest descriptions of China depicted the Chinese character in the most unflattering terms:

> They have many books on various subjects, yet are very deficient in true literature and science. . . The Chinese are distinguished for order, industry, and regularity; but their treatment of females, worshipping idols and general disregard of truth, are circumstances which lower them in the scale of nations, and rank them below the least civilized Christian communities.[21]

Geographies, like readers, also began to change at the end of the nineteenth century. They began to emphasize human development within the physical environment and to cite the relationships between races and groups, to discuss material resources, and to consider the effect of climate upon the development of the economy and society. The opening of Japan to trade in 1854 and the change in immigration patterns that brought great number of Asians to our shores evoked new views of the Asians. As part of this shift, the image of the Jew was also changed, and the description of him began to vary somewhat.[22]

Histories. History was originally part of the geography textbooks, but preoccupation with the story of the American War of Independence and later struggles stimulated interest in history as a subject itself. History books appeared in profusion after the War of 1812. The textbooks were concerned mainly with dates, political events, and wars. The use of pictures in history textbooks was more extensive that in all other books, except perhaps geographies. Portrait pictures were very popular, especially of war heroes, generals, and the like. In general, concern with economic, social or cultural matters was ignored in American history books.[23] The great weakness of these books was that, even as they later came to be written better, they remained a melange of listed facts and dates, with occasional narrative material interspersed between.

As a general rule, the authors ignored the development of American culture, social classes, labor, cities, and other non-political or non-military events. In these early histories, moreover, immigrants, Jews, and Asians were never even mentioned. The culture of the United States was Christian Protestant and history was written from that point of view. God appeared as the final and primary moving cause in all history. Religious toleration was always advocated, but generally in very abstract terms. Textbooks were full of comments about the terrible persecution of the English nonconformists, but almost nothing was said about the Puritans' lack of religious tolerance. Emphasis was placed upon our Puritan, New England heritage; much less was written concerning Spanish and French missionaries (who were Catholic). These facts are not **too** surprising when one considers that most history books were written by residents of New England. In fact, in books before the Civil War, anti-Catholicism was a prevalent theme. This began to be muted after the 1870's. Our studies showed less and less emphasis upon religion as we moved into the twentieth century and much more discussion of race. Nevertheless, the Christian bias was preserved in almost all texts. Typical of such attitudes was this statement: "There is no estabished religion in the United States. Every man worships God according to the dictates of his own conscience. But Christianity is the basis of the government and institutions, and public opinion is enlisted in its favor."[24]

In summary

In generalizing about the textbooks of the early nineteenth century, certain ideas persisted in almost all writing and teaching. Christian ethics and God permeated everything used in the schools. God was the fount of love and mercy, and the child must obey His laws as revealed in His Scriptures. Death was punishment for evil, but those who were good would receive salvation and release and mercy. Only Christianity preached true virtue, and only where the Christian religion dominated was progress possible, and civilization and morality able to flourish.

> Christianity is the only true religion. It is found in its truth and purity only where it is derived from divine revelation. This was given to our first parents, and again to Noah.
> . . .It was renewed in the Mosaic or Jewish religion, and was developed in its perfect form in the Christian religion.[25]

These were the texts used even as late as the period of the 1890's in which our detailed study began. Because of the conservatism of the period, we were not surprised to find that many changed very slowly. By the beginning of the twentieth century, however, the influence of John Dewey and other Progressives became increasingly pervasive, and many of his precepts are still found in today's textbooks. Therefore, we followed our examination of the textbooks of 1890-1920 with an extensive study of contemporary elementary texts and related materials in order to discover how or if educators' perceptions of ethnic minorities and intergroup relationships have changed. The comparison of the two sets of data did, indeed, reveal changes in public attitudes that are reflected in the instructional materials produced half a century later.

The importance and influence of the teacher in the classroom remained paramount. Even when the material remained biased, ethnocentric, and misapplied, his/her attitude, personality and sympathy could obviate all the weaknesses of the curricula. Evaluating the teacher's effectiveness in the past is at best a difficult task, but reminiscences such as this one of a young Chinese college student in the 1920's was an example of teacher rapport and success.

> The reason why I wanted to be teacher was because I looked up to a teacher as one who was very superior to me and somehow I idealized her. One is the teacher who taught my first grade in the English school. She taught the pupils well, encouraged us to the limit, helped us a great deal, sympathized with us, and she always seemed to us as if our mother was teaching us.[26]

The teacher was also influenced and to some degree directed by the changing precepts and goals in education. The teacher's manuals and editions we examined illustrated the ways in which educators themselves have adjusted to the changing mores of three decades.

NOTES

1. R. M. Elson, GUARDIANS OF TRADITION (Lincoln: Univ. of Nebraska Press, 1964), p. 4.

2. Philadelphia Public Schools, MANUAL OF THE GRADED COURSE OF INSTRUCTION IN THE PRIMARY SCHOOLS (Philadelphia: 1884), p. 64.

3. c. f. for a description of early geographies, Ralph H. Brown, "The American Geographies of Jedidiah Morse," ANNALS OF THE ASSOCIATION OF AMERICAN GEOGRAPHERS, 31, No. 3 (September, 1941), 145-267; Charles Carpenter, HISTORY OF AMERICAN TEXTBOOKS (Philadelphia: Univ. of Pennsylvania Press, 1963), pp. 265-70; Tyler Kepner, "The Influence of the Textbook upon Method," YEARBOOK OF NATIONAL COUNCIL FOR SOCIAL STUDIES, Fifth Yearbook (Philadelphia, 1935), 146-155.

4. John Frost, HISTORY OF THE UNITED STATES FOR THE USE OF COMMON SCHOOLS (Philadelphia: Biddle, 1837); bishop Davenport, HISTORY OF THE UNITED STATES TO BE COMMITTED TO MEMORY (Philadelphia, 1852).

5. Philadelphia Public Schools, MANUAL OF THE GRADED COURSE OF INSTRUCTION IN THE GRAMMAR SCHOOLS (Philadelphia, 1887), pp. 29-30; Kepner, pp. 157-63.

6. Altoona, COURSE OF STUDY (Altoona, Pa., 1907), p. 32.

7. Joseph M. Rice, THE PUBLIC SCHOOL SYSTEM OF THE UNITED STATES (New York: Century, 1893), pp. 14-38, 153.

8. Alfred L. Hall-Quest, THE TEXTBOOK (New York: Macmillan, 1920), p. 7.

9. Elson, p. 41.

10. Report of the Committee on the Study of Teaching in Intergroup Relations, INTERGROUP RELATIONS IN TEACHING MATERIALS: A SURVEY AND APPRAISAL (Washington, D.C. American Council on Education, 1949), p. 13.

11. Hall-Quest, pp. 82-83.

12. L. B. Monroe, FIFTH READER (Boston, 1871), p. ii.

13. Elson, p. 4; Lyman Cobb, NORTH AMERICAN READER (New York, 1835).

14. John A. Nietz, OLD TEXTBOOKS (Pittsburgh: Univ. of Pittsburgh Press, 1961), pp. 74-79.

15. Carpenter, pp. 85-87.

16. Harvey C. Minnich, WILLIAM HOLMES MCGUFFEY AND HIS READERS (New York: American Book Co., 1936), pp. 89-109.

17. Carpenter, pp. 85-87.

18. Charles Kingsley, THE HEROES OR THE GREEK FAIRY TALES (Boston, 1894), pp. xii-xiii; S. A. Edwards, A HAND-BOOK OF MYTHOLOGY FOR USE OF SCHOOLS AND ACADEMIES (Philadelphia: Eldridge & Brother, 1883), expresses the same ideas.

19. Carpenter, pp. 262-68.

20. Elson, pp. 181-87.

21. Augustus S. Mitchell, A SYSTEM OF MODERN GEOGRAPHY (1848, rpt. Philadelphia: E.A. Butler and Co., 1864), p. 207.

22. Carpenter, p. 268.

23. Nietz, pp. 268-69.

24. Elson, p. 58.

25. **Ibid.**

26. William C. Smith, THE SECOND GENERATION ORIENTAL IN AMERICA (Honolulu: R & E Research Associates, 1927), p. 17.

CHAPTER FIVE

THE INFLUENCE OF TEXTBOOKS

DURING THE GREAT IMMIGRATION PERIOD

Inasmuch as textbooks were (and are) second in significance only to the teacher as an educational force in the schools, the ways in which they were selected should have had great importance three generations ago. At that critical period of expanded immigration, however, textbook selection was more often based on an author's prestige (as a scholar more than as a textbook writer), the publisher's prestige, the efficiency of the publisher's sales force, the general appearance of the book (as in judging a book by its cover), wide adoption of a given text, and the book's cost.[1] Teachers were rarely consulted about the books they were to use. Little attention was paid apparently to either the degree to which the text content met the need for which it was intended or the quality of book production. Even less attention was paid to the question of whether the book would appeal to its users -- the students. Indeed, it was not unknown for publishers' salesmen to offer what amounted to bribes to the official responsible for choosing texts.

Shortly after the end of the first World War, it was urged that a new approach be taken. Each potential text was to be carefully examined in terms of the focus of its content, accuracy of content, balance of viewpoints, and the quality of its suggestions for teachers. As Maxwell wrote, a text ". . .should be selected wholly upon the worth of the book in the particular situation for which it is chosen, irrespective of prestige of publisher, author, wide use of the book, cost, etc."[2]

By the early 1920's, detailed "scorecards" for textbooks had been introduced to meet this call. Otis described one such scorecard. Of the total 1000 possible points, 110 were allotted to "local adaptability," 400 to subject matter, 120 to arrangement and organization, 170 to aids to instruction and study, 150 to mechanical features (book production), and only 50 to special features (authorship, publisher, preface, and publication date). Each of these categories had several items subsumed under it. For example, under subject matter, 65 points were tied to "child experience" (interests of the child, recognition of the play instinct, growth factor), and another 65 to "moral-civic values" (does not encourage prejudice, promotes loyalty and Americanism).[3] Another scorecard of that time listed the factor of interest, factor of comprehension, method of study illustrated, permanent value of the content, mechanical construction, plan and organization, and suggested helps to teachers.[4]

Two items are noteworthy with respect to these scorecards. First, the growing influence of progressive education was apparent in the inclusion of "interest to the children." One educator went so far as to note under "content" that, in geographies, "The children from a school in a foreign section of the United States will need to study Europe or the home of their ancestors from a different point of view than will the children of American parentage."[5] Second, there was a defensive attitude about the caliber of available teachers and the consequent concern with the quality of textbooks.

> We must recognize that our teachers are not as well prepared professionally as the teachers of some of the highly developed countries of Europe. With a poorly prepared corps of teachers, probably the only hope of improving instruction is by placing in the hands of the children the best textbook possible. The success or failure of our educational theories and methods in this country is largely determined by the type of textbooks used in the schools. The poorer the teacher, the better the textbooks need to be.[6]

This was not a point of view universally held, however. Another educator pointed out that "Good books cannot take the place of poorly prepared teachers. The teacher is, and always will, the most vital factor in the teaching process."[7]

With knowledge of this background of textbook selection criteria, or lack of them, at the end of the great immigration period, it was somewhat easier to comprehend the reasons for the variety of readers and history texts used during that period. The surprising fact is that these early texts were reissued through several editions with little modification, and continued to be adopted by school systems even into the 1920's, despite the changing attitudes toward text selection expressed in the professional literature. Until fifteen or twenty years ago, the comment was often made that it took as much as fifty years for new concepts to filter down from the educational scholars to the classrooms. Since the ideas of the Progressives had been published by 1900, let us see if this was the case with the textbooks used from 1890 to 1920.

Readers

Our search for ideas contained in the old readers encompassed readers and supplements that were published in the period 1864-1920 and used in the 1890-1920 period. Not all of them were graded, and few were part of multi-grade series such as we see today. In general, the level of reading taught even at the primer level was considerably higher than what is seen in contemporary readers. As for professional preparation, the teaching of reading was often included in a comprehensive "methods" text or "teacher's manual" rather than in a separate volume.

Purposes of the readers. At the turn of the century, reading and literature were considered the principal means by which children were introduced to their world, its values and its morality. Stories captured children's imaginations, gave form and focus to their first impressions, and were one of the earliest ways that stereotypes were created. Teachers and educators at the end of the nineteenth century perceived their function in teaching literature in these terms. Educators complained, however, that while an appreciation of the meaning and beauty of literature was the requisite for the successful teacher of reading, "in many parts of the country there are a surprising number who are called upon to teach with scarcely more than an elementary training in literature."[8] Furthermore, since the teachers were limited in both perspective and education, it rarely occurred to them to worry about whether their teaching created or stimulated prejudice.

Pedagogues perceived their function in teaching literature as one method of renewing and perpetuating moral and civic truths. A report of the Massachusetts Teachers' Association Committee of 1888 stressed the significance of literature in life: "Many a man owes a large measure of his success to some inspiring novel or essay, which first gave life to his feeble aspirations, and has exerted a healthful and elevating influence over his whole being."[9] A teacher's manual in Philadelphia stated that:

Teachers should frequently read to their divisions short, entertaining narratives, and make them the subject of familiar and instructive conversations with their pupils. So, also in lessons on animals, trees, and all works of nature, opportunities should be constantly improved to show the wisdom, power, and goodness of the Creator, and to inculcate the reverence that is due to Him, and a sense of dependence upon Him.[10]

Another manual suggested that

Pupils should commit some beautiful memory gem each week. Bring the pupils into fellowship with noble thoughts beautifully expressed and thus sow in their minds seed that will bear fruit in better English and taste for better reading and establish in thought higher ideals.[11]

In the various courses of study, teachers' guides, and the selection of books, there was at no time any interest or understanding expressed for the sensitivity or the needs of the immigrant children. None of the readers were selected with any ideal of teaching diversity or creativity. Indeed, the opposite was true.

It is not by direct moralizing that we best teach morals, but by incorporating into our courses of study and school activities those race materials and life processes which are in themselves the best expression and realization of moral conduct. . . We recommend the rich collection of race ethics and experience of the school course . . . as first enlarging and strengthening of their own characters, and second in equipping them with ample resources for influencing the development of the young.[12]

Thus, at the turn of the century, the tradition of education was permeated with the concept that schools were the vehicles of ethical training of the young. This goal remained a prevalent force in many school systems for decades, despite the fact that the progressive ideas of John Dewey were gradually being accepted at some of the teachers' colleges.

Virtues of the readers. From the Civil War to the 1890's, readers had been changed very little. Compilers were obsessed with creating reading skills that impart moral truths. For this reason, the McGuffey readers found enthusiastic acceptance, especially in rural areas of the United States (notably Ohio, Indiana, Illinois, Missouri, Michigan, Minnesota, Wisconsin, and Iowa). They attained the largest

sale and the widest distribution of any series that had yet been produced in America.[13] They taught the lessons of industry, thrift,
economy, kindness, generosity, courage, and duty. That the stories
were simplistic to the extreme did not matter, as long as they were
well written and conveyed the message. Tales contradicted the
reality of the children's experience, but that did not seem to disturb
parents, teachers, or even the children themselves.

Honesty was one of the lessons stressed in McGuffey's readers, but
honesty was always related to property. For example, a chimney
sweep, during the course of his work, was tempted to steal a watch.
He resisted the urge and was rewarded by being adopted by his em-
ployer. A boy broke a window while throwing snowballs. He had
been given a dollar as a gift, and though tempted to buy himself
a toy, he resisted the impulse and instead went to the owner of the
house with the broken window and offered to pay for the damage.
The owner was so moved by the boy's honesty that he gave him back
that dollar plus another. Laziness was excoriated in the story of
"Lazy Ned." Here was a boy so lackadaisical that, although he loved
to sled, he did not do so because he hated to climb up the hills. He
did not complete his homework and so had to leave school. Finally,
because he was lazy, he did not take care of the money his father
had left him, became penniless, and forced to beg for bread. The
moral of the story was quite clear.

Patriotism was extolled, and the traits of the founding fathers were
painted in the most glowing terms: George Washington was

> free from envy . . . If he had one passion more powerful than
> another, it was love of his country. . . First in war, first in
> peace, and first in the hearts of his countrymen, he was second
> to none in humble and endearing scenes of private life. Pious,
> just, humane, temperate, sincere, uniform, dignified, and com-
> manding, his example was edifying to all around him. . .[14]

No wonder generations of school children thought Washington was
a dull and wooden figure of history.

Gradually McGuffey's readers were supplanted (about the turn of
the century), particularly in urban sections, and new compilations
became popular. Readers were beginning to change. They had gradu-
ated from being a collection of secular material chosen at random
to being a series of **graded** readers, the aim of which was to instill

a combination of moral lessons and reading skills. Among the goals of the educators were to create school readers that

> . . .should not become the general encyclopedia for the other subjects of the curriculum -- nor the dredge of any one of them, it has its own message to bear and its own lessons to teach. Random selections, even of the highest intrinsic worth, will not accomplish this.[15]

The influence of progressive ideas also produced a whole range of supplementary reading books that were added to the reading series. The main stress, however, was to be placed on the introduction of good, classic literature and poetry. Many of the titles that were selected because of their moral and ethical content were delightful and enjoyable stories, hopefully still read by today's generation of children.

Even if the tales did not have intrinsic moral values, the teachers were still supposed to derive lessons from the stories. One book designed for the third or fourth grade was about ODYSSEUS, THE HERO OF ITHACA. The author explained:

> In no other works do children find the grand and noble traits in human life so faithfully and charmingly depicted as in Homer. Here all the domestic, civic, and religious virtues of the people are marvelously brought to life. . . The American can say that the child whose patriotism is kindled by the Homeric fire will the more gladly respond to the ideals set forth in the History of Columbus or Washington.[16]

In the early grades, oral reading and story telling introduced children to the nursery rhymes and jingles, such as the Old Woman and Her Pig, Little Red Riding Hood, Hiawatha, Cinderella, other fairy tales, and Aesop's Fables.[17] Mythology and folklore were found in increasing abundance in the readers, while the sectarian religious content diminished.[18] Reading aloud from good literature was also started in the early grades. "Memory gems" were chosen from the classics and assigned for memorization. Teachers werre urged to "convert their pupils to book lovers."[19]

As the children mastered the first primers, the stories remained simple, centered on nature, and included short rhymes and easy fairy tales. As the pupil learned more vocabulary, he was introduced to what could be considered the English and American classics: selections from Longfellow, Defoe, Dickens, Bryant, et al. Greek mythology, Norse legends, and many Bible stories were also included in the readers. Norton's HEARTS OF OAK was a reading series (six volumes) that illustrated this principle particularly well. The collection was devoted exclusively to literature. In fact, there was not one illustration in any of the books. The first readers consisted entirely of nursery rhymes, jingles, and Mother Goose, and then continued on to fables, myths, literature, and poetry. The series editor noted that literature "is one of the most efficient means of education of moral sentiment as well as the intelligence."[20]

The Bible as both literature and a source of moral teaching was used extensively by the teacher, and the tales from it were found frequently in these readers. The sessions of the National Education Association between 1857 and 1906 stressed ethical teachings as essential to the molding of children's character and for the inculcation of citizenship and patriotism. The Bible was hailed as a prime source of such teachings. In addition, association members felt that its mastery was necessary to understand properly all other literary forms.[21] It was not surprising, therefore, to discover Bible stories scattered throughout the readers that were then used to illustrate various moral precepts or as examples of good poetry. This practice created problems for Jewish children, especially those from an orthodox environment. It proved most disturbing for these children when the stories were illustrated or taught by the teachers in a sectarian fashion. This was particularly true in the presentations of the religious holidays of Easter and Christmas. Although the readers generally included Old Testament tales, sometimes they included a few from the New Testament, most often the Parables or the Sermon on the Mount. The relevance of these passages to the lives of non-Christian and/or Asian children is even more questionable, other than for the purpose of "Americanizing" all immigrants.

A book called STORIES OF OLDEN TIMES by Johannot that was highly recommended in many of the curriculum guides, reflected prevailing teacher attitudes. Designed for the fifth grade and above, the author stated that his purpose was to teach the principles of liberty and humanity.

> In the traditional stories and the truer records which follow, the pupil will see the play of the same emotions and passions, which actuate men at the present time and the careers of the great conquerors, Frederic and Napoleon, differ little essentially

from those of Alexander and Caesar. Tyranny remains the same forever, encroaching upon human liberty (and) limiting the field of human conduct.[22]

These stories were primarily about great heroes of history, and included one Bible tale and a story taken from Jewish history. Neither was identified as such, but they were selected to illustrate man's quest for liberty: the first was the story of Sennacherib (Kings, II), and the other was the story of Judas Maccabeus, characterized by the editor as the "Hebrew William Tell."

Among the supplementary materials, the popularity of the Kingsley edition of Greek mythology, first printed in 1853, continued unabated well into the twentieth century.[23] Another popular supplementary reader, designed also for the fifth grade, was a collection of British stories, the purpose of which was to instill a respect and love for English literature, a commendable goal. The book included excerpts from Addison, Lamb, Scott, Thackerey, and others. The choice of stories must have been edifying for the teacher, but for ten or twelve year old youngsters, they must have seem very dull, even though well written. We wonder how much children enjoyed this book or benefited from it! An examination of some of the supplementary readings suggested by teachers' guides and curriculum studies indicated, however, that many were chosen that had interest as well as literary value. One suggested course of study that "contained the moral ideas of the race" included these titles: Longfellow's HIAWATHA, Defoe's ROBINSON CRUSOE, Aesop's FABLES, Plutarch's LIVES, Scott's MARMION, Webster's SPEECHES, Franklin's AUTOBIOGRAPHY, Scudder's LIFE OF WASHINGTON, Hosmer's LIFE OF SAMUEL ADAMS, Hawthorne's GRANDFATHER'S CHAIR, Lamartine's LIFE OF COLUMBUS, Parkman's MONTCALM AND WOLFE, Coffin's BOYS OF 1776, Scott's TALES OF A GRANDFATHER, Stevenson's TREASURE ISLAND, Hale's MAN WITHOUT A COUNTRY, Cooper's LAST OF THE MOHICANS, Alcott's LITTLE WOMEN and LITTLE MEN, Pyle's ADVENTURES OF ROBIN HOOD, Barrie's PETER PAN, and Irving's RIP VAN WINKLE.[24]

The main objective of these readers and supplements was to present to the children the very best in literature. The books did, indeed, do just that. Sometimes mediocre stories were included, but on the whole, the quality was very high. On the other hand, many of the works were uninteresting and irrelevant to the children and perhaps beyond the understanding of the slower students. There was, in this period, little grasp of what children enjoyed reading and few scientific attempts to grade the selections according to the ages and interests of the students.

Emergence of nationalized texts. As we indicated previously, the regional bias and emphasis that had dominated the nation prior to and during the Civil War gradually began to disappear after peace came. The formal end of sectionalism coincided with the emerging centralization of government and the increased pace of industrialization that also led to growing nationalism, and a standardization of taste, culture, and fashion. The publishing industry and American education were also affected by these changes. Some regions, such as the South, had been particularly active in publishing works that were pertinent to their own particulary politics and prejudices. This was especially true in the writing of history textbooks. Even in the publication of readers, however, Southern companies had managed to produce their own versions prior to and during the war. For example, THE FIRST READER FOR SOUTHERN SCHOOLS was published in Raleigh, N.C., in 1864; Chaudron published a series of readers in Mobile, Alabama, also in 1864; Richard Smith wrote a text entitled THE CONFEDERATE FIRST READER (Richmond, Va., 1864); and Richard Stirling's OUR OWN FIRST READER FOR THE USE OF SCHOOLS AND FAMILIES (Greensboro, N.C., 1861-1864) was quite popular. These readers were used long after their publication dates, and did not differ significantly, except for their regional titles and orientation, from others used in the rest of the nation. When these readers were replaced, the new texts were those being used elsewhere in the country.

The publishing industry, like its counterparts in other fields, became great interstate or national businesses, and gradually the smaller companies had difficulty competing with the larger ones, such as Ginn, D.C. Heath, Lippincott, American Book Company, and Macmillan, that soon dominated the publishing market. Another factor that aided the growth of the larger companies was the increased willingness, in many areas, of school boards to provide free textbooks for the use of their students. As agents and salesmen discovered lucrative new markets, they had to learn to pander not only to the interests of politicians who influenced school boards, but they also had to conform to local prejudices, tastes, and desires if they were to convince the local authorities to purchase their wares. The result was that all textbook writers began to avoid any references that could be construed as controversial. The end products tended to become bland, homogeneous works that promoted a national ethnocentrism without regional, sectional, class, occupational, or racial

differences. The movement toward the mass produced and standard-
ized stereotypes of our society, popularly ascribed today to the influence
of the visual media, had its beginnings in the mass produced textbooks
that became so widely used after the Civil War.

> . . .The texts did serve as a warehouse for contemporary "truths"
> and as a source of authority for both teachers and parents.
> They thus performed a powerful and useful function, for whatever
> the faults of rote memorization, the intermingled facts and
> fancies contained in the early text books became fixed in the
> national consciousness.[25]

Some of the most noteworthy and widely used readers at the turn
of the century are listed below. Despite their early publication
dates, they were found in the schools three or more decades later.
One book, THE EUGENE FIELD READER, was published in 1905
and was still in use in a Honolulu school in 1940!

Baldwin's SCHOOL READING BY GRADES (1897) included fairy
tales and stories conveying moral lessons. At the more advanced
reading levels, there were many stories based on historical and biographical themes with less emphasis on literature. The sixth reader
included only English writers and those of the "classics."[27] The
SILVER-BURDETT READERS of 1902 included only British and
American authors.[28] The JONES READERS that did contain an
occasional Asian myth had been adopted by both the state of Texas
and the city of Chicago.[29] The CYR READERS were the "best sellers"
among the schools in the United States. They were also translated
into Spanish and sold in South America.[30] The content in the HEART
OF OAK books, edited by Charles Eliot Norton, was comprised of
more than three-fifths poetry, as well as fine literary selections.[31]
The BEACON READERS sold over a half-million copies.[32] Other
series were similar; some, however, stressed either nature themes
or moral lessons. These were THE NEW ENGLAND PRIMER, the
NEW FRANKLIN READERS, the SWINTON SERIES, NEW EDUCATION
READERS, and the Heath Series.[33]

The reading texts, of which the above are a small sample, did very
liittle to broaden the children's horizons or to introduce them to
new ideas or cultures. Supplementary readings, as we have indicated,
were largely literary, and there were others whose titles were found
on many suggested bibliographies. These books similarly did little
to bring in knowledge of other lands and civilizations. The following
titles suggest the nature of their offerings: J. Baldwin, FOUR GREAT

AMERICANS (1896); Mowry and Mowry, AMERICAN INVENTIONS AND INVENTORS (1900); W. F. Gordy, STORIES OF AMERICAN EXPLORERS (1908); A. M. Earles, CHILD-LIFE IN COLONIAL DAYS (1899); August Larned, OLD TALES RETOLD FROM GRECIAN MYTHOLOGY (1876); G. C. Eggleston, CAPTAIN SAM OR THE BOY SCOUTS OF 1814 (1876). (This was the story of Andrew Jackson's military campaigns.) Also read were F. Burnett's LITTLE LORD FAUNTLEROY (1894), G. Towle's HEROES AND MARTYRS OF INVENTION (1890), THE CHILDREN'S RED BOOKS (1908) -- a twelve volume series of fairy tales, and Helen Nicolay's biographies of American heroes.

There were, however, some rare exceptions. One was a marvelous little book of CHINESE FABLES AND FOLK STORIES that included charming real life tales of China's culture and civilization.[34] Another was THE FIRE-FLY'S LOVERS and OTHER FAIRY TALES. These stories were traditional legends of Japan that bore little resemblance to reality except in the names and illustrations.[35] Rudyard Kipling's THE JUNGLE BOOK did, indeed, portray other cultures, although the Western version of civilization was shown as superior. Another book by a popular author, A. A. Guerber, was entitled THE STORY OF THE CHOSEN PEOPLE. The title might lead one to thing that it was a series of stories concerning Jewish history; it was not that at all. The book was a collection of Old Testament tales -- the one exception being the story of Esther.[36]

The main emphasis of the entire reading program in the public schools between 1890 and 1910 was placed upon literary content. As noted, with few exceptions, there was no mention of other cultures in the nationalized readers. The uniformity of the illustrations, namely pictures of lovely blue-eyed boys and girls living in rural or suburban middle-class homes, served to stamp indelibly the image of "the American" in the minds of the children.

Early 20th century readers. Readers that were sold widely after 1910 did not differ radically from the older ones just described. In fact, frequently the content was almost the same, but there was a sharp divergence in goals. Less interest was expressed in teaching morality; the concerns had become more secular. The compilers were occupied with the task of inculcating patriotic and social conformity rather than religious or ethical beliefs. However, American social ideals still stressed ethical behavior. The "good" social values remained the same: perseverance, patriotism, honesty, love, beauty. LIterature was to acquaint the pupil with other American ideals as well: the dignity of work, belief in the equality of opportunity, and the notion that merit, not birth, determined an individual's worth. Americans were self-reliant, tolerant, and supported the twin goals of freedom and responsibility. These were values fully supported by both the Asian and Jewish immigrants.

Reading was, obviously, one of the most significant subjects taught.

One of the important problems before the schools consists not only in leading children to recognize America's past achievements, but also in bringing these to bear directly and indirectly upon the moulding of the thought, feeling, and action of every pupil.[37]

Moreover, the new emphasis was placed on a more subtle teaching of these virtues. Didactic materials, as in the formerly blatant morality tales, were to be avoided. "The growth oᶠ ideals comes through experience. Readers are an avenue through which the individual may experience the highest aspirations and deepest struggles of the soul, in the past and in the present."[38]

A book of poetry for the fifth grade included most of the selections of the ealier books; Longfellow, Helen Hunt Jackson, Browning, Bryant, and others, plus many new poems of "fancy and humor." Its avowed purpose was the

development of standards of taste and in the training of the capacity of appreciate and enjoy all forms of art. The teacher is not by any means to impose her aesthetic judgements and responses upon the minds of her pupils. Rather will she by judicious preparation and presentation strive to awaken the joy of spontaneous comprehension and emotional insight in their souls and hearts.[39]

The result was that the newer readers included a greater variety of stories, although they continued to stress British and American literature.

Changing times have always brought about changing goals. Dewey's disciples, who were concerned with preparing children for a work world and "Americanizing" immigrant children, stressed skills. "The way to Americanize all the various races of children growing up in this country is to let them live again the outstanding typical experience of the men and women who have built American society"[40] Teacher trainers became interested in **how** to teach and **how** children learn. Research was widespread, and techniques of pedogogy stressed the need to stimulate and interest children.

> In literature, in music, and in art the development in power of appreciation is undoubtedly from the simpler, cruder forms to those which we as adults consider the higher or nobler forms of expression. Mother Goose, the rhymes of Stevenson, of Field, or of Riley, may be the beginning of the enjoyment of literature which finds expression in the reading and in the possession of the greatest literature of the English language.[41]

As educators contemplated the relationship of experience to the learning process, they added more criteria to their choice of selections.

> Literature must be suitable. It must be properly graded... All material in the elementary grades where the mastery of the mechanics of reading is a major consideration, has been scientifically measured to determine the relative reading difficulty to be overcome.[42]

An editor of a series of readers said she had been "guided by her study of the most authoritative and up-to-date reports, investigations, courses of study, and surveys."[43] The new criteria in the selection of material now had as much emphasis as the previous concern for the learning of literature: these were the desire to stimulate and interest the children in reading, and to classify and grade the stories appropriately for the comparable age and class level of the children.

Teachers' editions emphasized the introduction of supplementary experience that would illustrate the stories. For instance, nature stories should be accompanied by classroom exhibits of flowers, animals, and trees that were in the stories. Interdisciplinary studies were suggested, and biography and fiction were added to lists that were interchanged in the history, geography, and reading lessons. Teachers were instructed, then as now, to provide a background or an explanation of each selection that was read in class. Lincoln's GETTYSBURG ADDRESS, one of the pieces in a fifth grade reader, necessitated the instructor's narration of the details of the Civil War, details of the battle of Gettysburg, and the reason for Lincoln's speech. Then it was necessary for the teacher to explain the meaning and even some of the vocabulary itself.[44]

Suggestions were also made in the teacher's edition to include community resources to enhance the child's learning. Visits to the police station, firehouse, stores, museums, and other local institutions were recommended. Of the 56 teachers' guides that we examined, only two suggested that the urban environment provided an excellent laboratory for the study of various cultures and immigrant groups. In one it was said that "The topic of migrations of peoples is very visible in the vicinity of the home of almost any child in America and close at hand study can be made of different cultures."[45] A second teachers' text suggested a whole lesson plan for the topic of "Immigration, one of the aspects of American life," to be used in the eighth grade. Among the aspects of the topic suggested for study was the condition of "City Congestion." And in the outline guide, the following background material was given to the teachers:

Old immigration more like own in language, religion, and ideals of government; many skilled workers. As a rule they do not live in separate groups. New immigration has made too little progress in education and representative government. The great majority are still unskilled workers. Very often they are clannish. It is important for the new immigrants to be taught. They are, for the most part, ignorant. They are mostly unskilled.

The guide further listed these books: THE AUTOBIOGRAPHY OF EDWARD BOK, Antin's THE PROMISED LAND, Steiner's OUR OLD WORLD BACKGROUND, and Riis' HOW THE OTHER HALF LIVES.[46] How the instructor handled this subject in the classroom without affecting the feelings of her immigrant students required more sensitivity than we suspect the average teacher possessed, with her limited resources.

Despite the increasing secularism of the schools and their texts, Bible stories continued to be included as "literature." One book, recommended as a source for oral reading, included Psalms 90, 103, the "Tale of the Prodigal Son," and the "Sermon on the Mount."[47] Another book used in some schools, though not the most popular, had been originally compiled for use in the YMCAs as part of their Americanization program. It contained mostly Bible stories from both the Old and New Testaments. Its rationale for the selection of these tales was based on the following idea:

In the United States of America, a nation built most definitely on religious foundations, it is due to prospective citizens that efforts to help them qualify for citizenship should include the communication of some knowledge of that religious consciousness which is a fundamental part of the heritage of our people.[48]

Emphasis continued to be placed on the teaching of stories of the holidays. The national festivals commemorated patriotic sentiments, and the religious fetes were celebrated joyfully in the classroom. As long as the holidays were introduced as secular occasions, no offense could be felt by non-Christians. Indeed, the stories in most of the readers **were** generally secular. "Crachit's Christmas Dinner" from Dickens or Clement Moore's "Night Before Christmas" were standard inclusions in the compilations. The story of Peter Rabbit was included to celebrate Easter or "resurrection" day as it was sometimes called. In addition, collections of Christmas or holiday stories were also used, both for silent and for oral reading. J. C. Dier's THE CHILDREN'S BOOK OF CHRISTMAS (Macmillan, 1911) was reprinted in 1925 and included some of the gospel stories. It also included tales of a Russian Christmas, a Siberian one, and one taken from Riis' book. It was beautifully illustrated. Frances Jenkins Olcott's GOOD STORIES FOR GREAT HOLIDAYS (Houghton Mifflin, 1914) ws reprinted in 1942. The stories were drawn from classic sources such as Ovid and Lucian. Other tales were from Hawthorne, Dickens, Anderson, and Grimm. the tales in Carolyn Sherwin Bailey's STORIES FOR EVERY HOLIDAY (Abingdon Press, 1918) were secular in tone, including Christmas and Easter. The emphasis was Western European in pictures and stories.

But, it was the teachers who determined **how** religious holidays were handled. Manuals and guides insisted that the teaching of holidays was very important. They suggested that the observance be very festive and special. Some guides suggested supplementing readers by reading or narrating the New Testament gospels, and thus instructing the children in the religious significance of the holiday. Others suggested that Christmas stories, chosen by the teacher, be read and recited, that a Christmas tree be decorated in class, and that pictures be hung honoring the holidays. Older children were to read special collections of Christmas stories and poems and, of course, sing the carols. "These exercises do not partake so much of the character of instruction as of entertainment and joyful festivity."[49]

If the readers and teachers showed little sensitivity toward the Jewish children's feelings about the religious aspects of holidays, an even greater violation of good taste and empathy was revealed by the inclusion of Shakespeare's MERCHANT OF VENICE as required reading in the eighth grade.[50] Shylock's speech (Act III, sc. 1) was considered to be a fine expression of emotion. Teachers were told that the proper analysis of this speech should illustrate how Shakespeare used it to "bring out his (Shylock's) peculiar character."[51] That the Shylock stereotype or the anti-semitic slurs might be offensive to Jewish children was never even considered at all. A Protestant, writing years later of his experiences in the Boston Latin school, commented on his English class. The majority of class members were Jewish. He wrote that his (non-Jewish) group, about 12 boys, "hated the Jews because they worked hard, because they were so relentlessly competitive, because their one thought was to force themselves ahead. . ." The curriculum, which was rigid in the eighth grade, included Burke's SPEECH ON CONCILIATION WITH THE COLONIES, THE DESERTED VILLAGE, and THE MERCHANT OF VENICE. For the latter, ". . .We read it scene by scene, we dissected it, we mapped out the plot and the subplots. . . The Jewish boys seemed impervious, however, just as they did to any of the not-too-veiled slurs coming from any of us." Each of the students took turns in reading the various speeches. Finally a Jewish boy was called upon to recite the famous passage of Shylock's apologia, "I am a Jew. Hath not a Jew eyes,..." and "suddenly to my embarrassed amazement I realized that his voice was trembling."[52]

It is obvious that the readers and supplementary books were oblivious to the needs, problems, or even the existence of urban immigrant groups. Readers were of very high literary quality, but stories that centered on rural or small town life rarely had any impact on or meaning for the city child. A story was related that a prominent educator of the time, G. Stanley Hall, presented the following story in a lecture:

> A class in a Boston school believed the real size of a cow to be the space occupied by its picture in their spelling books. This points a finger at the city child's ordinary ignorance of nature and country surroundings, and we should expect to find this ignorance intensified in the little Jewish children whose lives have been confined within such narrow city boundaries.[53]

Interviews with teachers confirmed Hall's observations. The scholarship of Jewish pupils ". . .is affected, I think by their ignorance of other surroundings than those to which they are habituated."[54] The choice of high quality literature frequently became a handicap also for these children. Not only were the stories and myths irrelevant to their experience, but the language itself must have been more difficult. There seemed to be little concern for compiling readers for children who needed remedial or additional help, or for those who were bilingual. Interviews with teachers revealed this failing. "As a rule, the Jewish children are quick in figures. They are attentive to school work. So many, even of American birth, hear a foreign tongue spoken so that the teaching of language is difficult." Another said quite frankly, "Only for the difficulty in learning English (Jewish children) would compare very favorably with American children."[55]

The readers and the curriculum lacked meaning for these children both in the choice of stories and the stress of middle class virtures (as defined by Protestants), but particularly in their treatment of groups sensitivities. The only mention of the Japanese or the Chinese was in the rare myth that accentuated the quaint and strange. Indeed, the salient fact is that all the readers emphasized western cultural values to the **exclusion** of all others. This attitude persisted with minor modifications until the 1940's. The result of this failure in the curriculum and a general lack of rapport led to school problems for the young. Truancy and drop-outs were common. Children were left behind in the grades, and it was not unusual to find big nine, ten and eleven year olds in the third grade. Many children did not even start school until past the age of seven, and many were absent often because of family problems and illness.[56]

Below are listed some of the more widely bought readers published after 1910 that continued to be used in the public schools into the 1930's and sometimes even later. The NEW BARNES READERS (1916) resembled the older compilations.[57] THE ELSON READERS (1920) included a delightful Japanese story, "Taro the Turtle" in the second grade.[58] In an earlier version of the same readers (1912), Book Three included a Japanese myth.[59] The WINSTON series' (1918) contents were almost the same as the earlier readers. One Chinese myth was included in the fourth grade reader.[60] The Searson and Martin collection included the usual literary selections and the "Lord's Prayer;" however, the fifth grade reader had a Chinese story, "A Bright Chinese Boy," and a charming Japanese tale, "Matsuyama's Mirror." The sixth grade reader concentrated on legends and tales of America. Eighth grade included St. Paul's speeches and also the "Prodigal Son" and Psalm 23.[61] The PETERS AND BRUMBAUGH METHOD READERS (1912) had a definitely progressive point of view and aimed their stories at entertaining children. The content was also middle class in its choice of illustrations of clothes and furniture.[62] STORY HOUR READINGS (1921) was used with other readers to encourage silent reading and to integrate more closely geography and history studies.[63] Mary Stoyell Stimpson's THE

CHILD'S BOOK OF AMERICAN BIOGRAPHY (1915, prt. 1930) represented some of the supplementary material used to enrich the reading programs. The figures in her book were all blonde and blue-eyed, and did not contain one visible immigrant from Eastern or Southern Europe or Asia. Walter Lefferts' NOTED PENNSYLVAN-IANS (1913) similarly ignored all immigrants including Haym Saloman; so did Eva March Tappan's HEROES OF PROGRESS, STORIES OF SUCCESSFUL AMERICANS (1921). However, her book did include Booker T. Washington. Other suggested books were SWISS FAMILY ROBINSON, MAN WITHOUT A COUNTRY, THE JUST-SO STORIES, BEN HUR, IVANHOE, AROUND THE WORLD IN EIGHTY DAYS, THE MILL ON THE FLOSS, ALICE'S ADVENTURES IN WONDER-LAND, TALES OF TROY AND GREECE, and PETERKIN PAPERS.

The readers, through illustrations and stories, created a system of values and a world for children that were all white, rural, small-town, and relatively well-to-do. It was a portrait of a society that revered specific values through its preoccupation with American and British literature. Indeed, much of this was commendable, for children were introduced at a young age to the best of the American literary tradition. Progressive teaching techniques, plus an instructor's sympathy and creativity, might have mitigated some of the alien elements of the stories for immigrant children, and could and did stimulate their interest when used. But as the truancy, drop-out, and retardation figures revealed, for too many the gulf between cultures was never bridged. Elsie Dinsmore, Tom Swift, Frank Merri-well, and Horatio Alger were heroes and heroines of the popular literature that was enjoyed by American children. These stories were distillations of the ideals proposed by the McGuffey readers. Their protagonists were white, middle class, competitive, and achiev-ers either on the playing fields of Yale or in the business world. The precepts in the books were always those of the virtues of the "Protestant ethic": hard work, honesty, and above all, success or victory. Children's popular stories buttressed the prevailing value system (ethnocentric) in a more pleasing and enjoyable fashion. As in the school books, there were no minority groups; there were no class differences; there were no cities; there were no major differ-ences in American life. Perhaps the only exceptions were the cowboy and Indian stories. These were stories that were adventuresome and romantic, largely untrue and certainly as unreal as the fairy tales the children read in the classroom.

As previously stated, the readers showed little or no concern for other cultures, with the exception of "Tales from the Arabian Nights" and occasional Japanese or Chinese legends. In many cases, casual inclusion of Bible and holiday tales was only another affront to Jewish students. Generations of school children were introduced to a sanitized, conformist, British-American world that differed completely from the reality of their daily experience, and that never introduced the students at a young impressionable age to the scope, the variety, the enormous vitality, and inherent values of differing literary traditions that already existed in the United States and other parts of the world. The values transmitted were those of western civilization only. Stress was placed on the traditions and values from the classical heritage and British literature. Future citizens had little knowledge of other cultures and developed many prejudices. Years later, a prominent anthropologist, Hsu, compared Chinese and American children's education and complained,

American school children entertain the idea that the world outside the United States is practically a jungle: China is a land of inscrutable ways and mysterious opium dens, and Africa a "dark continent" inhabited by cannibals and wild animals. Even Europe is a backward place, its only export a decadent culture and its present inhabitants an unprogressive lot whose ancestors stayed behind when their more intelligent and ambitious fellows departed for America. It must be emphasized that in recent years movements have been underway to correct these misimpressions to be found in American textbooks.[64]

What Hsu neglected to mention, of course, was the the Chinese and Japanese taught **their** children that peoples outside their own countries were "barbarians."

Whether Hsu's statement accurately described American texts in the late 1930's and 1940's is doubtful, but there is no question of the parochialism of American schools regarding other peoples and cultures, especially into the 1920's. Whether the prejudice and narrow provincialism observed in the post-World War I period can be attributed only to textbooks and the reading programs of the schools is questionable -- but, on the hand, the public schools had never become a force in the elimination or reduction of prejudice, or in the acknowledgement of the existence of cultural differences, either within the United States, or in the world.

Histories

We noted earlier that the readers used during the 1890-1910 period in most instances omitted reference to the existence of other cultures. Unfortunately, but to be expected, the histories also followed this pattern. Like the readers, the few histories in which other cultures were mentioned contained mostly negative comments. the incidence of positive or even neutral references to minority groups was, by comparison, negligible. The avoidance of controversy and contemporary issues in history texts appeared to publishers to be a necessity. As textbook publication became a major national industry, the tendency was to placate the various pressure groups and to please the widest possible variety of school boards and officials.

American histories. History was included in many courses of study before the Civil War, but it was not then generally required. After the Civil War, the growing nationalism and centralization of the nation saw the beginnings of a movement to promote civic and patriotic sentiments that gradually led to the requirement to study the Constitution of the nation, or to study about the United States as a whole, and often included the advice to study about a particular state and/or municipality. After 1860, 23 states passed legislation making United States history a required subject in the schools. During and immediately after the Civil War, southern states were especially anxious to use the schools as agencies to impart their own point of view, and during Reconstruction, many legislatures, pressured by the military government, used history to ease the intense sectional attitudes fostered during the War. As the country became more nationalistic, the academic organizations began to demonstrate a new and keen awareness of the importance of history as a separate required discipline. In 1876, a committee of the National Education Association recommended U.S. history for elementary schools, and "universal" history and the Constitution of the United States for the high schools.[65] In 1899, a committee of the American Historical Association advised a four years' course in history. The report encouraged continued revision in the history curriculum, and in 1909, a Committee of Eight wrote a curriculum guide for elementary schools that included European history as a prelude to the study of American development.[66]

More states, from 1900 on, insisted on the history requirement until the number grew from 23 to 34 such laws passed. Teachers were encouraged to teach patriotism and civics through history instruction, the celebrations of national holidays, and to put emphasis on reverence for the flag. "Keep continually before you the human element in history. . . . You are under a constant obligation to make the history course for the grades for life to those pupils who never go beyond the grades. . ."[67]

> The teacher should keep constantly in mind that the chief purpose of the instruction of history is to inspire the young with a broad, sound, generous patriotism, and to train them for the right discharge, in due time, of the duties of citizenship. . .Pupils should be taught in our political institutions, the source of freedom, the stability and the Power of the Nation.[68]

Thus history was used in the schools as a tool to propagandize the children. Nations throughout the world have used schools and history to teach their children loyalty to the state. They are taught esteem for the nation, a belief in its enduring sovereignty, its rights as a separate entity demanding their complete and sometimes unquestioning loyalty. History can be employed to teach them that their political system is superior, that through the exploits of their heroes their "race" is that of supermen, their economic productivity is greater, their social values more moral. In short, history can become the tool of economic, social, political, or religious groups who seek to impart their values to the young. Hence it was not an unusual pattern to discover in American educational development constant efforts on the part of various pressure groups to revise texts to teach a pet theory or to support prevalent laws and attitudes.[69]

> Our relations with the peoples of Europe, and the common origins of the civilization of the two continents, makes the history and growth of the civilization of the Aryan race of Europe, vital in importance to every student of history.[70]

Regional histories best illustrate this point. The South used history in its textbooks to teach children that the interests of slave-holders were both just and right. These texts attempted to present the South in a more favorable light and in general to avoid the portrayal of slavery as evil or uneconomic. Southerners agitated for texts that were different from those used in the North. Many of the national publishers were very willing to sell to an available market and were happy to prepare texts for southern use after Reconstruction. Some of these were: Jones, SCHOOL HISTORY OF THE U.S.; Venable, A SCHOOL HISTORY OF THE U.S.; Lee, HISTORY OF U.S.; James and Sanford, AMERICAN HISTORY; Evans, FIRST LESSON IN AMERICAN HISTORY; Estill, BEGINNER'S HISTORY OF OUR COUNTRY; and Mace-Petrie, HISTORY OF THE PEOPLE OF THE U.S.[71]

115

The most notable difference between northern and southern texts was a bias in the southern texts toward a more sympathetic view of the Civil War; stress was placed on the right of sucession and condemnation of Reconstruction. (In other ways, however, the texts resembled those used elsewhere in the nation.) A typical example of regional history was a book by McMaster, written as part of a whole series published by the State of California. The only difference between the California edition and the national edition was that more paragraphs were devoted to the Chinese question in the former as well as a special chapter at the back of the text dealing with the history of the state.[72]

The use of history as propaganda tended to be written on a national scale, extolling the American virtues and patriotism. One such example was a history by Brooks, CENTURY BOOK FOR YOUNG AMERICANS. This text was commissioned by the Sons of the American Revolution. Their avowed purpose was to embed in the minds of young people a more "exalted" patriotism, believing ". . .that the love of country is a lesson of reason not an institution of nature, and that it can be largely stimulated by proper teachings." The volume, therefore, became more civics text than a history book. While not mentioning either Jews or Asians or any specific minorities, it spoke of immigrants, commenting that while everyone was not born in the United States, all -- migrants or not -- have equal opportunity in the United States. "The emigrant in the crowded steerage is coming to the land of liberty full of anticipation and desire. . ."[73]

As seen in Figure 1, only a little more than half of the 122 American histories of the early period were found, in our examination of them, to mention immigrants. Less than 40 percent mentioned Chinese immigrants, despite their important role in the 19th-century economic development. Barely 10 percent of the books mentioned Japanese immigrants, and in only 6.5 percent of the books was reference made to Jewish immigrants. Earlier arrivals were mentioned more frequently, however, in these early histories.

One manual informed teachers that

> . . . history stimulates intelligent patriotism. If the public school is the "melting pot" in which we fuse the diverse and heterogeneous elements abounding in American life, then the study of American history is a most potent flame in this great process.

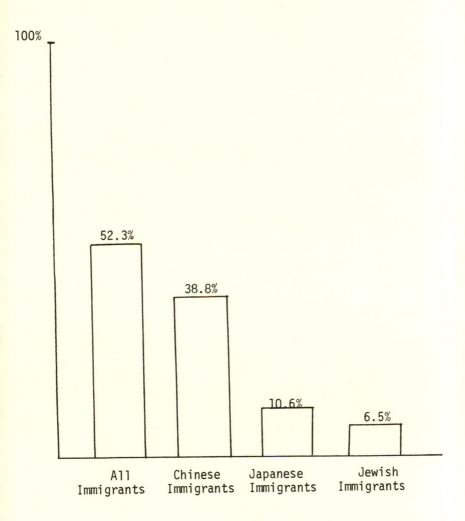

FIGURE 1   Early American Histories:
Mention of Immigrants (N = 122)

. . The little foreigner but recently arrived, who in broken English talks proudly of "what our Pilgrim Fathers have done," has felt the magic of this flame.[74]

History and civics brought to foreign children the only sources of indoctrination of the American traditions in the school system, and thus were very important.[75]

Influenced by John Dewey and stimulated by the scholarly quality of the historical writing, later education manuals urged the continual study of history because it was a valuable tool in the warehouse of instruction. They cited history as a necessary discipline in education -- it inspired judgment and analysis, and it let students reach rational objective observations.

While history kindles patriotism, when it is truthfully presented, it is also the best cure for a narrow provincialism, a provincialism which sees only one side to a question, that dislikes and sneers at all foreigners, that believes the false theory that "one's country is always in the right." It teaches anything history teaches balanced judgment. It is the remedy for the stupid partisanship which crushes independent reasoning and prevents reform.[76]

"History is taught to develop habits of effectually thinking, feeling, and acting with reference to the people, objects, laws, practices, institutions, ideals -- in a word to the important features of our complicated environment."[77]

Most of the early histories, both those written before the 1890's that were still being used in American schoolrooms and those written in the early 1900's, were dreadful. They were merely an unorganized collection of isolated names and dates, and they tended to be strung together with an inadequate narrative. Moreover, they emphasized almost exclusively political and military events. Urban change, labor problems, demographic changes, and cultural developments never existed for these authors. One example of these early texts is William Swinton's SCHOOL HISTORY OF THE UNITED STATES. It was written for younger students, and was simply a collection of numbered paragraphs in which significant names and dates were printed in bold-faced type. Students presumably memorized what the author considered to be essential data. Edward Everett Hale's HISTORY OF THE UNITED STATES was written in a more flowing narrative style and therefore was easier to read, but the emphasis continued to be on political events, dates, and military battles. A text by Edward Ellis, similar to the Hale text, was widely used.[78] Despite what we would consider major deficiencies today, such as poor and tiny print and dull narration, these early texts remained very popular for many years.

Obviously, the early textbooks as well as the later ones that gradually replaced them put a premium value on political campaigns and wars -- Indian, Civil, and Spanish-American. Because of this focus, they gave little time, space or discussion to topics such as immigrants, urbanism, or labor. Even the later texts, although written by historians or school teachers, were much the same. They had better and more profuse illustrations; they were written stylistically with a narrative that moved more fluently and that connected the political and military data in a more interesting and organized account. However, there was still very little mention of Asians, Jews, or other immigrants, and that in only a sentence or two. A typical example of these later texts, and one that was used widely, was the book by Ridpath. The work was divided into topics and written in a disjointed style. Minority groups were never mentioned, except for endless Indian wars. The only notice of immigration was an illustration of newcomers disembarking in New York.[79] A series of histories written by D. H. Montgomery was published by Ginn and Co., and was one of their biggest "sellers."[80] These books were a more literate and polished version of the Ridpath history. The content had a freer flowing, more readable narrative and was far more interesting. They contained many good illustrations, but these books were also primarily political histories, void of multicultural content.

Very gradually textbooks improved in quality as more scholars began to dominate the field of history writing. Authors such as McMaster, Andrews, Channing, Hart, Beard, et. al., expanded the scope of American history as they became sensitive to the broader aspects of history and included topics that encompassed more than political events. Their books evidenced interest in economics, urbanization, the labor movement, and even some of the social and cultural developments of the nineteenth century.

In spite of these improvements, if one judges by the texts, Jews did not play any kind of role in American history. The great migration of Jews to the U.S. began in the 1890's, and although Jews had participated in American life long before that, most of the authors reflected the bias of the Protestant majority and remained uninformed of their existence. Of the 122 American History texts examined, only eight or about 6.5% of the texts acknowledged the existence of Jews in the United States. When reference was made, it usually consisted of a brief statement. For example, "Jews came to Savannah and were given a home in the new colony."[81] That was the only note made in a book of 460 pages. Omissions were often deliberate because Jews were part of the controversy over immigration restrictions. In many cases, however, the authors did not recognize the contributions of Jews to American development, and therefore, simply ignored them.

One exception mentioned that there had been Jewish merchants in the colonies and that the "melting pot" had begun to function early in our history. Jews were also mentioned as a significant factor in the "second wave of immigration," including their role in the garment industry and in the labor movement.[82] The best account of Jews in the United States, in Beard and Beard, states:

> The Jews, then as ever engaged in their age-long battle for religious and economic toleration, found in the American colonies, not complete liberty, but certainly more freedom than they enjoyed in England, France or Spain. The English law did not recognize their right to live in any of the dominions, but owing to the easy-going habits of Americans they were allowed to filter into seaboard towns.

Then the account described the treatment of the Jews in the various colonies.[83] But such accounts were rare indeed!

References to Japan, on the other hand, were somewhat more frequent. Twenty percent mentioned either the opening of Japan or the Russo-Japanese War and the Treaty of Portsmouth. Even in these, the treatment was brief and superficial. In general, the small percentage of textbooks that discussed Japan used the narrative to enhance the prestige and importance of the United States. The United States brought Japan into active communication with the world. The United States was the peace maker, the arbitrator in the Russo-Japanese War. Japan became a great power because she copied American technological feats.

The descriptions of the opening of Japan were similar to the following one:

> Running his cannon mouths out of their portholes, Perry succeeded in persuading Japan to make a treaty permitting Americans

to trade with two of the Japanese ports. This resulted presently in the complete opening of the "hermit country" to the ships of all nations.[84]

A more ethnocentric viewpoint was expressed this way: "A treaty of commerce was made and from that day, Japan, copying American ideals and methods, has advanced until it is now the foremost nation of Asia." The author duly noted the Russo-Japanese War, and concluded with a favorable assessment of Japan because it imitated the United States.[85] A somewhat more sympathetic version was this one:

> . . .Perry led to our friendly but not too gentle knocking at the door of Japan in 1852. That hermit kingdom had received foreigners 250 years before, observed them with intelligent Asiatic eyes for a quarter of a century and then closed its ports firmly against all professing the Christian faith. . . What occured to turn hospitality to such black depths of distrust we can only conjecture. . .[86]

An older text described Japan as an empire of many large islands "occupied by a shrewd but peculiar people, who have always avoided anything to do with other nations."[87]

At the end of the nineteenth century, Japan had not yet become a major power in the Pacific that could threaten us. History books therefore treated Japan as of little importance, with only a reference or two as described. One source book included a description of Perry's reception in Japan, and another included a description of the Japanese coming to Washington. The one was picturesque and quaint; the other was merely descriptive of another important event in the daily recitation of names and dates that were unfortunately the substance of that book's organization.[88]

China was discussed less frequently and even more superficially than Japan. About 14% of the books mentioned the Boxer Rebellion or the Japanese-Chinese War. One author noted Marco Polo and his contact with a superior inventive culture,[89] and another described China after the conquest of Ghengis Khan. "The period afforded but a glimpse of a land of almond eyed, pig-tailed people, eager to learn the ways of the westerners, and possessed of certain arts and manufactures unknown to Europe. . ."[90] A few texts took care to note the United States' generosity in its donation of indemnity money to educate Chinese students in America, while ignoring the active discrimination practiced against their countrymen. The result of this education, according to one author, was that of "increasing the friendship of the Chinese for our country."[91] However, the author never mentioned the Chinese anger against the exclusion laws as it was expressed in the demonstrations and boycott in 1905.

All the authors who mentioned the Open Door Notes regarded them with favor. "It is safe to say that the United States will be at the geographical or what is the first stage, the commercial division of China."[92] For another, the Open Door Policy was the

> First fruit of the new place of America as a World Power. . . In this matter of Open Door, the immediate incentive of Ameri-can Policy was the wish to prevent the exclusion of American trade from rich Oriental provinces, but that policy fell in happily with the interests of civilization and humanity.[93]

Thus in general, the tone appeared to support the polic y as evidence of American greatness and humanity.

History textbooks devoted little space to Asian relations in general, and to China least of all. China remained at best on the periphery of American interests, and according to the texts, the Chinese were unimportant in the development of western civilization of which the United States was a part. Children reading and memorizing these texts. could have only a hazy impression of China and Japan. They could conceive of these countries only in terms of their relation-ship to the United States. The children's intellectual perceptions and values of non-western societies were judged and measured against those of the United States. These children were deprived of the opportunity to understand that **different** was not bad or inferior, but exciting and challenging, with inherent values of its own. The Asian children in schools were denied a pride in their heritage (that many acquired after school), and frequently were given ambivalent and conflicting feelings about themselves and their families.

Immigration, today considered an essential feature of American history, was handled with trepidation, if at all, in the texts. The new immigration was a source of controversy and scholarly debate, but 35% of textbooks examined did not even mention the subject. Most authors viewed it with great ambivalence. On the one hand, they visualized our nation as a haven for the oppressed, and saw the flood of newcomers as a source of producing energetic, ambitious, and creative citizens. One writer characterized this attitude in

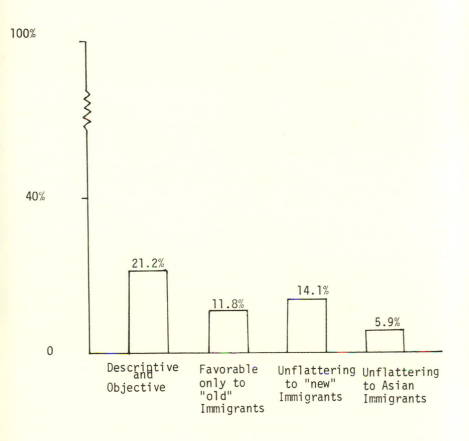

Figure 2. Early American Histories:
Reactions to Immigrants (N= 122)

the spirit of Frederic Jackson Turner: "In the crucible of the frontier the immigrants were Americanized, liberated, and fused into a mixed race, English in neither nationality nor characteristic."[94] But the words of Emma Lazarus, "Give me your tired, your poor,. . . the wretched refuse of your teeming shore. . ." also included a tone of superiority. By the end of the nineteenth century, however, feelings were changing. Earlier immigrants had already been absorbed or assimilated, had achieved mobility, and were treated in most books as an asset. In fact, many texts emphasized the "older" immigrants especially in their discussions of westward expansion. One, mentioning the contribution of immigrants to American life, included among his examples Michaelson and Gompers, although the author avoided mentioning that both were **Jewish** immigrants.[95] However, as Figure 2 shows, less than one-quarter of the early histories were descriptive and objective when they referred to immigrants. Twenty percent of the books were unflattering in their comments on "new" and Asian immigrants, with an additional 11.8 percent favorable only to "old" immigrants. Evidence of these views is seen in samples from the texts themselves.

Many books were willing to note the enormous growth in population and even mentioned the influx of new peoples from Southeastern Europe, noting in a negative way the change in the nature of the migrants.[96] Of the earlier immigrants, one writer said, "many foreigners. . .have made excellent citizens who have contributed to the national wealth and industry in a way that can hardly be praised too highly." These immigrants settled in the northern part of the nation.[97] Another author pointed out that the improvement of navigation had led many less desirable aliens to migrate to the United States, "and it is a question whether the extraordinary power of assimilation thus displayed can go on forever."[98] Still another claimed that the enormous migration into the North and West had upset and destroyed the older status quo in those areas where the newcomers settled. "The most worthless and vicious immigrants swelled the ranks of idleness and vice in the large cities." They did not venture into the South because there was no free land and southerners made no effort to recruit them. "They shrank from inviting among them the uncongenial newcomers from over the sea. These settlers, foreign in thought and feeling, widened the divergence of opinions and interest between the two sections of the republic."[99]

A number of books praised immigrants in general and noted their vast contributions to the development of the nation, and the added such comments as, "but within the past ten or fifteen years the general character of the immigrants has not been so good as formerly, the average intelligence and morals being much lower that it was before. . ."[100] And, "After the Civil War large numbers of paupers, criminals, and lunatics came to the United States and thus many European governments got rid of their burdens at our expense, while crime increased in America." This, claimed the author, justified the passage of restrictive immigration laws.[101]

A text used as late as the 1940's felt the "new" immigration posed a race problem. The old immigrants were similar in blood, language, and tradition, and thus were assimilated easily, but the new immigrants had not become American, had reduced the standard of living, and had made "the great cities breeding places for disease and crime and (offered) the unscrupulous politician cheap votes. . ." The author then pointed out the need for restrictive laws.[102] Immigrants, noted another writer, were always regarded with suspicion and hostility. He cited the attitudes during the older as well as the new immigration. "For many years we kept the door of America wide open. We asked no one where he came from. . . But there was always, among certain classes of native-born citizens, a suspicion of aliens."[103] A much smaller percentage of authors attempted to present a more balanced or sympathetic appraisal. "What America is to-day it owes almost entirely to European immigration, past and present. There is every reason to believe that this mixture of different nationalities, all of them improved by our free institutions, will make us a still greater and stronger people than we now are."[104] Others acknowledged that the immigration problem was complicated, and therefore, new laws alone were not the solution. "The public schools accomplish a great deal toward making the children of foreign descent good citizens of the country adopted by their parents. . ."[105]

A famous progressive historian discussed the new immigrants that settled in the cities, preserved their old world customs, and provided a cheap source of labor for business. He advocated Americanization of the newcomers.

> The revelation of the illiteracy in the army raised the cry, and demand was intensified when it was found that many of the leaders among the extreme radicals were foreign in birth and citizenship. . .All were agreed that they should be taught to speak and write the language and understand the government of our country.[106]

The enormous increase in immigration was inspired by those seeking economic improvement. Our nation experienced daily miracles as it embraced the political and social ideas of peoples of different races, "which have been absorbed into the nation and been so speedily transformed into American citizens, in sympathy with American ideals." If, continued the writer, we could continue to absorb the huge numbers coming to our shores the "result is not likely to be feeble or lacking in force, but an energetic, delicately constituted vigorous and forcible race. . . ."[107]

Asian immigration was always treated separately and almost always unfavorably. About 22% of the textbooks we examined included mention of Chinese immigration. Of the 22%: 63% of the texts were highly critical of the Asians or attempted to justify the discriminatory legislation; 10% of them tried to be objective; and the content in the remaining 27% was innocuous. Less space was spent on the Japanese immigrants, their privations and problems, and **none** defended or supported the Asians.

Very few of the authors gave any credit or even mention of the Chinese contributions to America, or of their work in building the railroads. On the contrary, the Chinese were portrayed as an undesirable element in the most unflattering terms. Restrictive laws that were passed against Chinese immigrants were in every case defended by the writers. In general the arguments against the Asians were based on the following principles: they were illiterate; they were not making America their permanent home; they were not able to assimilate; and finally, they had a lower standard of living and thus accepted lower wages. "The Asiatics worked for low wages, lived in squalid quarters on a few cents a day, and in general competed with the whites on terms which to the latter were intolerable. Their presence too, threatened to create another race problem."[108] Complaints about Chinese inability to assimilate were frequently of this tone:

. . .although the Chinese were much in demand as laborers it was objected that they lived by themselves, few of them learned English; they did not bring their families; they all intended to go to China in the course of time; and they were accused of working for lower wages than the white man.[109]

The justification of the restrictions was forcefully stated:

Though the law seems harsh, every nation undoubtedly possesses the right to expel from its shores any aliens whose presence may be considered dangerous to its interest, and likewise to refuse admission to all whom it may consider undesirable.[110]

"Accustomed to starvation wages and indifferent to the standards of living, they [the Chinese] threatened to cut the American standard to the point of subsistence."[111] Because the Chinese were willing to work longer for less wages, they aroused antagonism among the working men. "In California, particularly fierce race riots ensued. . ." that led to the passage of laws discriminating against the Chinese and eventually to the passage of congressional laws in 1882, 1892, and 1902.[112] "The Chinese live on almost nothing and work for so little that they arouse hate" -- this sentiment led to a movement to drive out the Chinese. "Chinamen were mobbed, beaten, and killed and a demand came from California and the West for their exclusion. . ."[113] Denis Kearney, a prejudiced agitator preached the "Chinese must go" and brought about the passage of exclusion laws that prevented "the coming of hundreds of thousands of men who would have brought about a race difficulty like the negro question in the South."[114]

The Chinese did not bring their families with them, for they did not intend to remain and become citizens. They showed little interest in American affairs and almost no inclination to adopt our customs. "It was feared that in time they might come over in such vast hordes as seriously to endanger our institutions."[115] One text, attempting neutrality, stated what was to become the popular stereotype of the Chinese. "In California and Nevada lived about 55,000 Chinese, a few of whom were brought East and became laundrymen, cooks, and factory hands."[116] Some authors simply listed the passage of restrictive immigration laws without justification or explanation.[117] A less prejudiced view, but nevertheless cautious in defending the law, was the following: "The increasing number of immigrants had caused consternation, not to say alarm. . .and it seemed desirable to take steps to restrict immigration."[118] One exception was a book by Barnes and Barnes that attempted to present a more objective view of the problem by including several quotes: one from a Chinese, who spoke of peaceful ways, hard work and the taxes they paid to the community; another quote in favor of unrestricted immigration; and a third that condemned Chinese laborers and defended the exclusion laws.[119]

Few texts showed concern with the Japanese problem, because it was a more contemporary issue. The Japanese had not come to the West Coast in large numbers until after 1900, and the diplomatic

127

problems had occurred after 1906. Thus the percentage of texts discussing these issues was very small. However, **all** of the authors who did write of the Japanese immigration condoned the United States' policies. "Were we to throw open our doors to the unlimited Japanese immigration we should be inviting a far more serious race problem than we now have with the Negro and the Indian."[120] Another account described how Japan became an important power after 1918, and with it the rise of racial prejudice that also appeared against the Japanese who had come to represent the "yellow peril." "Race prejudice played its part but the mainspring of the protest was the fear of economic competition." These factors led in 1906, to the San Francisco Board of Education segregation of Japanese students, and the Gentlemen's Agreement with Japan. Discriminatory landholding laws in California were also mentioned. "If our country could discover some means of attaining its purpose without branding Japanese as inferior. . . then perhaps we could restore friendly relations with Japan."[121]

One justification for Japanese exclusion was explained in these terms: "In 1907 the Japanese were excluded for the same reason as the Chinese -- it was believed their cheap labor would bring down wages of our own laboring men."[122] Other justifications of our attitudes were rationalized by noting that Chinese and Japanese students and businessmen were welcomed, but there was strong objection to receiving Asians in large numbers. "Doubtless there would be just such objections in Japan if scores of thousands of American laborers were to settle down there and compete with native laborers."[123] The most objective account simply stated that in 1911 the United States negotiated a treaty with Japan, but the Japanese had been offended by a clause that allowed the United States the right to exclude Japanese laborers in older contracts. "The new treaty omitted the objectionable clause; a private agreement was, however, made between the two countries, by which the United States still retains the right to regulate immigration from Japan."[124]

American histories were responsive to many public pressures and therefore taught the kind of American patriotism and ideals espoused by the various groups. These attitudes often appeared to contradict the idealism contained in the Bill of Rights, and conveyed messages that produced stereotypes.

World histories. World History textbooks were difficult to find. Schools simply did not consider world history important. What was called World History usually meant European history only, and that subject was stressed because American institutions were rooted there. Other cultures did not exist or were merely extensions of European imperialism. "Oriental" history meant the story of the Middle East. China, Japan, Indian, East Asia and Africa were barely mentioned in most narratives. In the few universal histories we found, the stories of non-western cultures were handled simplistically, inaccurately, and sometimes with patronizing language. The lack of interest in non-western cultures was further encouraged by the leading educational association, especially the American Historical Association. In a report 1899, the Committee of Seven objected to the exclusive study of American history and claimed that children derived a narrow simplified view of the world. The United States should not be "detached from its natural foundation -- European history." The following suggestions were made:

Grade III	The study of classic myths, Roland, King Arthur
Grade IV	Biographies of prominent people of history: Lycurgus, Solon, Darius, Pericles, Socrates, Plutarch, Romulus, Cato, Pompey, Caesar, Agricola, Alaric, Charlemagne, Luther, Henry IV, Gutenberg, Joan of Arc, Bayard, Clovis, Francis I, Richelieu, Alfred, Raleigh, Cromwell, Pitt, Nelson, Stephenson, Mohammed, St. Francis, Isabella, Columbus, Lorenzo di Medici, Galileo, Garibaldi, Rembrandt, William of Orange, Gustavus Adolphus, Peter the Great, as well as the American heroes
Grade V	Greek and Roman History
Grade VI	Medieval and Modern European History
Grade VII	English History
Grade VIII	American History

The justification for the above recommendations by the professionals was that "the substitution of a brief course in European history for a portion of the American now taught will conduce to a better appreciation of the important facts in American history. . ."[125] And since, "history teaching in the elementary schools should be focused around American history. . .America cannot be understood without taking into account the history of its peoples before they crossed the Atlantic."[126] Nowhere in any of the suggestions of curriculum changes was there a reference to non-western cultures or societies. In the few books on world history, the same bias was evident. Almost none of the books understood Chinese culture or the beauty and majesty of Chinese civilization. In many works, Japan was considered the superior culture, because the evaluation of these Asian societies was based upon how closely they resembled the United States. Sometimes a brief paragraph was included describing Confucius, the introduction of silk worms, or the building of the Great Wall, but in general the accounts were poor, disjointed, and insufficient.[127] One book described the opening of Japan and cited that country as being old -- "They knew nothing of the white man's inventions or ways of living. But in 50 years time they jumped a thousand years in civilization!"[128]

European histories mentioned Asia only in connection with imperialism -- European interests in China, the Opium Wars, the Japanese-Chinese War, and the Box Rebellion. One author wrote a patronizing assessment of Asian development that was probably more sympathetic than most:

> The enrichment brought to civilization by a renewed Japan should teach us the possible worth to the common life of the world of a renewed China and a renewed India. . . The expansion of Europe and the contact of the Christian West with the Confucian and Buddhistic East will be to give a new and richer content to civilization and a fresh impulse to the true progress of humanity.[129]

European history texts, like the American history texts, tended to be prejudiced in favor of Protestantism (versus Catholicism) and certainly favored Christianity over Judaism. The only discussion of Jews was in relation to their contribution of monotheism to civilization. Generally historical narrative tales of the Old Testament were read to illustrate these points. Often after these chapters, no mention was made of the development of Judaism or the Jews' fate in Europe. Post-Biblical history was ignored or only briefly mentioned (e.g., persecution by Inquisition in Spain). Many of the books narrated the sensitive story of the Crucifixion in a wholly sectarian manner that perpetuated two notions: one, the superiority of the new Christian faith, and second, the perpetuation of stereotypes that fed anti-semitism.[130] Some texts, anxious to avoid giving offense or arousing controversy omitted as much of the story as possible. Omission seemed the easiest and most popular means of dealing with religious matters. In fact, one methods manual complained that Hebrew history was at best most difficult to handle because of the religious content.

The easiest solution of the problem would be to omit any consideration of the subject, but Hebrew history is certainly important. . .and it would be strange to omit in a course on general history all consideration of the people to whom modern Europe owes its religious ideas, and many of its principles of conduct.[131]

Geographies

Geographies could not as easily avoid the mention of China, Japan, and other Asian countries, as seen in Figure 3. However, Asians were still not treated any more accurately or more adequately than in the other books. Jews were rarely mentioned; Israel as yet did not exist. Some books noted that Jews lived in Palestine, but spoke mostly about the Turks who ruled the land. In 1909, one geography described the major religions of the world and never mentioned Judaism at all.[132] Reference to immigrants was rare, whether "old" or "new".

At the beginning of the twentieth century, as the textbooks became better written, compilations by E.S. Tarr, McMurry, R.E. Dodge, A.P. Brigham, H.E. Frye, and Atwood became very popular and widely used. They emphasized human development, demonstrated the relationships between the races, and noted the effects of material resources and climate upon civic and social institutions. The result of this change in emphasis was that while geography study still retained much memorization, e.g., life forms, areas, topography, and climate, these drills were subordinated in an attempt to ascertain the influence of these physical factors upon all human activities.[133] "The purpose of geography teaching is to arouse in the pupil a desire to follow out each geographic lead to its logical end, to teach him where to seek geographic information and how to use it."[134]

Through the study of geography we may direct the student to current periodicals and newspapers of a good class, we may stimulate them to read books of travel and description and arouse a desire to travel, and at the same time we may train them into library habits. We may lead them to respect labor, to appreciate beauty in nature, and to an ethical point of view in the social phase of the study of the great commercial products.[135]

Figure 3. Early Geographies:

References to China, Japan, and Immigrants

(N = 53)

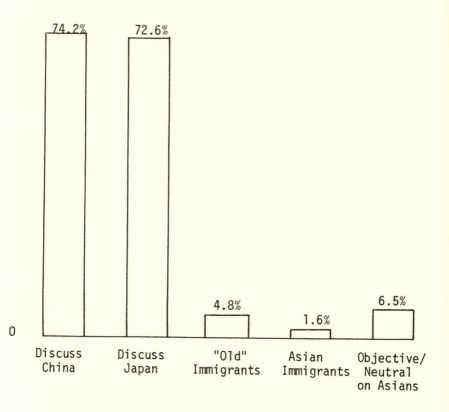

Most of the geographies were profusely and beautifully illustrated, and included many fine maps. In addition, the teachers' manuals suggested a large list of supplementary readings that could be used for history and literature as well. They included such titles as Dodge's HANS BRINKER, Marco Polo's TRAVELS, Miller's LITTLE PEOPLE OF ASIA, and Andrews' SEVEN LITTLE SISTERS.

A very large percentage of geographies had unflattering and inaccurate descriptions of China. This was especially true of the books that were published before 1910. These books exhibited more prejudice and were less objective than the books written later. All admitted that Chinese civilization was ancient, but some characterized it as static: ". . .we cannot say that the Chinese are a civilized people according to our standard for they are not progressive. . their way of doing things and thinking about things is to-day just as we find it in their books to have been 2,500 years ago."[136] The texts pointed out that several hundred years ago, the Chinese invented printing and gunpowder but for many years that part of the yellow race had made little progress. They had a few miles of railroads, and knew very little about machinery or the mining of coal. "They [the Chinese] could spin and weave fine silks long before the people of Europe knew how and they have long known how to make paper and beautiful porcelain dishes. . ."[137] According to several authors, the Chinese had developed a remarkable civilization, but their growth stopped. Not only did they not advance in the industrial arts, but they also did not adopt modern principles of hygiene.[138] A far more damaging assessment of the Chinese began:

> The Chinese surpasses all nations in patient endurance of labor. . . China is like a house built of bricks without mortar. . . Her people are not brave in battle. They have a strong race instinct which breaks out in massacres of foreigners. . .they have shown no public spirit, no national patriotism, no readiness to sacrifice self for an ideal. . . Mining has been almost impossible in China, lest, as the people ignorantly feared, the "earth-devils" be let loose.[139]

A series of geographies entitled HOME LIFE IN ALL LANDS was denigratory of other cultures, particularly those we would today call "Third World." One volume had as a sub-title, "Manners and Customs of Uncivilized Peoples," and China was included in this category. The accounts of life in China and Japan stressed the quaint and exotic, and the terms describing different customs included phrases such as "odd" food, "peculiar" customs, and "barbaric" laws.[140]

133

However, not all accounts in the geographies were so negative. A small percentage portrayed China in far more balanced and objective language.

China is another great land which has an old civilization. The Chinese made porcelain dishes long before our European forefathers did and plates and saucers are still called China. . . The Chinese had invented gunpowder, discovered how to make silk, paper, found out how to print and invented a kind of taxicab, while some of our ancestors were living a primitive existence, wandering in the forests of Europe and feeding on berries and wild animals.[141]

Japan was more often discussed in somewhat friendly and favorable terms. "Japan has made more progress than any other country in Asia. It has good schools. Its cities had great mills and factories." In describing Japanese customs, however, the differences between East and West were emphasized: ". . .isn't this a queer bed. . . It would amuse you to see the people of Japan eat rice. . ."[142] Phrases like those were hardly conducive to creating respect for cultural differences. As in the histories, the Japanese were admired because they had imitated the West and the United States.

The people of the yellow race living on the islands of Japan have made more progress than any other branch of the race. They are eager to learn how the white men do all kinds of work, and they have been wise enough to adopt many customs of the white race. The Japanese are a brave and active people. They have fine ships of war, as well as ships for trading.[143]

Other authors characterized the Japanese as the "English of the East" or as the "Yankees of the East."[144] Japan is the most progressive nation of the Far East because of the willingness of the Japanese to profit by the experiences of the more advanced nations." The textbooks devoted much space to the industrial development and modernization of Japan.[145]

The subject of immigration was again mentioned infrequently in the texts. Included only in the studies of the United States, the subject was generally covered in the descriptions of the major cities. And in some accounts, of course, immigrants were never mentioned at all. The children in the city of New York, claimed one author, came from all over the world, including China and Japan. Some would live in tenements, and some in the country. The account concluded: "If the children enter your school, you will surely welcome them as you would like to be welcomed, if you were a stranger in a strange land. They now belong to our great American family."[146] Although many texts admired Japan and treated China haughtily, those geographies that talked of the Asian immigrants regarded them with the same disdain revealed in the American histories. A description of San Francisco contained this item: "An interesting portion of this city is the section called 'Chinatown.' Many thousands of Orientals landed in the city, living huddled together in hovels, almost like rats."[147] Geographers, like the historians, constantly reiterated that the Chinese lived on so little that they depressed the wage scale: ". . .the habits of coolies are such that in all civilized communities their existence in large numbers has been found socially undesirable and injurious."[148] But never did explanations follow these unwarranted accusations. Textbooks repeated the same complaints. The Asians did not make good citizens; they did not adopt our ways. One writer described the Chinese in San Francisco: "Here may be seen opium dens, idol temples, theatres, dirt, squalor and wickedness. . ."[149] Another stated that Asians differed in religion and custom, and that the problems of assimilation were far greater than for Europeans. "The fear is that should we permit the Asiatics to come here as freely as we permit other races, we would soon have on our hands a Japanese problem and a Chinese problem, quite as serious as our present-day negro problem."[150] Others defended the exclusion laws against the Japanese since, according to these authors, they could not possibly assimilate and therefore, restrictions were "probably the kindest policy for both races."[151] The influence of the explicit and implicit meanings of such material upon the young, impressionable minds of both majority and minority school children had long-lasting effects.

In Summary

The general impression of schools and teaching in this period was that readers retained high literary quality; the histories and geographies, though not as well written, were designed for "good" readers. The values imparted by all the books and many schools were very narrow and ethnocentric. Changes were occurring throughout this period, but those that were positive were very slow in reaching the classroom. Texts written at the end of World War I were still a part of many curricula in the 1940's. Some were reprinted. Others were edited and new chapters were added to bring the books up to date.[152] Thus in some cases, inaccuracies, prejudices, and misinformation were transmitted to more than one generation. The sad effects of these inadequacies were revealed in a study made in 1958. Impressions about China were asked of 181 persons who were articulate and highly educated. Few remembered learning much about Asia in school, and what they recalled was similar to the few paragraphs that we have already described.[153] The prejudice against Asians, the Japanese especially, played its role in the incarceration of the Japanese in World War II. Prejudice and stereotypes cannot be attributed to the schools alone, but generations of children were educated with little appreciation of Japan's or China's intrinsic cultural values, and with no respect for the Japanese and Chinese immigrants. As for the Jews, they played a small role in American schools, and teachers remained insensitive to the needs of Jewish as well as other immigrant children. Ethnocentrism dominated the textbook and classroom alike.

NOTES

1. C. R. Maxwell, "The Selection of Textbooks," SCHOOL AND SOCIETY, 9 (January 11, 1919), 44-52.

2. **Ibid.**, p. 51.

3. E. M. Otis, "A Textbook Scorecard," JOURNAL OF EDUCATIONAL RESEARCH, 7 (February, 1923), 133-34.

4. H. L. Donovan, "How to Select Textbooks," PEABODY JOURNAL OF EDUCATION, 2 (July, 1924), 7.

5. C. E. Cooper, "A Method for Judging and Scoring Textbooks in Grade School Geography," JOURNAL OF EDUCATIONAL METHOD, 4 (1925), 330.

6. Donovan, p. 2.

7. Cooper, p. 333.

8. Manfred J. Holmes, ed. "Training and Improvement of Teachers in Elementary and Kindergarten," NATIONAL SOCIETY FOR THE STUDY OF EDUCATION (Bloomington: Public School Publishing CO., 1908), p. 14; S. H. Clark, HOW TO TEACH READING IN THE PUBLIC SCHOOLS (New York: Scott, Foresman, and Co., 1898) p. 18; Frederick Gates, "The Country School of Tomorrow," PUBLICATIONS OF THE GENERAL EDUCATION BOARD, Occasional Papers, No. 1 (New York City, 1921), pp. 1-15.

9. Rebecca H. Shankland, "The McGuffey Readers and Moral Education," HARVARD EDUCATIONAL REVIEW, 21 (Winter, 1961). 64.

10. Philadelphia Public Schools, MANUAL OF THE GRADED COURSE OF INSTRUCTION IN THE PRIMARY SCHOOLS (Philadelphia, 1884), p. 64.

11. Altoona, COURSE OF STUDY (Altoona, 1907), p. 3.

12. Charles A. McMurry, COURSE OF STUDY IN THE EIGHT GRADES (New York, Macmillan,1906) II, 5-6.

13. Rudolph R. Reeder, THE HISTORICAL DEVELOPMENT OF SCHOOL READERS AND METHODS IN TEACHING READING (New York: Columbia Univ. Press, 1900), p. 51.

14. For more on McGuffey's Readers, c.f. Harvey C. Minnich, WILLIAM HOLMES MCGUFFEY AND HIS READERS (New York: American Book Co., 1936); Shankland, pp. 60-72; Henry H. Vail, A HISTORY OF THE MCGUFFEY READERS (Cleveland, 1910); Richard D. Mosier, MAKING THE AMERICAN MIND: SOCIAL AND MORAL IDEAS IN THE MCGUFFEY READERS (New York: Russell and Russell, 1965); Alice M. Ruggles, THE STORY OF THE MCGUFFEY'S (New York: American Book Co., 1950); E. V. Estensen, "McGuffey, A Statistical Analysis," JOURNAL OF EDUCATIONAL RESEARCH, 39 (February, 1946), 445-57.

15. Reeder, p. 60.

16. Mary E. Burt and Zenaide A. Ragozin, ODYSSEUS, THE HERO OF ITHACA (New York: Scribner's Sons, 1898), p. iii.

17. Emilie Poulsson, IN THE CHILD'S WORLD (Springfield: Milton Bradley CO., 1893); R. R. Robinson, TWO CENTURIES OF CHANGE IN THE CONTENT OF SCHOOL READERS (Nashville: George Peabody College for Teachers, 1930), p. 46.

18. Robinson, p. 47.

19. Sarah Arnold, "How Reading is Taught in Boston," Eva D. Kellogg, ed., TEACHING READING IN TEN CITIES (Boston: Educational Publishing Co., 1900), p. 24-28.

20. Reeder, pp. 58-60.

21. Edgar B. Wesley, N. E. A. THE FIRST HUNDRED YEARS (New York: Harper and Row, 1957), p. 50.

22. James Johonnot, STORIES OF THE OLDEN TIME (New York: American Book Co., 1889), p. 4.

23. see page 133 **supra.**

24. McMurry, COURSE OF STUDY, II, 6, 38-57; Claude A. Phillips, MODERN METHODS AND THE ELEMENTARY CURRICULUM (New York: Century Co., 1923), pp. 41-57; Altoona, COURSE OF STUDY, p. 1.

25. Richard C. Spitzer, "Discovering America," AMERICAN EDUCA-TION, 21, No 7, (1975), 26-27.

26. EUGENE FIELD READER (New York: Scribner's Sons, 1905). Written on the fly-leaf: property of the Kapalama School (Honolulu), 1940.

27. James Baldwin, SCHOOL READING BY GRADES: SIXTH YEAR (New York: American Book Co., 1897).

28. Vincent A. Davis, THE LITERATURE OF ADVANCED SCHOOL READERS IN THE UNITED STATES, 1785-1900 (Chicago: unpublished dissertation, Univ. of Chicago, 1934), p. 115.

29. Thomas B. Lawler, SEVENTY YEARS OF TEXTBOOK PUBLISHING, 1867-1937, A HISTORY OF GINN AND COMPANY (Boston: Ginn and Co., 1938), p. 187-90.

30. **Ibid.**; Ellen M Cyr, CYR'S FIFTH READER (Boston: Ginn and Co., 1899).

31. Lawler, p. 188.

32. **Ibid.**

33. NEW FRANKLIN FIFTH READER (New York: Sheldon and Co., 1884); THE NEW ENGLAND PRIMER (Boston: Ginn and Co., 1900); Swinton's PRIMER AND FIRST READER (New York: American Book Co., 1883); HEATH SECOND READER (Boston: D.C. Heath, 1901); THE BEACON PRIMER (Boston: Ginn and Co., 1912); A. J. Demarest and William M. VanSickle, NEW EDUCATION READERS, Book 4 (New York: American Book Co., 1901).

34. Mary Hayes Davis and Chow-Leung, CHINESE FABLES AND FOLK STORIES (New York: American Book Co., 1908).

35. William E. Griffis, THE FIRE-FLY'S LOVERS AND OTHER FAIRY TALES OF OLD JAPAN (New York: T. Y. Crowell, 1908).

36. A. A. Guerber, THE STORY OF THE CHOSEN PEOPLE (New York: American Book Co., 1896).

37. E. Ehrlich Smith, THE HEART OF THE CURRICULUM (Garden City: Doubleday, Page and Co., 1925), pp. 131-32.

38. Phillip, p.40.

39. Oscar Gerson, POETRY FOR THE GRADES, Grade 5, (Philadelphia: Franklin Publishing and Supply Co., 1918), p. ii.

40. Charles A. McMurry, HOW TO ORGANIZE THE CURRICULUM (New York: Macmillan, 1924), p. 20.

41. George D. Strayer and Naomi Norsworthy, HOW TO TEACH (New York Macmillan, 1918), pp. 134-135.

42. Robinson, p. 51.

43. Emma M. Bolenius, BOYS' AND GIRLS' READERS, 6TH GRADE (Boston: Houghton, Mifflin, 1919).

44. William Chandler Bagley, CLASSROOM MANAGEMENT, ITS PRINCIPLES AND TECHNIQUES (1917, rpt. New York: Macmillan, 1918), p. 204.

45. David Snedden, SOCIOLOGICAL DETERMINATION OF OBJECTIVES IN EDUCATION (Philadelphia: J. B. Lippincott Co., 1921), pp. 235-36; Samuel H. Ziegler, THE SOCIAL STUDIES IN THE JUNIOR HIGH (Cleveland, 1923), p. 34.

46. Smith, HEART OF CURRICULUM, pp. 123-26.

47. Claude M. Fuess, SELECTIONS FOR ORAL READING (New York: Macmillan, 1916).

48. Mary C. Barnes, EARLY STORIES AND SONGS FOR NEW STU-
DENTS OF ENGLISH (New York: Fleming H. Revell Co., 1912),
p. iv; Phillips, p. 14 recommends the stories of Joseph, Moses,
and David as being very suitable for the 3rd, 4th, and 5th grades.

49. McMurry, HOW TO ORGANIZE CURRICULUM, p. 140; H. Rugg,
"Do the Social Studies Prepare Pupils Adequately for Life Activi-
ties?" Twenty-Second Yearbook of the NATIONAL SOCIETY
FOR THE STUDY OF EDUCATION, p. 4; John Wayland, HOW
TO TEACH AMERICAN HISTORY (New York: Macmillan, 1914),
p. 48.

50. McMurry, HOW TO ORGANIZE, p. 352; Phillips, p. 55.

51. Clark, HOW TO TEACH READING, pp. 205-207.

52. Francis Russell, "The Coming of the Jews," ANTIOCH REVIEW,
15 (March, 1955), 35-36.

53. Charles S. Bernheimer, THE RUSSIAN JEW IN THE UNITED
STATES (Philadelphia: John C. Winston, 1905), p. 189.

54. **Ibid.**

55. **Ibid.**, p. 203

56. Selma Berrol, "The Schools of New York in Transition, 1898-1914,"
URBAN REVIEW, 1 (December, 1966), 17-19.

57. Herman Dressel, May Robbins, and Ellis Graff, THE NEW BARNES
READERS, Book 1 (New York: A. SA. Barnes Co., 1916).

58. Elson and Runkel, ELSON READERS, Book II (New York: Scott,
Foresman, and Co., 1920), p. 52.

59. William H. Elson, THE ELSON READERS, Book 3 (New York,
1912), pp. 28-31.

60. Sidney Firman and Ethel Maltby, THE WINSTON READERS,
4th Reader (Philadelphia: John Winston, 1918).

61. J. W. Searson and George E. Martin, STUDIES IN READING,
Grades 5,6,7,8 (Chicago: University Publishing Co., 1914).

62. THE PETERS AND BRUMBAUGH METHOD READERS (Philadelphia: Christopher Sower Co., 1912).

63. E. C. Hartwell, Story Hour Readings (New York: American Book CO., 1921).

64. Francis L. K. Hsu, AMERICANS AND CHINESE, TWO WAYS OF LIFE (New York: Henry Schuman, 1953), pp. 87-88.

65. Bessie L. Pierce, PUBLIC OPINION AND THE TEACHING OF HISTORY IN THE UNITED STATES (New York: Da Capo Press, 1970), pp. 78-82.

66. THE STUDY OF HISTORY IS SCHOOLS, REPORT TO THE AMERICAN HISTORICAL ASSOCIATION BY THE COMMITTEE OF SEVEN (New York: Macmillan, 1899).

67. Philadelphia Public Schools, MANUAL OF THE GRADED COURSE OF INSTRUCTION IN THE GRAMMAR SCHOOLS (Philadelphia, 1887), p. 30.

69. c. f. Jacques Driencourt, LA PROPAGANDE NOUVELLE FORCE POLITIQUE (Paris: Armand Colin, 1950).

70. COURSE OF STUDY FOR THE PUBLIC SCHOOLS IN THE CITY OF ATLANTIC CITY, NEW JERSEY (Atlantic City, 1905).

71. Pierce, PUBLIC OPINION, pp. 160-64.

72. John Bach McMaster, NEW GRAMMAR SCHOOL HISTORY OF THE UNITED STATES, California State Series (Sacramento, 1903).

73. Elbridge J. Brooks, THE CENTURY BOOK FOR YOUNG AMERICANS (New York: Century Co., 1894), pp. iii. 16-17.

74. Calvin N. Kellner and Florence E. Stryker, HISTORY IN THE ELEMENTARY SCHOOL (Boston, Houghton Mifflin, 1918), pp. 2-3; Charles A. McMurry, SPECIAL METHOD IN HISTORY: A COMPLETE OUTLINE OF A COURSE OF STUDY IN HISTORY FOR THE GRADES BELOW THE HIGH SCHOOL (New York: Macmillan, 1905), p. 7.

75. Zeigler, **op. cit.**, p. 12; COURSE OF STUDY OF ATLANTIC CITY, p. 45.

76. Kellner and Stryker, p. 2.

77. A. I. Gates, "The Psychological vs. the Chronological Order in the Teaching of History," THE HISTORICAL OUTLOOK, 11 (1920), 228.

78. Charles Carpenter, HISTORY OF AMERICAN TEXTBOOKS (Philadelphia: Univ. of Pennsylvania Press, 1963), pp. 204-208; Edward Everett Hale, HISTORY OF THE UNITED STATES (New York: Chautauqua Press, 1887); Wiliam Swinton, A SCHOOL HISTORY OF THE UNITED STATES (New York: American Book Co., 1893); Edward S. Ellis, COMPLETE SCHOOL HISTORY OF THE UNITED STATES (Philadelphia: Porter and Coates, 1892).

79. John Clark Ridpath, PEOPLE'S HISTORY OF THE UNITED STATES (Philadelphia: Historical Publishing Co., 1895).

80. Lawler, pp. 105-108.

81. Lawton B. Evans, THE ESSENTIAL FACTS OF AMERICAN HISTORY (Chicago, Sanborn and Co., 1915), p. 101.

82. Charles A. Beard and William C. Bagley, A HISTORY OF THE AMERICAN PEOPLE (New York: Macmillan, 1920), pp. 2., 505.

83. Charles Beard and Mary Beard, HISTORY OF THE UNITED STATES (New York: Macmillan, 1921), pp. 11-12, 585-86, 410-11.

84. Edward Eggleston, THE NEW CENTURY HISTORY OF THE UNITED STATES (New York: American Book Co., 1904, p. 287; c.f. similar accounts in Reuben Thwaites and Calvin N. Kendall, A HISTORY OF THE UNITED STATES FOR GRAMMAR SCHOOLS (Boston: Houghton Mifflin, 1912), p. 319; Susan P. Pendleton, NEW SCHOOL HISTORY OF THE UNITED STATES, revised (Richmond, 1900), p. 242; John McMaster, NEW GRAMMAR SCHOOL, p. 484.

85. Everett Barnes, SHORT AMERICAN HISTORY BY GRADES (Boston: D. C. Heath, 1908), pp. 226, 233, 251; c.f. Matthew

P. Andrews, HISTORY OF THE UNITED STATES (Philadelphia: J. P. LIppincott, 1914), p. 250; Wilbur F. Gordy, A HISTORY OF THE UNITED STATES FOR SCHOOLS (New York: Scribner's Sons, 1898), p. 301.

86. Helen Nicolay, OUR NATION IN THE BUILDING (New York: Century Co., 1916), p. 405.

87. G. P. Quackenbos, PRIMARY HISTORY OF THE UNITED STATES (New York: Appleton, 1866), p. 189.

88. Albert B. Hart and Anne Chapman, SOURCE-READERS IN AMERICAN HISTORY, No. 3 (New York: Macmillan, 1903), p. 86; Quackenbos, PRIMARY HISTORY, p. 191.

89. Thwaites and Kendall, p. 467.

90. Edwin E. Sparks, THE EXPANSION OF THE AMERICAN PEOPLE (Chicago: Scott, Foresman, and CO., 1900), p. 89.

91. A. B. Hart, ESSENTIALS IN AMERICAN HISTORY (New York: American Book Co., 1912), pp. 561-62.

92. Sparks, EXPANSION OF AMERICAN PEOPLE, p. 448.

93. Willis M. West, HISTORY OF THE AMERICAN PEOPLE (New York: Allyn and Bacon, 1918), pp. 640-41.

94. John Higham, STRANGERS IN THE LAND (New Brunswick: Rutgers Univ. Press, 1955), p. 122.

95. Emerson David Fite, HISTORY OF THE UNITED STATES (New York: Henry Holt and Co., 1916), p. 505.

96. McMaster, NEW GRAMMAR SCHOOL, p. 428.

97. Charles K. Adams and William P. Trent, A HISTORY OF THE UNITED STATES (Boston: Allyn and Bacon, 1903), p. 537.

98. Harry Pratt Judson, THE GROWTH OF THE AMERICAN NATION (New York: Chautauqua-Century, 1895), p. 340.

99. Susan L. Pendleton, NEW SCHOOL HISTORY OF THE UNITED STATES, P. 239.

100. Gordy, HISTORY OF UNITED STATES, PP. 394-95.

101. **Ibid.**

102. David Saville Muzzey, AN AMERICAN HISTORY (Boston: Ginn and Co., 1911), p. 622; c.f. Frederic A. Ogg, NATIONAL PROGRESS, 1907-1917 (New York: Harper, 1918), pp. 120-125.

103. D. H. Montgomery, AN ELEMENTARY AMERICAN HISTORY (Boston: Ginn and Co., 1904), p. 243.

104. Thwaites and Kendall, supplement, p. i.

105. Oliver P. Cornman and Oscar Gerson, A BRIEF TOPICAL SURVEY OF UNITED STATES HISTORY (Boston: D.C. Heath, 1901), pp. 134-36; D. H. Montgomery, THE STUDENT'S AMERICAN HISTORY, Second revised edition (Boston: Ginn and Co., 1916), p. 599.

106. Beard and Beard, pp. 410-11, 585; Beard and Bagley, pp. 505-11.

107. Andrew C. McLaughlin, A HISTORY OF THE AMERICAN NATION (New York: Appleton, 1899), p. 538-39.

108. Fite, p. 433.

109. A. B. Hart, SCHOOL HISTORY OF THE UNITED STATES (New York: American Book Co., 1918), pp. 391-92; McMaster, NEW GRAMMAR HISTORY, p. 444.

110. Fite, P. 458.

111. Mary and Charles Beard, p. 583; L. B. Evans, P. 428; Henry W. Elson, SIDE-LIGHTS ON AMERICAN HISTORY (New York: Macmillan, 1908), p. 468; Waddy Thompson, A HISTORY OF THE UNITED STATES (Boston: D. C. Heath, 1904), pp. 453-54.

112. Matthew P. Andrews, p. 365.

113. William M. Davidson, A HISTORY OF THE UNITED STATES (Chicago: Scott, Foresman, and Co., 1902), pp. 488-89.

114. A. B. Hart, ESSENTIALS, pp. 518-19.

115. Gordy, p. 398; c.f. John Fiske, A HISTORY OF THE UNITED STATES FOR SCHOOLS (Boston: Houghton Mifflin, 1894), p. 360; John P. O'Hara, A HISTORY OF THE UNITED STATES (New York: Macmillan Co., 1919), p. 381: Eva March Tappan, OUR COUNTRY'S STORY, AN ELEMENTARY HISTORY OF THE UNITED STATES (Boston: Houghton Mifflin, 1902), p. 237.

116. A. B. Hart, SCHOOL HISTORY, p. 376.

117. William H. Venable, A SCHOOL HISTORY OF THE UNITED STATES (Cincinnati: Wilson, Hinkle and Co., 1872), p. 245.

118. McLaughlin, p. 509.

119. Mary S. Barnes and Earl Barnes, STUDIES IN AMERICAN HISTORY (Boston: D.C. Heath, 1893), pp. 388, 405-06.

120. Elson, SIDE-LIGHTS, P. 468.

121. Ogg, pp. 207-212; O'Hara, pp. 381-82; Beard and Beard, p. 584.

122. D. H. Montgomery, THE LEADING FACTS OF AMERICAN HISTORY (New York: Ginn and Co., 1920), p. 243.

123. A. B. Hart, SCHOOL HISTORY, p. 376; Beard and Bagley, p. 509 mentions the Gentlemen's Agreement.

124. Thwaites and Kendall, p. 467.

125. Committee of Seven, AMERICAN HISTORICAL ASSOCIATION, pp. 163-69.

126. **Ibid.**, p. 170; c.f. McMurry, SPECIAL METHOD, pp. 25-32; Henry Bourne, TEACHING OF HISTORY AND CIVICS IN THE ELEMENTARY AND THE SECONDARY SCHOOLS (New York: Longman, Green, 1902), p. 192.

127. John D. Quackenbos, SCHOOL HISTORY OF THE WORLD (New York: American Book Co., 1889), p. 25; Hendrik Willem Van Loon, THE STORY OF MANKIND (New York: Macmillan, 1923), pp. 217, 232-41, 443.

128. V. M. Hillyer, A CHILD'S HISTORY OF THE WORLD (New York, 1924), pp. 145-46.

129. Philip Van Ness Myers, MEDIEVAL AND MODERN HISTORY (New York: Ginn and Co., 1905), p. 692; Henry E. Bourne, A HISTORY OF MEDIEVAL AND MODERN EUROPE (New York: Longman, Green and Co., 1905), pp. 471-72.

130. Stuart E. Rosenberg, THE SEARCH FOR JEWISH IDENTITY IN AMERICA (New York: Anchor Books, 1965), p. 122.

131. Bourne, TEACHING OF HISTORY, p. 199.

132. Charles Morris, HOME LIFE IN ALL LANDS, MANNERS AND CUSTOMS OF UNCIVILIZED PEOPLES, Book II (Philadelphia: J.B. Lippincott and Co., 1909), pp. 301-04.

133. Mendel E. Branom and Fred K. Branom, THE TEACHING OF GEOGRAPHY (New York: Ginn and Co., 1921), p. 51.

134. Jane Perry Cook, "Primary Aims in Geography Teaching," JOURNAL OF GEOGRAPHY, 9 (1911), 203.

135. Bertha Henderson, "Cultural and Training Value of Geography," JOURNAL OF GEOGRAPHY, 14 (1915), 100-101.

136. Jacques W. Redway, THE NEW BASIS OF GEOGRAPHY (1902, rpt. New York: Macmillan Co., 1914), p. 115.

137. Alexis Everett Frye, GRAMMAR SCHOOL GEOGRAPHY (1895, rpt. Boston: Ginn and Co., 1902), p. 36.

138. Frank M. McMurry and A. E. Parkins, ADVANCED GEOGRAPHY (New York: Macmillan, 1921), pp. 409-426; Leonard O. Packard and Charles P. Sinnott, NATIONS AS NEIGHBORS (New York: Macmillan, 1926), pp. 458-461.

139. Edward Van Dyke Robinson, COMMERCIAL GEOGRAPHY (Chicago: Rand McNally and Co., 1910), pp. 310-323.

140. Charles Morris, HOME LIFE IN ALL LANDS, HOW THE WORLD LIVES, Book I, 16-28, 82-84, 124-126, 176-77, 180-222; Book II, 70-78, 112, 147-151.

141. James Fairgrieve and Ernest Young, THE NEW WORLD AND THE OLD (New York: Appleton and Co., 1925), pp. 359, 378.

142. Alexis Everett Frye, ELEMENTS OF GEOGRAPHY (Boston: Ginn and Co., 1898), p. 156.

143. Frye, GRAMMAR SCHOOL, pp. 36, 172; McMurry and Parkins, pp. 420-26.

144. Robinson, pp. 302-10; Rose B. Clark, UNIT STUDIES IN GEOGRAPHY (Yonkers-On-Hudson: World Book Co., 1924), p. 195.

145. Packard and Sinnott, pp. 170-171; J. Russell Smith, HUMAN GEOGRAPHY, PEOPLES AND COUNTRIES (Chicago: Winston and Co., 1920), p. 456; c.f. Morris, II, 70.

146. George A. Mirick, HOME LIFE AROUND THE WORLD (Boston: Houghton Mifflin and Co., 1918), pp. 156-157.

147. Frank M. McMurry and Ralph Tarr, AN ADVANCED GEOGRAPHY (New York: Macmillan, 1908), p. 151.

148. Carpenter, HISTORY OF TEXTBOOKS, pp. 277-78.

149. R. Elson, GUARDIANS OF TRADITION (Lincoln: Univ. of Nebraska Press, 1964), p. 164.

150. Ezra Thayer Towne, SOCIAL PROBLEMS (New York: Macmillan, 1916), p. 53.

151. Bessie Pierce, CIVIC ATTITUDES IN AMERICAN SCHOOL TEXTBOOKS (Chicago: Univ. of Chicago Press, 1930), p. 161.

152. c.f. Beard and Bagley; Muzzey; Ogg.

153. Harold R. Isaacs, SCRATCHES ON OUR MINDS (New York: John Day Co., 1958), pp. 92-108.

CHAPTER SIX

TEXTBOOKS, TEACHERS, AND TEACHING TODAY

Changes have occurred in both teaching methods and content of instructional materials during the almost forty years since World War II. These changes can for the most part be attributed to the varying influence of four main factors. First, a major revolution has resulted from technological advances. This has brought forth an abundance of audio-visual aids of varying quality, quick and easy reproduction of printed material, and rapid computation of mathematical data. Children born during the post-war baby boom, now adults, grew up with television as part of their daily lives. Fascination with the wonders that could be seen as they happened, as well as with the drivel that was shown, reduced reliance on the printed word. Anxiety grew, especially after Sputnik, about "Why Johnny can't read," although there was less concern about the content he could not decode.

A second influence on education in these recent decades has been the tremendous increase in international interaction. American servicemen during the Second World War, and millions of tourists since the war, became aware of places and peoples outside the United States. Teachers learned about techniques used successfully by their colleagues in other countries, and adapted those methods to their classrooms. (The outstanding example of this was the adoption of the "open classroom," originally used in England, as a setting for learning.) At the same time, people were moving within the country (migration) and between countries (immigration) at a more rapid rate than had been true in the pre-war years. Again, this brought about an increased interchange of ideas between localities and between countries. Furthermore, changes in the immigration laws, passed in 1965, brought an influx of the previously restricted Asians to the United States. Just as pre-1880's immigrants were characterized as "old" immigrants and post-1880's were "new," so the lifting of restrictions made a division between "old" Asians and "new."

The conditions under which the latter came differed markedly from the familyless Chinese workers of the late nineteenth century and the Japanese "picture-brides" of the early twentieth century. The "new" Asian immigration has meant new challenges for the schools, for it is less possible today for the child to evade school or eventually to survive economically without knowing how to speak and read English. The needs of these children differ from those of 50 or 60 years ago, and the ways in which those needs are met must similarly differ.

A third major factor on teaching and textbooks has been the overflow of side effects from the civil rights movement of the 1960's. No longer were blacks, Spanish-speaking, and other cultural groups willing to accept slurs, omissions, and/or distortions in the textbooks or the classroom. This led to the development of new criteria for textbook selections, which will be discussed later in this chapter. The civil rights movement and subsequent legislation led to professional and lay concern with curriculum content, also to be discussed in this chapter. These changes mandate the sharpening of teacher competence in the area of the culturally different, thereby necessitating comment and evaluation of teacher education.

Finally, today's teachers are better prepared to teach than were those of the pre-1920 period. They have had to meet more stringent requirements to obtain certification, and have frequently gone beyond the bachelor's degree in their education. Thus, in combination with the rise of other media, there should be less reliance on textbooks as the major teaching resource. However, as a result of interviews with public school teachers and administrators, we suspect that the average classroom teacher is still quite dependent on the textbook. Two visiting Australian educators, in fact, commented that "In almost all of the history classes we observed, the textbook has played a dominant role. It seems to be the main guide to the organization of content which teachers employ."[1] Evidently publishers have found this to be true also, since they still demand of authors that teacher manuals be provided complete with detailed objectives, lesson plans, directives for questioning and activities, and test questions. Even in the public school systems, the development of new curricula evokes the preparation of curriculum guides with very detailed information on what is to be taught and how. Administrators have found that their teachers feel more comfortable relying on such specifics, using the guides as "crutches," rather than using their own research and creative abilities to initiate appropriate activities to meet course objectives.

In order to appreciate the magnitude of changes that have occurred, we present a description of texts in the immediate post-war period. The results of evaluative studies done at the time by several researchers, as well as our own study of texts, are presented in the light of contemporary selection criteria. Since it is impossible to consider texts in a vacuum, these data are followed by discussions of educational goals, and multi-cultural and teacher education.

The post-war years

En route from the texts of the great immigration period to the texts of today, we scanned several readers of the intervening decades. Not only were they oriented to the suburban/rural white middle-class, but they were bland to the point of stifling any normally inquisitive child's desire to read. Furthermore, they were unchanging from one generation (the 1930's) to the next (1950's). Texts were reissued every few years with few if any modifications in their content. In one instance, a first-grader had the same "Dick and Jane" reader that his mother had had 24 years earlier! Another example of reprinting carried to the extreme was the reader PARADES (Scott, Foresman, gr. 6) that we read in the 1956 edition. This book was originally published in 1910, and subsequently reprinted unchanged in 1912, 1919, 1921, 1928, 1932, 1936, 1946, and 1956.

Commercial children's literature, such as the rhythmic yet simple books by Dr. Seuss, and many informative books published as "Golden Books," were more stimulating to learning and the imagination for pre-schoolers than were the readers these children encountered in the primary grades. Even these, however, were not much more multi-ethnic than the readers and other texts used in the schools. The American Council on Education published in 1946 the results of several studies on the treatment of Asians in a variety of elementary and secondary school textbooks. These were characterized by omissions of historical events and of countries, errors of fact, and disproportionate stress on China. References to Japan, of course, were colored by the country's aggressions leading up to and during the Second World War. A more recent study, ASIA IN AMERICAN TEXTBOOKS, published in 1976 by the Asia Society, found similar omissions and errors, as well as continued emphasis on a Western-centered approach and the perpetuation of stereotypes.[2]

Even today, it should be noted, Asian countries other than China and Japan are only occasionally mentioned in secondary school textbooks, and rarely if ever at the elementary level. Such references are most often connected with events in American military history. For example, in describing the Phillipines, the Islands were acquired in the Spanish-American War of 1898 and were promised independence in 1934 that was granted in 1946. In between, the Phillipines were occupied by the Japanese in World War II and freed by MacArthur, the "hero of Bataan and Corregidor." As for Korea, it was the scene of the United Nations' "police action" from 1950 to 1953. From that time, it remains divided into the Communist North and the "democratic" South. Viet Nam was the scene of an unpopular war and great United States' losses between 1960 and 1974. It is now partitioned into the Communist North and the conquered South. So much for Asian history in the textbooks. What is not even mentioned, however, is that Filipino immigrants suffered many of the same deprivations experienced by the Chinese in terms of family life when they came to the mainland.

In 1952, it was noted by Trager and Yarrow that

> Primers and pre-primers tend to depict family and neighborhood life in completely static, unreal terms. Every family is named Jones, Smith, or something equally Anglo-Saxon. . . . The assumption is that there is only one kind of church, that "everybody" goes there, and that everybody is Protestant. . . An Oriental person is often in "native" costume and with a "pigtail." Unless the story is exotic or about faraway places the Oriental is rarely present, and, when he is, he has the role of the ubiquitous laundry-man.[3]

These views were confined in our own limited examination of 1950's and early 1960's readers (N = 19). Further, with regard to the assumption of "only one kind of church," a study made in 1963, based on an analysis of 120 elementary social studies textbooks, found these books to be biased in favor of Protestantism over Catholicism and of Christianity over Judaism. "Definitely sectarian, they ignore the pluralistic character of American life." Other studies concluded in the same period confirm these observations.[4]

A survey in the mid-1950's of texts used in 25 Western countries revealed that these books presented a distorted and fragmented view of Asian history and important figures, much as was true in the United States. The viewpoint was distinctly European.[5] Even the American social studies text of the early 1960's avoided controversial issues such as group differences for fear of community disapproval, because of teacher ignorance and/or incompetence, and because of publisher avoidance. However, they were also devoid of the racist theories of history that had permeated the histories of the nineteenth century. In a survey of these texts, it was found that there were more errors of omission than commisison.

> It is not that other peoples are portrayed as racially inferior. Rather, there is the repetitive, sing-song refrain that the United States, its allies, and the countries of its origin in Western Europe represent most of what is good.[6]

An inflated patriotism, seen earlier, continued to be characteristic of the American History texts of the 60's.

Avoidance of controversy has not been the only difficulty in writing good textbooks. Vocabulary has to be controlled both in level of word difficulty and sentence length, particularly at the elementary grade levels. (This is, however, a problem today as well at the secondary and college levels.) Integrated content and illustrations, depending on the locale, were to be included in only some text editions even during the 1960's. Alternate formats were used for the "lily-white" editions adopted by some school districts. Another problem, one that contributes even now to the blandness of many elementary texts, is the committee authorship of these books. The result of such effort is that ". . .the textbooks children study are totally lacking in individual style, private opinion, and personal passion."[7] These assorted difficulties form a large part of the reason why today's textbooks, too, may appear to be "uninspiring" and ideologically sterile, although they tend to be colorful and profusely illustrated. These are factors to be considered as the publisher ponders on whether to invest half a million dollars or more per book in production. A series destined for several grades obviously represents an even greater financial risk, thus mandating greater caution, prudence, and foresightedness on the part of the publishers.

Textbook selection

The civil rights demonstrations of the early 1960's, and the legislative and executive "War on Poverty" of the Johnson administration forced educators and publishers to take a new look at the textbooks being used in the schools of the nation. Their principal concern was the "all white" content of readers, histories, and other texts. By the time of the Congressional hearings on minorities in textbooks in late summer of 1966, some changes had already occurred in content and illustrations to introduce blacks into them. Even so, a number of publishers testified that they were still producing two versions of many texts. One was the newly integrated version, frequently a risky venture; the other, a continuation of the "lily-white" edition. This practice was defended on very basic economic grounds -give the customer what he wants.

Included in the record of the 1966 hearings were state regulations for book purchases under Title II of the Elementary and Secondary Education Act of 1965, and the guidelines from several states for textbook selection. On paper, these all appeared to be very inter-group-relations-oriented. In practice, the testimony of publishers, state superintendents of schools, black leaders, and others indicated that any progress made in the textbook treatment of minorities tended to be at the secondary level.[8] However, the Chandler Reading Program and the Bank Street Readers (Macmillan) did attempt to provide multi-ethnic reading content for younger children. Subsequent examination of curriculum guides developed in the 1970's similarly reveals that ethnic studies or multi-cultural curricula also tend to be taught principally at the secondary level. However, attitudes are more malleable in earlier grades -- a strong rationale for modification of the elementary level curriculum guides and texts.

There is considerable evidence to support the assertion that many, possibly most, teachers deviate little from the content of textbooks and the accompanying teachers' editions. Therefore, if the texts do not propose "controversial" topics such as cultural pluralism (or even admit to the existence of minority groups), there is a danger that pupils may not be exposed to such topics at all.[9] At the same time, texts that **do** try to avoid prejudice need to be accurate without being dryly statistical, to avoid common stereotypes without creating new and unrealistic ones, and to reflect high-quality historical scholarship, rather than unwarranted generalizations and false optimism.[10] A criticism of both history and literature texts has been that "The prevailing emotions of the people involved are not revealed; hence, the events never come to life."[11] Portrayals of Asian-Americans, for example, rarely mention their strong family units, low rates of delinquency and crime (true until quite recent years), or achievements. This is not to say that every volume in a series of texts must contain material relevant to the Asians, the Jews, or any other specific group, favorable or unfavorable. However, through supplementary readings, televised or filmed material, or other techniques, the young student needs to be made aware that "Persons do not live as footloose individuals; they carry on as members of functional groups playing significant roles in society."[12] As members of society, moreover, they need to be seen in group settings as family members, in occupational settings, and even growing up, in texts as well as supplementary sources. These are portrayals common in elementary social studies curricula that tend to move from studies of the family to the community, to the nation, and then to United States history and a smattering of world history.

Selection criteria

Several states have developed selection criteria for textbooks, whether for statewide adoption or as guidelines for local school district selection committees. These criteria are then used to evaluate texts in current use or offered for future adoption. In an introductory statement in 1971, the California Task Force to Reevaluate Social Science Textbooks, Grade Five through Eight, expressed its philosophy concerning this group of texts:

> Because teachers and the textbooks they use exert influence on the intellectual growth and self-determination of the individual, it is essential that the materials the school provides do indeed give the student the opportunity to develop an image deeply rooted in a sense of personal dignity and also to grow in his respect for an understanding of all aspects of American society.[13]

The Task Force evaluated both the quantity and quality of content on minority groups, and checked for distortions and inaccuracies. They also took note of ethnocentrism, as well as insensitivity toward various groups or omission of these groups where their inclusion would be appropriate.

Michigan educators similarly searched for representatives of various minority groups; departure from the white, middle-class, rural/suburban orientation; recognition of religious needs; mention of immigration and immigrants; and other evidence of sensitivity to cultural diversity and pluralism.[14] In Pennsylvania, a checklist is suggested that provides for ratings (Superior, Acceptable, Unacceptable, Not Pertinent) and page references on 18 items:

1. Includes materials on minorities where relevant.

2. Reflects respect for personal and cultural differences and the worth and importance of the individual

3. Offers factual, realistic, mature treatment.

4. Gives balanced treatment of past and present.

5. Presents accurate, pertinent information.

6. Comes to grips with issues and problems.

7. Presents varied points of view.

8. Develops concepts of pluralistic society.

9. Shows cultural diversity in illustrative materials.

10. Includes cultural diversity in text materials.

11. Emphasizes both positive and negative aspects.

12. Avoids distortion and bias.

13. Avoids use of name-calling or emotionally charged words.

14. Supports generalizations with the specific and the concrete.

15. Avoids stereotyping.

16. Aids in building positive attitudes and understandings.

17. Distinguishes between fact and opinion.

18. Gives attention to holidays, festivals, religious observances of various minority groups.[15]

These three samples of contemporary approaches to textbook selection are typical of those in use in other states. They also served as bases for the development of the criteria applied in this study.

Results of evaluative studies

There have been a number of studies in the past several years that evaluated the portrayal of minorities in textbooks, some sponsored by state departments of education as part of their cyclical reviewing program, a few by independent researchers, and others sponsored by major organizations such as the American Jewish Committee, Anti-Defamation League of B'nai Brith (both of these extending their concern beyond the Jewish people), and National Education Association. Despite the protestations at the 1966 Congressional hearings, it is apparent from these studies that significant omissions and errors continued to be published throughout the 1960's and into the 1970's. However, it must also be noted that the conclusions given are based on limited surveys, with the number of texts and teacher editions per study ranging from eight to sixty.

The reading texts of the 1960's varied somewhat in content and quality. Collier (1967) examined 25 multi-ethnic readers for the primary grades from four publishers, copyrighted 1960 to mid-1965. Although she was primarily concerned with Negro (sic) references in these books, she found that children of other minority groups, as well as some of the black children, had few opportunities to identify with characters or settings of the stories. Also, a kind of bland happiness pervaded the stereotyped family situations, which even the children could recognize as unrealistic. She concluded that much needed to be done to meet the needs of **all** children in the basal readers.[16] Of 73 elementary level readers from twelve publishers that we read, copyrighted 1965-69, only a few reflected multicultural content.

MORE ROADS TO FOLLOW (Scott, Foresman, 1965, gr. 3), and THE NEW TIMES AND PLACES (also Scott, Foresman, 1962, gr. 4-1), included the only stories in this group of texts that suggested an awareness of the problems facing the immigrant child. "Out of her shell" (gr. 3) reflects the shyness of a Danish girl in an American classroom, her cultural pride, and the development of an eventual mutual acceptance and respect by the young heroine and her new classmates. The fourth-grade reader story, "Star Pupil," focuses on the problem of a non-English-speaking girl and how the class helped to teach her a new language (English). MORE ROADS TO FOLLOW also includes a story involved with a traditional Chinese New Year parade in San Francisco ("Soo-Pung measures up"), and has a story set in Japan. CAVALCADES (Scott, Foresman, 1965, gr. 6) contains an entire section with stories of immigrants and immigration. There are Haiku poems as well as Mary Antin's poem, "Homeless Birds," and a story of Chinese immigration, "To the City of Golden Hills," included to promote understanding of the "Oriental strand in the tapestry of peoples who looked for a better life in a new land."[17]

McGraw-Hill's SKYLINE SERIES (1965, gr. 2-4) is mildly multi-ethnic in stories and settings. The Ginn 360 series (1969, multi-graded), though strong on creativity and curiosity, is somewhat weak on actual multicultural content. A few illustrations include what might be Asians, but these lack sufficient clarity for sure identification.

LAUNCHINGS AND LANDINGS (American Book Co., 1968, gr. 6) contains a biography of "Emma Lazarus: Champion of Immigrants," and a story about "Hatsuno's Great-grandmother" that occurs in the present. The American Book series, in general, presents an attempt to include stories that include "foreign-sounding" names, occasional non-American settings (most often these are AmerIndian or Eskimo), more urban content, and information from a variety of sources -- science, myths, biography, and history. With one or two exceptions, references to Asians are remote in time and/or location. The Teacher Edition suggests questions designed to provoke thought on some of the "exceptions." For example, "Learning a new language" (IDEAS AND IMAGES, g. 3-2) asks: "If we get a new student in our class that (sic) does not speak our language, what could we do to help him?" The story "Best Friend" (KINGS AND THINGS, gr. 5) is the tale of a Chinese-American girl who moves from San Francisco's Chinatown to an "All-American" community on the peninsula south of the city. The teacher is urged to ask: "What do you think about Judy's adjustment to the new community, to a new name, and to living in a predominantly non-Chinese community for the first time?" The idea of retaining pride in her ancestry is expressed more than once in the story.

The 1966 Harper & Row multi-disciplinary readers showed some movement in the direction of multicultural content. Most successful of those examined in this series was FROM FARAWAY PLACES (gr. 3), in which the theme was that children of different national origins told stories of their ancestral lands. Japan was one of eight countries represented. The concluding section, "Americans All," emphasized ancestors and native lands in general. Harper & Row's two readers at the upper elementary levels in this period, FROM PILOTS TO PLASTICS (1969 and 1974, gr. 7) and FROM STARS TO SCULPTURES (1969, gr. 8), had stories set in India (both British and independent) and old Siam in the former, and an excerpt from THE RAFT, a World War II novel, with two brief references to the Japanese as the enemy, in the latter. Of 384 figures identified in illustrations in both books, only 18 were clearly Asians. Each book also contained a biography section. The Danny Kaye biography used a Yiddish word occasionally, and mentioned that he had conducted the Israeli Symphony, but otherwise gave Jewish children less reason for group pride than stories of blacks gave to that group. The biographical data on architect Louis I. Kahn, reproduced from a biographical reference source, listed his Jewish religion, but again offered little in the way of opportunity for ethnic pride. The accompanying teacher's manual for each of these texts gave little direction for discussion of these different cultures or attaining affective objectives other than creating "empathy with story characters" on the part of the students. The "sin of omission" was also seen in a time-line given in FROM PILOTS TO PLASTICS. This listed independence in India in 1947 and a liberal government taking office in Bolivia in 1952, but omitted Israeli independence in 1948 and the Communist regime's take-over in China in 1949, events certainly equal in importance to India's independence.

In the case of most readers of the late 1960's, however, "integration" meant blacks and whites, but not other groups, in the illustrations. Often the integrated illustrations were surface changes only. That is, there was no change in the story line that could be related to the racial differences shown. Several series remained rural, white, and middle-class in outlook. Religion was completely avoided, as were all references to Christmas or Easter-related topics or symbols. There is an occasional reference to a **"Sunday** suit," implying a universal need to have a good suit to wear to church, but otherwise even oblique references to religion are omitted entirely.

Social studies texts published in the late 1960's had not yet caught up with cultural pluralism either. There was not much more content referring to Asians or Jews than there had been two decades earlier. The 15 Teacher Editions that we examined were equally weak in this area. Comments from three evaluative studies substantiate the concern with omissions and errors, and are offered in the order of their publication.

Michael Kane's review of the treatment of minorities in 48 social studies high school texts, published in 1970, is widely regarded as a landmark effort. Kane included comparisons with the earlier Anti-Defamation League study (1960) and the report of the American Council on Education (1949). His evaluative criteria included **inclusion** (information about minority groups as relevant), **validity** of statements, **balance** of negative and positive views, **comprehensiveness** to eliminate stereotyping, **concreteness** as opposed to generalizations and platitudes, **unity** of information about a group to increase meaningfulness, and realism about social evils.[18]

With respect to the treatment of Jews in high school world history texts, Kane found continued emphasis on the ancient Hebrews with less attention paid to modern Jewish history or the centuries between ancient and modern history, except for discussions of the State of Israel and its people. Presentations of the crucifixion story, difficult to handle in a way satisfactory to all, and medieval and modern European history as tied to the Jews of these periods, were still generally replete with distortions. American history texts were found to be even weaker, with very few references that ". . .convey a realistic sense of the diversity of the American Jewish population and thus of their similarity to other peoples of this nation."[19] Kane concluded that, as of 1969, textbooks were still contributing to the development of anti-semitic stereotypes and behaviors.

Asians fared even more poorly, according to Kane. They were not even included in ten of the thirty texts he examined, and the criteria of comprehensiveness and balance were not met in any of the texts that mentioned Chinese- or Japanese-Americans. Two textbooks referred to these groups in contemporary society in less than a page each, and two others contained one photograph of an Asian each.[20] Views of the Japanese tended to be more sympathetic than portrayals of the Chinese immigrants mostly because of references to the Japanese-American internment during World War II. Kane found no improvement in the treatment of Asians from earlier textbooks, and he himself omits any comment on the complete omission of references to Asians other than Chinese and Japanese.

If Kane came to such negative conclusions about **high school** history texts, it is not surprising to read the disturbing findings of surveys on **elementary** level books. The report of the California Task Force in December 1971, previously mentioned, stated that **none** of the 15 basic social studies tests or 45 supplemental texts and teachers' editions they examined was in compliance with the California State Code on content regarding minority groups. Since California has a state-wide text adoption policy, such a negative finding had serious implications for teachers, authors, and publishers. In a general comment, the Task Force averred that

. . .the books generally reflect. . .a pervasive ethnocentrism in both framework and content, an insensitivity to people of various ethnic groups. . . Some of the most flagrant abuses occur in the Teachers' Guides and Teachers' Editions, which often confound the previously mentioned deficiencies by providing prejudicial supplementary material and by instructing teachers as to what answers and conclusions they are to extract from supposedly inquiring students.[21]

A sample of comments on the content in books evaluated for use in grades five through eight follows, with specific reference to Asian-Americans:

Kenneth Bailey et al. THE AMERICAN ADVENTURE (1970)
  Very little (and that, negative) on Asians in America.

Frank J. Cappellutti and Ruth H. Grossman. THE HUMAN ADVENTURE (1970)
  Little on Asia; what is included jumps from 3rd century B.C. to 1912 A.D.

June R. Chapin et al. QUEST FOR LIBERTY: INVESTIGATING UNITED STATES HISTORY (1971)
  Misinformation on Chinese.
  "There is the implication that all Chinese, Japanese, and Jews go to college these days and have no problems. No mention whatever is made of Filipinos."[21]

Frederick M. King et al. CONCEPTS IN SOCIAL SCIENCE: THE SOCIAL STUDIES AND OUR COUNTRY (1970)
  Nothing on Asian-Americans; implied negativism toward Jews.

Frederick M. King et al. CONCEPTS IN SCIENCE: THE SOCIAL STUDIES AND OUR WORLD (1970)
  Criticisms of references to Chinese history (p. 41 of report).

Gerhard N. Rostvold et al. VOICES OF EMERGING NATIONS (1971)
  "This book is very negative in its use of the word 'different.'"[23]

Martin W. Sandler. PEOPLE MAKE A NATION (1971)
  Although considered a "model text" in many ways, "No mention of Japanese-Americans, treatment of Chinese on two pages not well done."[24]

Staff of the Center for the Study of Instruction. THE SOCIAL SCIENCES: CONCEPTS AND VALUES, PURPLE (1970)
  Section on immigration does not include Asians.

Perpetuation of myths on Asian-Americans; ignores Filipinos and Koreans.

Totally unacceptable in portrayal of Asian-Americans.

Referring to p. 314 of text: "By perpetuating the myth of the Asian 'model minority,' the textbooks reinforce complacent attitudes in the general public that hinder efforts to deal with the very real problems of gang warfare, inadequate housing, drug abuse, poor health conditions, and chronic unemployment."[25]

Staff of the Social Studies Curriculum Center. THE AMERICANS (1970)

"This book lacks any mention whatever of Mexican-Americans or Asians."[26]

Carl G. Winter et al. VOICES OF THE AMERICANS (1971)
(Designed for the slow to average student)
Nothing on Asian-Americans.

Ralph Sandlin Yoke, et al. EXPLORING REGIONS OF THE EASTERN HEMISPHERE (n.d.)

Many errors and omissions noted in treatment of Asians.

"Essentially, Asian societies in this textbook serve as no more than foils for appropriate contrasts with Western endeavor and enterprise. Whether they be the monomaniacal Japanese ruthlessly emulating American ways from industrialization to ecological disaster, the Chinese Communists portrayed as the antithesis of The American Way, or the Koreans, Filipinos, and Asian women who remain part of the invisible and faceless teeming hordes, 'Man in Asia' remains as simple, contrite, and expendable. . ." as it was to Americans in the early 1900's.[27]

Michigan's Department of Education evaluated eight primary level (grade 2) social studies texts, published between 1965 and 1971, with somewhat similar results.[28] In most schools, the focus of the social studies curriculum in second grade is the community.

Anderson. COMMUNITIES AND THEIR NEEDS (1969)
White, middle-class orientation
No mention of immigrants
Little attention paid to religion

Brandwein. THE SOCIAL SCIENCES: CONCEPTS AND VALUES (1970)
No Orientals in section on the United States although they are

present in the discussion on the world
Middle-class focus
No mention of religion
Open-ended questions

Davis. OBSERVING PEOPLE AND PLACES (1971)
Multi-social; realistic
Open-ended questions

Goetz. AT HOME IN OUR LAND, 2nd ed. (1965)
White, middle-class, and rural
Unrealistic

Hanna. INVESTIGATING MAN'S WORLD: LOCAL STUDIES (1970)
Reflects a diverse and pluralistic society
One drawing may be of an Oriental child
No mention of religion

King. COMMUNITIES AND SOCIAL NEEDS (1968)
Too little diversity shown within United States
Unrealistic
Avoidance of problems
Weak attempt to be multi-ethnic

McDonald. ONE PLUS ONE: LEARNING ABOUT COMMUNITIES (1971)
No Orientals pictured
Urban, multi-racial, multi-ethnic`
Churches and synagogues mentioned once
Senior author claims there is a picture of a parade in Chinatown

McIntyre. EXPLORING OUR NEEDS, rev. ed. (1969)
Middle-class and white-oriented
Innocuous, bland, unrealistic
No mention of religious needs

In terms of contemporary state selection criteria, only one of the texts appears to be satisfactory.

Two studies published in the mid-1970's reveal that the blatant prejudices extant even in the texts of the early 1960's have been toned down, but not eliminated. A study of sexism and racism in popular basal reader series used in Baltimore, and published in 1976, found that:

The five series reviewed. . . generally underrepresent minority groups; fail to deal honestly with socio-economic oppression; portray minorities more frequently in fantasy or history than in realistic contemporary settings; give inaccurate interpretations of the cultural achievements and heritage of minority groups; and perpetuate ethnocentric bias in favor of white culture, values, and standards. Such biases alienate minority children from textbooks and education, discourage pride in their own heritage and culture, and conversely, encourage assimilation into the dominant culture.[29]

The Baltimore project included two series from Ginn and Company (1964 revised edition, 1969 Reading 360 series); the Macmillan Bank Street Series (1971 revised edition); SRA basal reading program (1971 revised edition); Scott, Foresman OPEN HIGHWAY series (1965-68); and a follow-up with the Scott, Foresman NEW OPEN HIGHWAY series (1973-74), Scott, Foresman READING UNLIMITED READING SERIES (1976), and the Macmillan Series R Reading Program (1975). In the follow-up it was concluded that ". . .while some of the **most overt** racism and sexism is gone, **more subtle,** covert forms remain -- and these are dangerous **because** they are subtle."[30] White ethnocentrism and avoidance of current controversies were still present.

In the other study, a task force in Springfield, Ohio, examined the history texts used in that city (1975). Of 11 books studied, 6 were unsatisfactory, 3 less than satisfactory, and only 2 were satisfactory. "Eurocentrism" was a frequent source of criticism in these books. In one of the unsatisfactory texts, PEOPLE USE THE EARTH (Silver Burdett, 1972, gr. 3), the task force cited the following omissions:

Pages 77-85 discussing Israel do not explain how the Jews came to receive that land, nor the displacement of the Palestinians who lived there. Some background could be provided to third graders to help them better understand the Middle East situation at the present time. Within these same pages there is only one group picture which shows the variety of racial background of Jews. All of the other pictures (both group and single) depict European Jews.[31]

Our own examination of this text indicates that this criticism is valid, but that it appears to be more the result of a disjointed presentation of content found in this and other Silver Burdett texts than an act of intended discrimination.

1970's texts

Increasing pressure on both educators and publishers in the decade since the 1966 Congressional hearings to produce texts appropriate to a pluralistic society should be reflected in books presently in use. To ascertain whether this has occurred, we examined pupil and/or teacher editions of readers and social studies books published in the period 1970-76. We found considerable variation in quality and quantity of content with respect to immigrant history, Asians and Jews.

Of the readers, the Harper & Row multi-disciplinary series offers the most cause for positive comment. Not only do the readers increase in multi-cultural content over earlier editions we had seen, but several of the teachers' editions contain a special paper on "Reading and the Spanish-speaking child" that could easily be applied to other cultural groups as well. Points stressed in the paper include the importance of the child's self-concept and recognition of the child's cultural heritage. Although this is part of a guide to teaching reading, several helpful views of culturally different children are also expressed. Attention is paid, for example, to the lack of simple "academic experiences which people assume are common to all children" among the children of poverty. There are warnings for the teacher to avoid generalizing about **any** group. Mention is also made of the conflict that minority group children face when they know that education is important, but feel that they must reject a part of themselves in order to attain an education.[32] The point is made that those children who refuse to both face the conflict and try to resolve it constructively are the children who ultimately drop out of school.

Suggestions to the teacher are valuable to the cause of multi-cultural education, if they are read by the teacher. For example, in the teachers' guide for COMING TO CROSSROADS (Harper & Row, 1982, gr. 5), the story "Open Road to Eagle," which concerns one black boy in a Boy Scout troop, suggests that the teacher encourage the children to write about an experience or situation in which they felt out of place. Sensitivity to the plight of the non-English-speaking child is seen in "The Day for English," a story in TRAVELING THE TRADE WINDS (1972, gr 4). Here, the teacher is encouraged to ask pupils, "How do you suppose Candita felt? (Elicit from pupils that Candita must have felt alone in a strange, new land where she could not understand the language.)"[33] It is also suggested that children who speak a language in addition to English say something

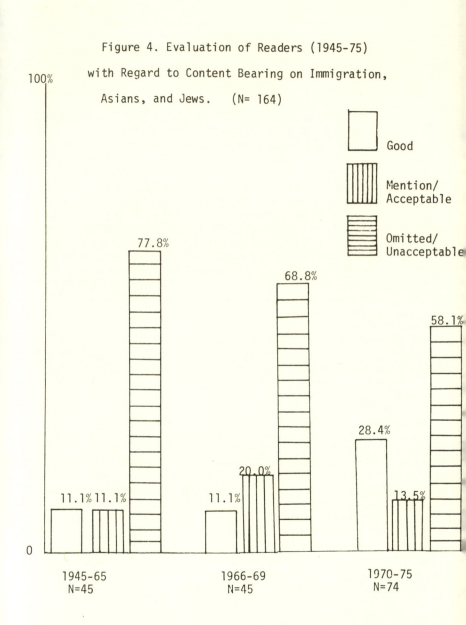

Figure 4. Evaluation of Readers (1945-75) with Regard to Content Bearing on Immigration, Asians, and Jews. (N= 164)

Good

Mention/ Acceptable

Omitted/ Unacceptable

100%

77.8%

68.8%

58.1%

28.4%

11.1% 11.1%

11.1%

20.0%

13.5%

0

1945-65
N=45

1966-69
N=45

1970-75
N=74

166

to the class in that language, perhaps speak about some customs of their heritage, and show a "native costume" if it is available. The tone of this suggestion is somewhat condescending, and a more constructive approach would be appropriate. "The coins of Lin Foo," a one-act 16th-century Chinese play, in addition to promoting a discussion of the play form and China of that time, provokes the topic, "Discuss the advantages and disadvantages of maintaining cultural traditions in a strange country."[34]

A social studies segment in FROM SKYSCRAPERS TO SQUIRRELS (1973, gr. 2) has, as one type of community, life in Haifa, and as another, a secular view of life on a kibbutz. Hebrew print is shown and observance of the Sabbath as a day of rest in Israel is discussed, although without any reference to its religious significance. The teacher is instructed to ask the children about similarities and differences between their lives and communities and those in Israel. This is one of the rare instances where Jewish children encounter content in the public school that they also meet in the religious school.

Not all of the Harper & Row readers are equally good in reflecting cultural pluralism. For example, FROM MYSTERIES TO MICROBES (1975, gr. 3) omits any mention of the role of Chinese laborers in building the railroads in the West in a story about "Railroads Yesterday." Other texts in the series (1972-75) ignore Asians and Jews completely in print and almost completely in illustrations. On the other hand, rapid adaptation to change is seen in FROM LIONS TO LEGENDS (gr. 6). The 1974 Teacher Edition, designed to accompany the 1973 pupil text, makes no references to Asians or Jews. Yet the 1975 pupil edition substitutes a biography of Golda Meir for one of Rachel Carlson, and includes in the mathematics section an informative article on how Japan converted to the metric system to replace the earlier "flat" article on metrication.

The uneven content of readers is seen also in a Webster McGraw-Hill series, READING FOR CONCEPTS (1970). There are several scattered references to various Asian peoples or countries in Books B - E (gr. 2-4) and Book H (gr. 6), but very few in Book A (gr. 1) or Books F and G (gr. 5). An interesting omission is noted in connection with a section called "Greetings to you" (gr. 2); "In another part of the world people say 'Shalom (sha-lom).' The word 'shalom' means peace."[35] Neither the language nor the people who speak it are identified, although other languages and countries are named. In the fifth grade Book F, there are two brief articles on immigration history that refer to the British and the Dutch exclusive of other peoples. Despite these negative aspects, there are many positive cultural group references in the series.

In Lippincott's basic reader series (McCracken/Walcutt, 1975), there is little, if anything, with which Asian or Jewish children can identify in the eleven pupil texts. Nothing in the teachers' editions suggests constructive use of the contents in any way except the teaching of reading. Similarly, in an eight book series published by Cambridge (READING AND SPEAKING, 1973), all instructional objectives are oriented to reading skills exclusively. Such ethnic content as is present reflects blacks in the illustrations and Spanish names of story characters. Asians are rarely seen in the illustrations, and neither Asians nor Jews are included in the printed text. Of four Houghton Mifflin primary readers, only one (REWARDS, 1971, gr. 3) reflects concern with individual differences and with Asians. These are apparent in a sympathetic story about a Japanese boy without grandparents in this country, "Meet Miki Takino," and in a selection on Hawaii, which ". . .is called a 'melting pot' because its people come from many other countries and all live happily together."[36] Macmillan's THE MAGIC WORD (1970, gr. 6) has a section on the growth of language that includes text and illustrations dealing with Chinese ideograms and Japanese and Hebrew letters. There are, in addition, stories on a Chinese boy in China; several with content involving blacks, American Indians, and Eskimos; one with a Puerto Rican hero; and a concluding story on "The Outsider," which concerns a black girl in Hawaii, and explores her feelings about being the victim of real and imagined prejudice. These stories can be used to heighten sensitivity to other cultures as well by an astute teacher.

In addition to basal readers, there is an extensive variety of supplemental texts. from a series called TEACHING PICTURES (Cook Publishers, 1973), one can select the package called "Living together in America," which is ungraded but is directed to elementary schools students. Among the groups included are Chinese, Japanese, Jews, and even Appalachian people. The author is careful to distinguish between old and contemporary situations, mentions restrictions on the immigrant groups, and is critical of these past practices. Reasonably positive statements are made concerning each group.

SRA (1970) has a series of paperbacks called AMERICA: LAND OF CHANGE that has a low reading level (gr. 4-7) but content appropriate to grade 6 and above. The teachers' guide specifically urges open-ended, inquiry-oriented discussion of the issues presented.

These include religious freedom, the internment of the West Coast Japanese during World War II, prejudice against the early Chinese and Japanese immigrants, and the "melting pot" v. the "salad bowl" views of different groups in this country. The texts themselves are not as useful. For example, the paperback focusing of "Growth" of the nation refers solely to Europeans in the discussion of immigrant poverty and omits, in its section on transportation, any mention of the Asian workers who helped to build the railroads in the West (and the railroad itself). The paperback on "People" centers almost exclusively on Europeans, with some emphasis also on blacks and Puerto Ricans. The chapter on "newcomers" (1815-1914) cites the Jews once and the Asians not at all. In the 128 pages of this book, there are four sentences on anti-Jewish discrimination and less than one-half page on the Chinese, Japanese, and the exclusion laws.

A six-volume supplementary reading series ("Triple I") issued by the American Book Company (1970) is unusually sensitive to cultural patterns. Each volume has a section on self-image, interpersonal relationships, the world of work, inter-social relationships, and values. The teachers' editions offer strongly supportive suggestions for activities that will enhance student pride, such as having students look into their own ethnic heritages, report on various other groups, and study the contributions to society of all groups of people. It is also stressed that

> The teacher is the vital key in helping each child build pride in his racial or cultural group. Care should be taken to accent similarities so that children will understand that similarities far outweigh differences.[37]

The stories in these books reflect a wide variety of ethnic groups and themes.

An ungraded reader, COUNTRIES AND CULTURES (SRA, 1970) also has a wide variety of reading selections appropriate to multicultural education. Included are stories on Confucius, life on a kibbutz, an Israeli fisherman at the Sea of Galilee, Burmese monks in Thailand, Tokyo, Japanese girls, the Grand Canal of China, and the Chinese Water People of Hong Kong and Kowloon. Examples of Haiku and Vietnamese poetry are also given. This reader lacks illustrations, however, which reduces the effectiveness of its messages. SRA has also published two filmstrip series to supplement the readers. "American Sampler" (1974) has one filmstrip concerned with ethnic heritage. "Families around the world" (1974) has a filmstrip for each of eight countries. The one on China deals with the effects of the Cultural Revolution in Communist China. The one on Japan, centered on a family in Tokyo, urges discussion of traditional Japanese attitudes and suggests activities for learning about Japanese culture. In the third relevant filmstrip, about a family in Tel Aviv, activities are encouraged that will promote learning the significance of various Jewish religious ceremonies.

Among the social studies texts, the series developed by the Social Science Staff of the Educational Research Council of America, and published by Allyn and Bacon, is superior in its approach to history. It includes parallel time charts for Western **and** Eastern civilizations. Facts are given from the time of primitive man to present history, giving students a solid foundation for further work in the social sciences. This series is clearly the most sensitive of the social studies texts read to cultural pluralism and diversity. Recurrent themes focus on a culture as a mixture of values, traditions, ideas, habits, and institutions, from the first grade text on "Our Country" through the "Challenges of our Times" series for grade seven. There is constant interweaving of Jewish and Asian history throughout the texts wherever appropriate. Immigrant history is introduced in the 1974 revision of "The Making of our America" at third grade level, and reintroduced in "Prejudice and Discrimination" at the seventh grade level. At the lower level, one objective raises the question, "Why did older Americans often dislike new immigrants or treat them unfairly?"[38] This balanced presentation is apparent also in the seventh grade text, where children are encouraged to imagine the self-image of the immigrant child in a situation that is unwelcoming.

One of the "Area Studies" (geography supplements) in the series focuses on the Lands of the Middle East, including "Israel" a western nation in an Arab world," and a chapter on the political scene in the Middle East as of 1971. In the latter, both Arab and Israeli views are given. This book poses a marked contrast to a parallel book published by Sadlier which, in 17 lines, notes that Israel is neither Arab nor Moslem, and that there are Arab-Jewish "differences." A third regional geography, published by Fearon (1974) commits several errors: a map shows Israel's pre-1967 borders without elaboration; the section on Israel is introduced with the statement that "This small nation was created in 1948 by Jews from all over the world," when it was in fact created by United Nations action; and the impression is given that most Israelis are farmers on a kibbutz or moshav, when the fact is that such workers constitute only a small percentage of the population.

Another theme that recurs in the Allyn and Bacon series is the potential outcome of culture conflicts: acculturation, assimilation, genocide, or relatively harmonious diversity. The evils of negative prejudice and discrimination are repeated throughout the narratives of history from ancient civilization to the present, with the Holocaust under the Nazis frequently compared to other instances of genocide by victors during the centuries.

A second social studies series that is successful in emphasizing cultural pluralism is the Holt Databank System (1972), which has a variety of texts and supplementary audio-visual aids to learning. The materials for kindergarten through grade two offer sharp contrast to the second grade texts examined in Michigan (supra). The three levels of materials are successively entitled "Inquiring about Myself," "Inquiring about People," and "Inquiring about Communities." The text content, largely pictorial at this stage, includes a variety of peoples in everyday pursuits as well as culture-related activities. At each of these levels, the "Teacher's Planning Calendar" suggests basic and special activities tied to holidays or special events of different cultural groups. Since the teacher has considerable latitude when it comes to utilizing these supplementary activities, it is imperative that he or she have the sensitivity and knowledge to encourage their implementation. Texts at the higher levels of the Holt System similarly are supportive of cultural pluralism and intergroup understanding. As part of the American history presentation, there is a 30-page section on immigrant history, divided into the 1790-1890 and 1890-1920 periods. Several groups are mentioned, including the Japanese (in California) and the Jews (in New York). Using examples of families for human interest, the texts and filmstrips present the reasons for immigration, difficulties faced, discrimination, and becoming a citizen.

A third social studies program that stresses universality rather than difference is the controversial "Man -- A Course of Study" (MACOS), developed by Jerome Bruner and others.[39] Typically used at the fifth grade level, MACOS employs a variety of ethnographic materials to present an anthropological model for studying general human culture and the concept of human universality. It attempts to use a neutral stimulus (an Eskimo culture) as a basis for inter-cultural understanding and respect. Although the student materials do not include either Asians or Jews, these groups and others are included in the supporting teacher materials as background for discussion. Similarly, "The Family of Man," an elementary social studies program for Kindergarten through grade 6 developed at the University of

Minnesota, attempts to teach concepts relevant to cultural diversity and universality. In this curriculum, however, cross-cultural studies are employed rather than a "neutral" culture. As always, the effectiveness of these curricula depends upon the teacher's willingness to read and use the supporting materials and to initiate meaningful discussion/activities related to them.

At the sixth grade level, ELEVEN NATIONS (Ginn, 1972) includes the study of China, India, Israel, and Japan as well as European countries. Although there are omisisons of historical data, there is a clear attempt in the Teacher's Edition to have the teacher convey the concepts of the poerful influence of a religious heritage and tradition, the consequences of change on a people, and culture shock; causes for immigration; and evidence to counteract stereotypes and prejudice. In general, the Teacher's Edition tries to reinforce similarities as well as differences among the nations studied.

One of the newer history textbooks, written in a more conventional manner and designed for the early junior high school level, and presently used in the Philadelphia schools, is Sandowsky and Hirshfield's MAINSTREAMS OF WORLD HISTORY. This text is especially strong in its presentation, both accurate and sympathetic, of African and Asian civilizations. Its balanced perspective in regard to Western civilization includes relevant references to the role and position of Jews in different historical periods.

In most of the other readers and social studies texts, there is little mention of Asians in their native lands or in this country, a line or two about immigrant history, and virtually nothing about Jews. This "sin of omission" is conspicuous also in the teacher editions. When reading several of the soical studies texts, in fact, one is struck by the fact that the NEW YORK TIMES crossword puzzles include references to Asian and Jewish data far more often than some of the texts do. It is difficult to locate Asians in the illustrations as a certainty, although one might infer their presence from stereotyped drawings of children with straight black hair, cut in bangs across the forehead. Even this attention to Asians is minimal, certainly far below the number of figures than can be identified as either black or Spanish in origin. Our observation of this phenomenon confirms the report of Weitzman and Rizzo (1974) that found only 160 Asian figures in 7680 people shown in elementary texts in five subject areas.

A substantial improvement in references to immigration, Asians,

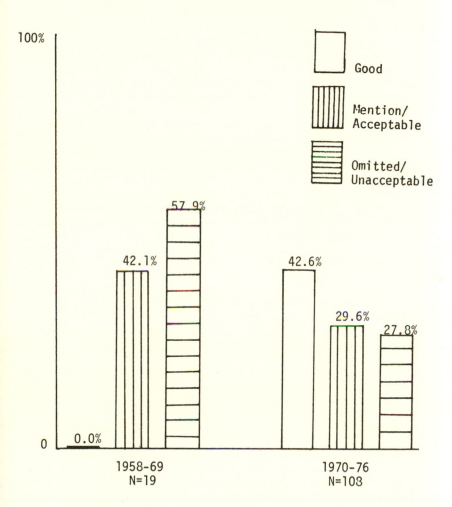

Figure 5. Evaluation of Social Studies
Texts (1958-76) with Regard to Content Bearing on
Immigrants, Asians, and Jews (N=127)

and Jews is seen in Figure 5, where there were no "good" references in the 1958-69 sample of social studies texts and 42.6 percent in the 1970-76 sample. At the same time, omissions and unacceptable references were reduced form 57.9 percent to 27.8 percent in the same pair of samples.

By the mid-1970's, one could conclude that there was some effort to integrate textbooks in both content and illustrations, but there was frequently a "forced" air about the effort that reduced its effectiveness. Little was being done to promote mutual respect and understanding in either pupil or teacher editions, with the exception of the books cited for positive efforts, at the elementary level.

By the early 1980's, changes in textbooks became more evident. Educators, authors, and publishers began to develop and introduce more balanced and meaningful text content in atempts to respond to the demands of an acknowledged multicultural society and the corresponding need for a more appropriate curriculum. By 1983 we found increased multicultural content in stories, more narratives reflecting the contributions of a wide variety of immigrant and minority groups to both American history and modern society, and more multi-ethnic illustrations. Stereotypy was less prevalent, although still to be found in some texts. Teachers' manuals, however, provided suggestions for elaborating on textbook content and offering affective insturction relevant to a pluralistic society. The situation is thus demonstrably better in this most recent decade than it was one or six to ten decades ago.

It should be noted, as was commented upon in the Michigan study, that there continues to be omission of any content dealing with the religious needs of any people in most of the books examined. This reflects, on the one hand, an insensitivity on the part of the authors, and, on the other hand, an awareness on the part of the evaluators of the role of religion as a social institution within local communities, and the fairly common involvement of people with some religious group, not necessarily Protestant. The one book in which religion is discussed in a comparative way is FOUR WORLD VIEWS, part of the Allyn and Bacon series, at the fifth grade level. One of the views concerns Judaism in its traditional and modern modes. Hinduism and Confucianism are two of the other religions presented, with a comparison of traditional Chinese views of people contrasted with those of the Chinese Communists. The inclusion of the Greek view provided an interesting balance. Mention of religion in general or in a comparative manner would not constitute a violation,

174

in these contexts, of the principle of church-state separation.

Children's literature

Not all of children's reading is in textbooks. Frequently the teacher recommends juvenile trade books for supplementary reading. Although this was not an area in which we did extensive research, we believe it appropriate to comment on conclusions of survey's of children's literature since this is a learning resource.

Beginning with books for pre-schoolers, there was a gradual increase in minority group content, principally blacks and Puerto Ricans, in the period 1935-1970.[40] Gast also found that children's fiction, for Kindergarten through grade eight, had fewer negative stereotypes when dealing with minority groups in the 1945-1962 period than was true in books of earlier years, although there were still occupational stereotypes such as the Chinese cook and Japanese gardener.[41] It was interesting that Gast found the Chinese characterized as lower class and relatively unassimilated, whereas the Japanese were perceived as middle-class and more assimilated, although both groups were portrayed as displaying American middle-class virtues. There were not, however, very many available books featuring teen-agers of either group. Indeed, in a three-and-a-half page list of books for primary level readers, divided by ethnic group, there were very few on Chinese-Americans (3), Japanese-Americans (2), Jewish folklore (1), or involving the Jewish religion (8).[42] By contrast, Banks lists one primary and 5 intermediate level books on ChineseAmericans, and 5 primary and 9 intermediate level books on Japanese-Americans. For the upper grades, there are at least four books relevant to Jewish immigrants, one on Chinese-Americans, eight on Japanese-Americans, and two on Filipino-Americans (a group not included elsewhere).[43]

A survey of "notable" trade books in the area of social studies for children in Kindergarten - grade eight, copyrighted 1975, reveals only 8 books of 131 that focused on Asians or Jews. Of these, 4 were primarily informative (on Hong Kong, Malaysia-Singapore, Thai culture, and problems of Soviet Jews), 2 were literary (fables from the Buddha and Japanese folk tales), 1 was on ancient Japan, and the last was a novel based on the Israeli-Arab conflict. Of the 20 books listed under "Pluralistic cultures in our society" in this survey, none referred to Asians or Jews in this country.[44]

That the situation is not limited to these groups is apparent in two reviews of children's literature published in 1983. Neito found that in 56 books dealing with Puerto Ricans, assimilation, racism, sexism, and an ethnocentric colonialism were still dominant themes.[45] Similarly, Sims found that children's fiction, although improving, still provides too few positive images for black children.[46]

Such meager offerings scarcely permit fulfillment of some of the values of reading multi-ethnic literature, as enumerated by Carlson in 1972:

Gaining an identity with one's own culture
Gaining a positive self-concept
Cultural contributions of ethnic groups
Sense of identity with other peoples
Geographical concepts and customs
Intercultural relations, and others.[47]

Apart from these newer books, there have been several popular series read by generations of children since the series first appeared in the early 1900's. These include THE BOBBSEY TWINS, NANCY DREW, ROVER BOYS, TOM SWIFT, and the HARDY BOYS series. Despite some revisions in the 1950's, they continue to be racist, ignoring reality.[48] These trade series would never appear on teachers' recommended reading lists, yet they were and are widely read by elementary school children, complete with stereotypes and ethnocentrism.

Young people who read children's fiction

. . .should be helped to realize that the diverse yet worthwhile values and characteristics of the minority group should be coveted and retained. . . Literature should be used to prevent or heal bruised egos -- a malady so common amongst children and youth who are culturally different.[49]

These are not the only virtues of reading multi-ethnic literature. As adults know well, reading a good novel about other people or other time periods enhances understanding of history, different customs, vocabulary (English and other), and life styles. There is no reason why children's literature cannot do the same for school children.

Goals of education

Schools today are trying to meet a variety of demands and expectations that stem from different philosophical bases. There are those who urge a return to the essentials of a liberal education in order to preserve our national position of technological and political supremacy (the "back-to-basics" movement in elementary education). Others stress the primacy of the individual -a child-centered vs. a subject- or society-centered curriculum. A third segment of society favors alternatives to traditional education, or even the elimination of schooling as we know it altogether. The result of trying to integrate these disparate viewpoints is usually the promulgation of a policy statement that includes the educational equivalent of "motherhood and apple pie."

To review briefly related policy statements of an earlier day, consider those published in 1918. The National Education Association's Commission of the Reorganization of Secondary Education enunciated what came to be known as the "Seven Cardinal Principles." These goals for education included: health, worthy home membership, competence in the fundamental learning processes, vocational efficiency, worthy use of leisure time, and ethical character.[50]

Little change was noted when

> The Educational Policies Commission, in 1961, iterated the traditional obligation of the school to develop in students the ability to think and to reason. This is basic to the achievement of other goals of education; health, worthy home membership, vocational competence, effective citizenship, worthy use of leisure, and ethical character.[51]

A more contemporary list adds to these basic goals. The Ten Goals of Quality Education adopted by the Pennsylvania State Board of Education in 1965 made a few significant additions to those above. According to the statement of Goals,

Quality education should:

1. help every child acquire the greatest possible understanding of himself and an appreciation of his worthiness as a member of society.

2. help every child acquire understanding and appreciation of persons belonging to social, cultural and ethnic groups different from his own.

177

3. help every child acquire to the fullest extent possible for him, mastery of the basic skills in the use of words and numbers.

4. help every child acquire a positive attitude toward the learning process.

5. help every child acquire the habits and attitudes associated with responsible citizenship.

6. help every child acquire good health habits and an understanding of the conditions necessary for the maintaining of physical and emotional well-being.

7. give every child opportunity and encouragement to be creative in one or more fields of endeavor.

8. help every child understand the opportunities open to him for preparing himself for a productive life and should enable him to take full advantage of these opportunities.

9. help every child to understand and appreciate as much as he can of human achievement in the natural sciences, the social sciences, the humanities and the arts.

10. help every child to prepare for a world of rapid change and unforeseeable demands in which continuing education throughout his adult life should be a normal expectation.[52]

In a non-governmental approach to the question of educational goals, teachers in the field were polled by Phi Delta Kappa, an honorary society in education. Those polled on 18 goals of education ranked fifth

Learn to respect and get along with people with whom we work and live.

A. Develop appreciation and respect for the worth and dignity of individuals.

B. Develop respect for individual worth and understanding of minority opinions and acceptance of majority decisions.

C. Develop a cooperative attitude toward living and working with others.[53]

178

The eleventh ranked goal was

Learn how to respect and get along with people who think, dress, and act differently.

A. Develop an appreciation for and an understanding of other people and other cultures.

B. Develop an understanding of political, economic, and social patterns of the rest of the world.

C. Develop awareness of the interdependence of races, creeds, nations, and cultures.

D. Develop an awareness of the processes of group relationships.[54]

The remaining goals are similar to those given in other lists cited. Like the others, citizenship, health, basic and vocational skills, use of leisure time, are among the major goals perceived by these educators.

Such policy statements, reflecting an intellectual perspective, are interpreted differently by local school boards to conform to the specific pressures within their communities. Thus, schools continue to present diverse patterns, with some giving lip service to the goals and others making some real effort to conform to the spirit and letter of the statements. The presence of the second Goal in the Pennsylvania statement, or the 5th and 11th in the Phi Delta Kappa poll, regarding respect for ethnic/cultural differences is idealistic, and possibly impressive to some. Yet these, too, are implemented in varying ways. The curriculum guide, as we have seen, may stipulate that certain values be conveyed, resource materials be used, and "enrichment" activities be employed, but it is the classroom teacher who ultimately determines whether what is learned is surface or meaningful, truly respectful of others or not.

Multi-cultural education

In most cases, even today obviously, the study of non-Anglo-American groups is an exercise in exotica. The emphasis tends to be on differences from ourselves, whether because of race, climate, economic interdevelopment, or customs. The attitude often conveyed from teacher and/or text to child is "Aren't they quaint?" Or "strange"? Or "inferior"? Little attention is paid to the role of these groups

179

as figures on the stage of history, as contributors to the world's or our country's arts and sciences, or as human beings of intrinsic interest -- unless they are Western European, or ancient (Greeks and Romans), or bearers of folk tales. Yet even seventy years ago, some Americans recognized that immigrants could enrich this country's life. Jane Addams believed that

> . . .if these people are welcomed upon the basis of the resources which they represent and the contributions which they bring, it may come to pass that these schools which deal with immigrants will find that they have a wealth of cultural and industrial material which will make the schools in other neighborhoods positively envious.[55]

"These people" were primarily non-Western European immigrants, not the Asians or blacks or Spanish-speaking people. Nevertheless, Addams' statement maintains its veracity if we only look beneath the surface.

If we examine the arts alone, American music has a unique flavor developed from the spirituals and songs of the blacks into blues, jazz, and the modern classics of Gershwin. A further interesting development is the wedding of this musical idiom and the Jewish Sabbath Eve liturgy by Charles Davidson. "Fiddler on the Roof," a musical based on the culturally-oriented stories of a Jew (Sholom Aleichem) has been translated into almost twenty languages, including Japanese, and has been enjoyed by audiences all over the world because of the universality of its message and experiences. Fine arts have profited from the works of Diego Rivera in Mexico, and architecture from the work of I. M. Pei. Nobel prizes in literature have been awarded to Asians, Latin Americans, and others who are **not** Western European in heritage. However, our school children, particularly those away from urban centers, are rarely exposed to these contributors and their work. Our teachers, having themselves had little contact with these resources, can do little to change the situation without further learning on their part.

If a constructive multi-cultural curriculum is put into the classroom practice with well-prepared teachers and appropriate learning materials, then a society in which cultural pluralism is recognized as a reality can flourish. The curriculum must be honest and realistic in content, however.

Students must be exposed to a curriculum which will enable them to develop valid comparative generalizations and theories about American ethnic groups. Students need to know that immigrants in all periods experienced rejection, hostility, and psychological shock upon their arrival in America. However, they should also be aware of the significant ways in which the immigration of these groups was different.[56]

Students need to learn, as they are growing up, that all was not "rosy" for any group, that this country could and did make people miserable through antithetical attitudes and behaviors, but that despite these errors, progress was made by various groups.

Ultimately, what is wanted from a multi-cultural curriculum is the development of what Orlando Taylor calls "trans-cultural respect and awareness."[57] Education cannot accomplish this alone; the role of the family as primary shaper of attitudes is too well-entrenched. However, eyes can be opened, questions can be raised in children's minds as to the validity of prejudices learned earlier, and movement toward this ultimate goal can be initiated. To achieve even the initiation of such movement, however, means that teachers have to be prepared and knowledgable so that they can provide information and be truly involved in the development of a meaningful multi-cultural curriculum.

Teacher education

It is virtually impossible, as we have seen, to consider any form of educational media without considering the teacher as well. In reporting surveys of selection criteria and of textbooks by others and ourselves over the past thirty years, there is recurrent mention of the teacher's role, the teacher's knowledge, the teacher's attitudes. Although we certainly found considerable improvement in the contents of textbooks with respect to Asians and Jews in the readers and social studies texts of the past six years, we also found that there is a great need to expand the horizons of prospective (and in-service) teachers beyond what is presently part of the teacher education curriculum.

The analysis of textbooks

. . .is especially revealing about the treatment of the Far East because most American teachers have not had special training in the field of Asiatic studies. The textbook, in too many cases, is the major reservoir of information for teachers and pupils alike about an area of the world which has not, until recently, or even now commonly, been treated adequately or objectively in institutions of higher education and in centers of teacher training.[58]

That statement, published in 1946, unfortunately stands as equally true more than three decades later. Not only the few teachers been exposed to any aspect of Asian studies, but few have had the opportunity to gain an informed background about any ethnic group other than their own, except perhaps the blacks or Afro-Americans. Neither ethnic studies nor cultural pluralism courses are required in teacher education curricula or state certification requirements, with rare exceptions. California **did** pass a law in 1969, to be effective in Fall 1974, requiring in-service ethnic studies courses for professional staff in all school districts that had one or more schools with 25% or more minority enrollment. Unhappily, the statute provided no funds for such courses, no penalties for non-compliance with the law, and no mandatory attendance requirement for school personnel.[59] Unfortunately, this is the case in a large state with many ethnic groups in its population; it is scarcely surprising, then, that most other states have **no** requirements for teaching teachers that there are many diverse groups about which they should have knowledge. (There are such requirements in individual school districts in Michigan, Minnesota, and some other states.) Teacher education has not even communicated enough in present programs to make teachers sensitive to the ways in which they may inadvertently embarass students by not being attuned to cultural differences. One notable exception is the requirement at the University of Michigan School of Education that pre-service teachers satisfy a multi-cultural requirement prior to the practice teaching experience.[60]

It is not enough today to mention isolated incidents of black history or biographies of an occasional non-white leader, or tell teachers that they should be devoid of prejudice and avoid discriminatory acts. Nor is a focus on one cultural group an adequate basis for teaching children from many groups. Banks believes that it is essential that teachers study ethnic groups in a comparative framework, gaining a ". . .working knowledge of the role of ethnicity in American life and about the histories and the problems of the various ethnic groups before he or she can implement a sound ethnic studies program."[61] The teacher, as part of developing this working knowledge, needs to examine his or her own attitudes and behaviors toward various ethnic groups. Also, of course, the teacher must become sufficiently informed about and sensitive to inaccuracies and biases in teaching materials to be able to correct such errors as they come to the class' and/or the teacher's attention.

An examination of ten current methods texts, designed to prepare teachers to teach elementary social studies, is encouraging. There appears to be, in the methods texts published between 1970 and 1978, some progress from earlier volumes that included the Far East only under "geographical concepts," discussed "Anglo-America" as a firm reality, and had no references to anything ethnic, or the topics of immigration, melting pot, or cultural pluralism. The texts vary in quality, of course, from those preaching acceptance of cultural differences to those that actively promote the integration of cultural pluralism into the classroom. In brief, this limited survey can be summarized in the following comments concerning both positive and negative aspects of their contents.

W. L. Chase and M. I. John. A GUIDE FOR THE ELEMENTARY SOCIAL STUDIES TEACHER, 2nd ed. Allyn and Bacon, 1972.
>Stresses the development of patriotic feelings and appreciation
>Urges acceptance of other people, but in **their** countries primarily.
>Nothing on immigrants, melting pot, or cultural pluralism in the United States.

Marjorie A. Crutchfield. ELEMENTARY SOCIAL STUDIES: AN INTERDISCIPLINARY APPROACH. Charles E. Merrill, 1978.
>Good chapter on multiethnic education

M.C. Gillespie and A.G. Thompson. SOCIAL STUDIES FOR LIVING IN A MULTI-ETHNIC SOCIETY. Charles E. Merrill, 1973.
>Sees the social studies as a potential vehicle for developing "the competencies demanded for effective living in a multiethnic society."[62]
>Suggests interdisciplinary approaches: modules, unit teaching (as "The multi-cultural U.S.A.")
>Mentions components of a multi-ethnic classroom.

A.J. Hoffman and T.F. Ryan. SOCIAL STUDIES AND THE CHILD'S EXPANDING SELF: TEACHING WITH A PSYCHOSOCIAL APPROACH.
>Suggests several individualized instruction "packages" on persecution, differences and communication, intolerance, and ethnic origins and values.

Also suggests a group role-playing activity on ostracism (similary to that in the film, "Eye of the Storm.").

J. Jarolimek and H.M. Walsh, eds. READINGS FOR SOCIAL STUDIES IN ELEMENTARY EDUCATION, 3rd ed. Macmillan, 1974.
Good selection of readings generally in this field.
Several good articles dealing with melting pot and/or cultural pluralism in elementary social studies.

J.R. Lee. TEACHING SOCIAL STUDIES IN THE ELEMENTARY SCHOOL. Free Press, 1974.
General suggestions for instructional approaches appropriate to chapters on attitudes and values, psychology, and the social studies, American issues, film and the study of other peoples.

John U. Michaelis. SOCIAL STUDIES FOR CHILDREN IN A DEMO-CRACY, 6th ed. Prentice-Hall, 1976.
Discusses value of ethnic and intercultural studies to all children Some stress on teacher evaluation of texts and instructional media as well as teacher guidance of students "to detect unfair treatment, demonstrate how it may be avoided, and learn how to avoid it in their own behavior."[63]
Nothing on immigrant history, melting pot, or cultural pluralism.

M.E. Ploghuft and A.H. Shuster. SOCIAL SCIENCE EDUCATION IN THE ELEMENTARY SCHOOL, 2nd ed. Charles E. Merrill, 1976.
Includes a chapter each on "Multicultural and intergroup studies" and "Religion and social science education."
Curriculum outlines for studies of Chicanos and comparative religion are included as sample units.
Very limited survey of currently available social studies text series.

W.R. Ragan and J.D. McAulay. SOCIAL STUDIES FOR TODAY'S CHILDREN, 2nd ed. Appleton-Century-Crofts, 1973.
Mentions intercultural education as a means of removing preju-dice and discrimination.[64]
Focus in discussion of group differences seems primarily socio-economic, secondarily racial (in the sense of black).
Resource reading list for teachers does not include any books

on Asian-Americans or religiously different.

No mention of immigrant history, melting pot, or cultural pluralism.

D.J. Skeel. THE CHALLENGE OF TEACHING SOCIAL STUDIES IN THE ELEMENTARY SCHOOL. Goodyear Publishing, 1970.

"Ease of transportation, which permits more travel and contact of peoples from around the world, places pressure on the social studies to provide understanding of different cultures. The mobility of people into our communities from other countries adds emphasis to this task."[65]

Concepts included as recommendations: minority group history, minority group contributions to common heritage, understanding of meaning and effects of prejudice, use of culturally different children (and their parents) as resource persons.

Stresses interpersonal sensitivity and concern.

These examples provide an idea of what is already available for the traditional methods course in social studies. Much less appears to be encompassed in methods course texts for reading, language arts, and children's literature. Some attention is paid in **these** texts to the difficulties of the "bilingual" child with respect to reading and writing, but virtually nothing is said about amplifying the content of stories read, about exploring the feelings of some of the characters, or of relating the stories to real-world problems. An exception is Huck's book on children's literature (1976), which manifests an unusual amount of concern for realism, perspective, avoidance of stereotypy, and sensitivity in children's books. Her discussion under the heading of "Living in a pluralistic society," part of chapter 7 in her text, is especially recommended for the ideas and the analyses of stories it contains. Rudman's "issues approach" to children's literature study (1976) includes chapters on blacks and native Americans as examples fo minority groups. She points out that the ideas and suggestions presented should be transferable to any minority group.[66]

In the more specific ehtnic studies/cultural pluralism course, as well as in the general methods courses, it is important that the coursework providing a carefully thought-out pattern for acquiring information and developing affective objectives, a pattern that could be applied to any group at any level, wherever the teacher might be located.

The content of such a program must be interdisciplinary, as was suggested for the multicultural curriculum at the elementary grades. It must draw upon American, immigrant, and appropriate world history; religious studies; sociology, anthropology, psychology, economics, and other social and behavioral sciences relevant to the group(s) being studied. Geography, for example, might enter the course both in terms of locating the countries of origin of different groups and then at a more local level in identifying the regions or neighborhoods in which the various groups settled and why.

A wide variety of experiences should be included in the program. Coursework should not be limited to lectures and textbooks, helpful though these may be. In urban or near-urban communities, there should be ample opportunity for field trips to an ethnic enclave where members of the ethnic group can be met and conversed with, where foods can be tasted and stereotypes tested. Discussion with a leader of the ethnic groups, with an open question-and-answer session, can provide more of the "feel" of the group than any printed words, as well as offering an insight into and understanding of the group's value system and customs. In a university community, foreign students are often willing to discuss their countries and their own adjustment to American customs, their experiences at a human relations level, their culture, and so on. Where these resources are not available, perhaps local residents of different cultural heritages can serve as guest speakers on the traditions and beliefs of their ancestors. The more direct contact that teachers can have with people of diverse backgrounds, the more sensitive they will be to the commonalities as well as differences among humans.

Films and other audio-visual materials are frequently useful in recreating the past, as immigrant history is discussed. Similarly, the reading of memoirs, ethnic literature, and published accounts of public reaction to various groups can contribute to the greater understanding of cultural pluralism that is the goal of the program. A particularly rich source of information on the contemporary concerns of different ethnic groups would be ethnic newspapers, if available in English. Discussion of dual allegiance problems, as in the prolonged conflicts in Ireland and the Middle East, or in the case of the two Chinas, might also be helpful in demonstrating the "pull" that one's heritage has even when one is a third- or fourth-generation American.

Finally, if effective translation of the teacher education program to the classroom is to occur, it would seem advisable to have non-teaching cultural pluralism or ethnic studies in the classroom will produce both a united educational front to the community and an increased allocation of funds to purchase or develop appropriate teaching materials. Secondly, minority group parents would be more encouraged to interact with the school if they knew that they would be welcomed by school receptionists and administrators alike with respect for their humanity, sensitivity to their values and customs, and sincere concern for the welfare of their children.

A principal theme to be conveyed in the teacher education program is that to be different does not imply inferiority or superiority. This is, after all, the essence of a society in which cultural pluralism is accepted and respected. If this is truly the goal of society today, rather than assimilation or amalgamation, this is the message that teachers will have to bring, in word and action, to their classrooms.

As can be seen from this presentation of the contemporary school scene, the demands on teachers and textbooks are more complex than they were at the turn of the century. Since there is an intrinsic time-lag in publishing, it is imperative today for the teacher to be attuned to the crises and trends that affect what and how she teaches her students, for textbooks cannot be as quickly responsive. For most of the students, the teacher's interpretation of the text's printed passages is the one that endures. This is a serious responsibility, especially in so sensitive and meaningful an area as multicultural education.

NOTES

1. M.J. Elliott and K.J. Kennedy, "Australian impressions of social studies theory and practice in secondary schools in the United States," SOCIAL EDUCATION, 43 (1979), 294.

2. ASIANS IN AMERICAN TEXTBOOKS (New York: Asia Society, 1976).

3. H.G. Trager and M.R. Yarrow, THEY LEARN WHAT THEY LIVE (New York: Harper and Brothers, 1952), pp. 358-59.

4. Arthur Gilbert, "Reactions and Resources" in Theodore Sizer, ed., RELIGION AND PUBLIC EDUCATION (Boston: Houghton Mifflin, 1967), p. 53.

5. R. Fenton, "Asian History Through Western Glasses," UNESCO COURIER, May, 1956.

6. Hillel Black, THE AMERICAN SCHOOLBOOK (New York: William Morrow, 1967), p. 96.

7. **Ibid.**, p. 38.

8. BOOKS FOR SCHOOLS AND THE TREATMENT OF MINORITIES, Hearings Before the Ad Hoc Subcommittee on De Facto Segregation of the Committee on Education and Labor, House of Representatives, 89th Congress, August 23 - September 1, 1966.

9. A. Miel and E. Kiester, Jr., THE SHORTCHANGED CHILDREN OF SUBURBIA (New York: American Jewish Committee, 1967), p. 55.

10. N.C. Polos, "A Yankee Patriot: John Swett, the Horace Mann of the Pacific," HISTORY OF EDUCATION QUARTERLY, 4 (1964), 479; c.f. R.S. Mock, "Racial and Religious Prejudice in American Literature Textbooks," INDIANA SOCIAL STUDIES QUARTERLY, 22 (Autumn, 1969), 15.

11. Mock, p. 15.

12. L.P. Miller, "Materials for Multi-Ethnic Learners," EDUCATION-AL LEADERSHIP, 28, No. 2 (1970), 130.

13. K.S. Washington, et. al., TASK FORCE TO RE-EVALUATE SOCIAL SCIENCE TEXTBOOKS GRADES FIVES THROUGH EIGHT (California State Board of Education, Bureau of Textbooks, 1981), p. 1.

14. W.W. Joyce, "Minorities in Primary-grade Social Studies Text books: a Progress Report," SOCIAL FOUNDATIONS, 37 (1973), 219-33.

15. GUIDELINES FOR TEXTBOOK SELECTION: THE TREATMENT OF MINORITIES (Harrisburg: Pennsylvania Department of Public Instruction, 1969), p. 6.

16. M. Collier, "An Evaluation of Multi-ethnic Basal Readers," ELEMENTARY ENGLISH, 44, No. 2 (1967), 152-57.

17. CAVALCADES, Teachers' Edition (Glencoe: Scott, Foresman, 1965).

18. Michael B. Kane, MINORITIES IN TEXTBOOKS: A STUDY OF THEIR TREATMENT IN SOCIAL STUDIES TEXTBOOKS (Chicago: Quadrangle Books, 1970), pp. 5-6.

19. Ibid., p. 49.

20. Ibid., pp. 122-23.

21. Washington, "California Task Force," p. 2.

22. Ibid., p. 51.

23. Ibid., p. 45.

24. Ibid., p. 53.

25. Ibid., p. 37.

26. Ibid, p. 54.

27. **Ibid.**, p. 56.

28. Joyce, **op. cit.**

29. "Sexism and Racism in Popular Basal Readers, 1964-76," (New York: Racism and Sexism Resource Center for Eudcators, 1976), p. 5.

30. **Ibid.**, p. 39.

31. "Springfield, Ohio: A Battle for Multicultural Texts," Interracial Books for Children BULLETIN, 6, No. 1 (1975), pp. 1, 6-7.

32. TRAVELING WITH TRADE WINDS, Teachers' Edition (New York: Harper & Row, 1972), pp. T17-T18.

33. **Ibid.**, p. T196.

34. **Ibid.**

35. READING FOR CONCEPTS (New York: Webster McGraw-Hill, 1970), p. 102.

36. REWARDS (Boston: Houghton Mifflin, 1981), p. 215.

37. I AIM, ASK, AND ACT (Cincinnati: American Book Co., 1970). P. T-7.

38. THE MAKING OF OUR AMERICA, Teachers' edition (Boston: Allyn and Bacon, 1974), pp. 151-58.

39. MAN - A COURSE OF STUDY (Cambridge: Education Development Center, Inc., 1970).

40. J.E. Bernstein, "Minority Group Representation in Contemporary Fiction for American Children Between the Ages of 3 and 5." URBAN REVIEW, 5, No. 5 (1972), 43.

41. D.K. Gast, "Minority Groups in Children's Literature," ELEMENTARY ENGLISH, 44, No. 1 (1967), 12-23.

42. M.P. Archer, "Minorities in Easy Reading Through Third Grade," ELEMENTARY ENGLISH, 49, No. 5 (1972), 43.

43. J.A. Banks, TEACHING STRATEGIES FOR ETHNIC STUDIES (Boston: Allyn and Bacon, 1975).

44. SOCIAL EDUCATION, 40 (1976), 238-44.

45. S. Nieto, Children's literature on Puerto Rican themes - Part I: The messages of fiction. INTERRACIAL BOOKS FOR CHILDREN BULLETIN, 1983, **14** (1 & 2), 6-9.

46. R. Sims, What has happened to the 'all-white' world of children's books? PHI DELTA KAPPAN, 1983, **64** 650-653.

47. R. K. Carlson, Emerging Humanity: MULTI-ETHNIC LITERATURE FOR CHILDREN AND ADOLESCENTS (Dubuque: Wm. C. Brown, 1982), pp. 11-18.

48. Interracial Books for Children BULLETIN, 6, No. 1 (1975), 1,5.

49. P.J. Cianciolo, "A recommended Reading List for Children and Youth of Different Cultures," ELEMENTARY ENGLISH, 48, No. 7 (1981), 782.

50. Lita L. Schwartz, AMERICAN EDUCATION: A PROBLEM-CENTERED APPROACH, 3rd ed. (Washington: University Press of America, 1978), p. 46.

51. **Ibid.**, p. 51.

52. CITIZENS COMMISSION ON BASIC EDUCATION REPORT (Harrisburg, 1974), pp. 22-23.

53. H. Spears, "Kappans Ponder the Goals of Education," PHI DELTA KAPPAN, 55 (1973), 31.

54. **Ibid.**, p. 32.

55. J. Addams, "The Public School and the Immigrant Child," JOURNAL OF PROCEEDINGS AND ADDRESSES, National Education Association, 1908, p. 102.

56. Banks, p. vii.

57. L. Baca and K. Lane, "A Dialogue on Cultural Implications for Learning," EXCEPTIONAL CHILDREN, 40 (1974), 556.

58. TREATMENT OF ASIA IN TEXTBOOKS (Washington: American Council on Education, 1946), p. 3.

59. E.V. Blaylock, "Article 3.3: California's Answer to Cultural Diversity in the Classroom" PHI DELTA KAPPAN, 57 (1975), 203.

60. G.C. Baker, "Multicultural Education: A Priority for the Future," THE INNOVATOR, University of Michigan School of Education, 7, No. 9 (July 4, 1976), 16.

61. Banks, pp. 116-17.

62. M.C. GIllespie and A.G. Thompson, SOCIAL STUDIES FOR LIVING IN A MULTIETHNIC SOCIETY (Indianapolis: Charles A. Merrill, 1973), p. 18.

63. J.U. Michaelis, SOCIAL STUDIES FOR CHILDREN IN A DEMO-CRACY, 6th ed. (Englewood Cliffs: Prentice-Hall, 1976), p. 345.

64. W.R. Ragan and J.D. McAulay, SOCIAL STUDIES FOR TODAY'S CHILDREN, 2nd ed. (New York: Appleton-Century-Crofts, 1973), pp. 114-15.

65. D.J. Skeel, THE CHALLENGE OF TEACHING SOCIAL STUDIES IN THE ELEMENTARY SCHOOL (Pasedena: Goodyear Publishing, 1970), p. 19.

66. M.K. Rudman, CHILDREN'S LITERATURE: AN ISSUES APPROACH (Lexington: D.C. Heath, 1976), p. 174.

CHAPTER SEVEN

SUMMARY, UPDATE, AND CONCLUSIONS

In review

The Progressive movement, which so strongly influenced government and teaching policies in the early decades of this century, stressed as its cardinal purpose the ideal that the immigrant should be Americanized or assimilated into the mainstream, and used this as its most stringent guideline for action. "Melting-pot" to these well-meaning, decent, political and educational reformers meant homogenization. Most of the criticisms, angers, and frustrations over the "new" immigrants, including the Asians and the Jews, were directed at their inability to be absorbed or their clannishness. Even when economic rivalries, as in the case of the Japanese and the Chinese, were the major causes of hostility and rejection, the inability to assimilate was the constantly reiterated rationale for restrictive and discriminatory legislation.

In referring back to commission reports, legislation passed at both the state and federal levels, attitudes reflected by newspapers, magazines, and reformers' speeches over the continuity of cultural traditions in the early twentieth century, one realizes: how **could** textbooks read any differently concerning the immigrant, the Jew, the Oriental?[1] If the community consensus favored the melting-pot concept, why should teachers' guides, curriculum studies, or criteria of text selections have ever been sensitive to ethnic differences? Indeed, it was surprising that the schools displayed any more sympathy and less obvious prejudice than the general population. Textual criticism was muted compared to newspaper articles or official reports. In fact, texts were more noted for their omission of any consideration of "undesirable aliens" than for any negative references to them. The texts of the 1890-1920 period in reading, history (American and world), and geography, were characterized first by omission of Asians and Jews, second by inaccuracies and errors regarding these groups, and third by a pervasive ethnocentrism. Teachers' manuals took a condescending attitude toward immigrant children, stressing the need to teach them cleanliness and "American" ways. Although memoirs are not totally accurate reflection of the past, bitterness and anger, to our surprise, were not expressed by the immigrants over the schools' treatment of immigrant children.

In summary, while the public school systems exercised little understanding of ethnic problems or concern with pupils' sensitivity, they were, in spite of themselves, far ahead of the community. Indeed, to have expected teachers, writers, and publishers to issue books or teach facts that criticized existing laws and existing policy, was to have expected more than was realistic. What school board, what principal, could permit such criticism at the elementary and junior high levels without creating a threat to law and order? How could Boards of Education, writers of curricula, or educators devise guidelines for sympathetic treatment of ethnic diversity when no one believed in it?

As has already been shown, "racism" had become a respectable doctrine. Darwin had been ensconced in the social sciences, and the intellectual elite had rewritten sociology and history to emphasize the unique character and superiority of America's Teutonic or Anglo-Saxon institutions and peoples. They were alarmed lest the "inferior" new immigrants could not adjust to urban life or assimilate "traditional" American concepts. The president of Brown University wrote about immigration as a danger,

> So enormous is the influx of foreigners that we were threatened with a fatal emasculation of our national character. The manner in which we have incorporated alien elements heretofore is among the wonders of history, but it is at least a question whether we can continue to do this always. It seems in part, therefore, a healthy sentiment which has by the law of 1882 excluded Chinese labor immigrants.[2]

A more sympathetic scholar noted,

> This ceaseless immigration has had its dangers and still presents its difficulties, but if all the foreign elements can be assimilated into our life, the composite nation that results is not likely to be feeble or lacking in force but an energetic, delicately constituted, vigorous and forcible race. . .[3]

Organizations appeared on the American scene that represented a revival of nationalistic sentiment. They were symptomatic of continuing antipathy to the "new" immigrants. Because many of the members and leaders were intellectuals, action taken was often in the form of "educational" campaigns to inform Congress and the public of the dangers of unlimited immigration. Not everyone agreed with their viewpoint, but even those who supported, sympathized with, and loved the immigrants never publicly defended their right to ethnicity.

Social workers, educators, and progressives claimed that the deplorable conditions of the slums and urban decay were not the result of immigration, but of untrammeled industrialization and exploitation of the workers. They also passionately claimed that the children of the new immigrants would be acculturated through the **public schools.** Though the reformers admitted that charges of the older ethnics' persistent loyalty to their heritages were true, they insisted that this factor had continued because not enough **effort** or **money** was being provided to speed the process of assimilation. Social workers therefore advocated not only that the schools "Americanize" the children, but also that action programs be established to educate the adult immigrant. Policies and expenditures had already been implemented through the settlement houses and visiting nurse associations. Education was felt to be the cure-all for all social problems, and many cities did develop extensive adult education centers to help the immigrant.

Social workers and reformers alike were determined to stampede the immigrants into citizenship, into speaking English, and into feeling a great devotion for existing American institutions. They were equally determined to force them to abandon their old memories, their old traditions, and their old loyalties.[4] Apparently no one cared about the upheaval in homes torn between old country traditions and new world learning, or the feelings of inferiority drummed into the immigrant child's being until, if ever, he became "Americanized." The Asians by their appearance, and the Jews by their religious observances, never quite reached that state and therefore suffered the pangs of negative self-concept and feelings of inferiority throughout the school years and even into adulthood.

Since the 1920's, the United States has experienced traumatic changes, most notably those of the great depression and the Second World War. The flow of immigrants from Europe almost stopped in the 1930's and early 1940's, except for the few intellectuals who fled from Hitler's Europe. The internal movement of migrants did not cease, however. New residents appeared in the old ghettos: rural blacks, appalachian whites, Puerto Ricans, and in the Southwest, the Mexican-Americans. Concern with assimilation did not end. As affluence, more education through the "G.I. bill," and the post-war industrial development occurred, blacks began to achieve middle class status in ever larger numbers, and their demands grew for greater equality and civil rights. They developed their own cultural institutions within their communities, and increased their pride in their heritage and identity. The decolonization of Africa stimulated greater self-awareness. As the blacks' interest in their past traditions increased, others began to search for **their** own roots: Second and especially third generation Americans looked backward to their origins and cultural patterns, exemplifying Hansen's "law." As the tempo of social change produced challenges to the existing value systems, many examined their past to discover new ideals and security based on their own historical identity. Interest in minorities grew and Americans began to explore the possibilities of a "pluralistic" society rather than that of the "melting-pot."[5]

Continuing acts of discrimination, somewhat less blatant overall than those of 25 or 50 years ago, have challenged this interest. As we have shown, such acts increase in periods of crisis. Economic recession or depression, leading to lay-offs in order of seniority, which conflict with non-discrimination hiring mandates, lead to civil disorder in some minority groups. Also noted earlier, political crises lead to violence against a scapegoat group. A recent political candidate's unfortunate choice of words, "ethnic purity," with regard to housing patterns, had an initial negative impact on his campaign for a presidential nomination by his party. After decades of interfaith commissions, interfaith proclamations, interracial activities, and pressures of every kind for intercultural tolerance at the very least, the hostility and discrimination still in evidence make the workers in the cause of cultural pluralism shake their heads in wonder at the impermeable attitude structure of so many people.

To some extent, the resulting ambivalence and contemporary disillusionment have led to a new ethnicity. As a result, non-black minority groups in the 1970's followed the lead of the blacks of the 1960's. They drew inward to form pressure groups on their own behalf, waving the threat of votes over recalcitrant legislators. Ethnic consciousness-raising revived the conflicts between ethnic identity and acculturation in a new generation.

Kallen, as early as 1915, had advocated "cultural pluralism."[6] In his conception, culturally different groups would co-exist within the larger society, sharing in common some of the values, customs, and practices of that society, while maintaining their own holidays, foods, and other ethnic characteristics. In contrast, many of the activists of the 1960's and early 1970's advocated a cultural pluralism that was really a cultural separatism. To them, cultural pluralism meant autonomous minority groups within the larger society. This conception led to the rapid development of black studies courses, teaching of Swahili, the contention that only members of a given minority should or could teach children of that group, and similar moves toward a separatist society. Such an extreme position has been deplored by many, including Harry Broudy[7] and James Banks,[8] both leaders in the educational world.

The majority group member, having heard of or witnessed discrimination, has other sources of ambivalence. On the one hand, he wants everyone to have an equal chance, believes that civil rights legislation is necessary, and urges non-discrimination in college admissions and employment opportunities. On the other hand, he resents the reverse discrimination and quota systems that follow. The **De Funis** case exemplified the difficulties inherent in attempts to be "fair." Further, if he is a teacher at any level, he is torn between giving the poorly-prepared minority group student the grade said student has earned and giving him one that will maintain the student's positive self-concept **and** grade-point average. If academically honest, the instructor is called "racist" and "anti-" whatever. If less than honest, his colleagues upbraid him for lowering standards, and he feels the same way himself. Furthermore, if he lowers standards, he is indulging in a form of racism that anticipates lower performance levels because the minority group **is** inferior and incapable of meeting normal academic expectations. The inner turmoil becomes indigestible.

Until the past five to ten years, Asians and Jews had the lowest delinquency rates of all minority or majority groups. There were so few of their youths in detention centers or prisons that this "accomplishment" was held up to other groups as a role model. This is no longer true. Asian and Jewish adolescents have accommodated to the drug culture, the desire for "kicks," anti-establishment behavior, and anti-education positions in increasing numbers. This parallels the rise in divorces in these groups, and the decline of the power of the cultural group. Tradition no longer binds, and the older generation fears complete assimilation of their children and grandchildren

197

through intermarriage. The great melting pot may yet produce an homogenized American, but at what cost to the minority cultures?

Supreme Court decisions in the areas of church-state separation and school desegregation have led to a whole new series of questions and challenges for educators. The textbooks, curricula, and educational goals have all been mandated to change to reflect concern for minorities. The schools are to provide social and economic equality, **not** equality of opportunity. The schools, through their programs, are to be the agencies by which culturally different children can achieve social mobility. The dependence of society on the school as the agency of social miracles has not changed in fifty years. The changing goals have been reflected in the programs of the elementary and secondary schools, the open admissions at many colleges, equal opportunity subsidies quotas in recruiting for professional schools, in government programs such as the War on Poverty, Upward Bound, Get Set, and Head Start. These are programs designed to enable culturally different children to succeed academically.

Today's educators have rejected the progressives' notions of homogenizing minority children and have adopted different criteria and aims for education. All children are equal and the schools and their intellectual opportunities must be available to **all**, no matter how ill-prepared or receptive. Each child is a unique individual and many teachers have suggested that current grading and testing standards are unfair and biased against the poor, the culturally different, and the under-privileged. John Dewey's philosophy has been tempered by the teachings of the new psychologists -- Piaget, Maslow, and Bruner.[9]

The success of these efforts has been debatable. Upward mobility came to minorities in earlier years only when their children had absorbed the values of the majority culture. The Asians and the Jews of the past did not follow completely the same hard road as some other immigrant groups because, as we have shown, these two societies shared traditions and values that were not too dissimilar from those of the dominant culture. The push for education, the push for social development, came from within the groups. Agencies were established by these groups to preserve their own cultural values, which often helped sustain the bruised egos of their young, perpetuating pride in their own identities. That does not mean that there was not alienation, despair, and self-hate, but these feelings were not strong enough to destroy the community bonds, and the cultural power of the ghetto was potent enough to provide comfort for many of the estranged. These groups did **not** develop the "riotous manifestations" of latent rage that Erikson imputes to those viewed as "pseudospecies," but did to some extent". . . incorporate the derisive opinion of the dominant 'species' into its own self-estimation."[10] The efforts of the Chinese, Japanese, and Jewish immigrants, moreover, tended to combat successfully the threat to individual development of ". . .various combinations of guilt and rage which prevent true development, even where knowledge and expertise abound."[11] The community prescribed constructive achievement and political restraint, thus channeling the energy generated by guilt and rage into positive actions. Even when outraged by some thoughtless or deliverate evidence of discrimination, the elders of these communities counseled calm and a "low profile," and the youth obeyed.

The immigrant groups of today, like many of their predecessors, tend to lack these supportive institutions, and therefore are more dependent upon the schools and social agencies to help their children acculturate to the majority society. Unlike the practices of the progressive era, we have become somewhat more tolerant of the culturally different. This has been helped by the broader knowledge of other groups engendered by world travel, greater education, and the influence of the mass media. All of these new attitudes should be reflected in the textbooks, study materials, and classroom practices about various cultures of the third world -- about the Japanese, Chinese, Koreans, Filipinos, Mexican-Americans, and the Jews. It is imperative that educational media contain these changes in a meaningful form, such that they teach understanding and reduce prejudice.

Classroom practices

The feelings that one has about oneself, the self-concept, have much to do with one's performance as an individual and as a student. Much has been written in recent years about the need to include this aspect, the affective side of life, as well as cognitive education in the schools. In the realm of the social sciences, for example, this may mean clarifying values held, toward other peoples as well as toward oneself. The child comes to school with some attitudes and values already in the process of development. In accord with today's emphasis on affective education, and as an integral part of studying other cultures, the teacher is supposed to ask the children why they feel the way they do about each group -- that is, to clarify their feelings. In questioning the source of the values held, the teacher can use superstitions and old wives' tales to illustrate illogical sources of values, without condemning the children's values (if contradictory) or their origins. Through the use of a variety of instructional techniques and media, the teacher is to provide information that will guide the children to a more rationally based system of values.

A case in point is the MACOS program, cited earlier. In an evaluative study of this program,

> Some children failed to see any commonality between their own culture and the Eskimo culture. Thus, children tended to respond to studies of people from another culture in one of two ways. . .The child who takes the attitude "We are superior" is setting one standard for all cultures, and that standard is his own culture. The child who takes the attitude "They have their ways, and we have ours -- there is not much in common between us" is maintaining that every human group is unique and cannot be judged from outside. Both attitudes deny the universality of mankind.[12]

A third, albeit unlikely, reaction might be neutral; that is, the study of Eskimo culture might be perceived as simply one more element in the curriculum with as much affective stimulation as the multiplication tables.

Although to some extent the students' reactions depend on their own degree of dogmatism or the rigidity of their value system, what appears to be more important, indeed crucial to the reduction of ethnocentrism, is the social-emotional climate established by the classroom teacher. In Martin's study

> The individual classes that showed the greatest gains in tolerance toward Eskimos. . .were the classes in which observers reported the highest frequency of positive teacher statements about the culture and in which the teacher permitted pupils to express their initial negativism and later to openly discuss their reasons for those feelings.[13]

This conclusion has far-reaching implications for teacher education.

There is some concern that the discussions that are part of the MACOS program or others like it will lead to a kind of conformity and confused thinking -- all in the name of "social adjustment" -- that is every bit as undesirable as the lack of awareness and sensitivity demonstrated in the texts and methods of 50 years ago. Some of the affective education programs are adopted with minimal teacher preparation for coping with the painful truths and feelings that arise in classroom discussions. In this case, more harm than good is the result. In other affective programs, the goals are such that those who achieve them may adjust well to the demands of the school, but are poorly prepared to cope with the independent thinking and initiative required in the real world. Dewey said that learning is not a preparation for life; it is life. Therefore, homogenizing behavior in school may well be a disservice to the learner.

> The motive of making children safe for schools seems to permeate much of the affective movement today. We want youngsters to be happy and cooperative and agreeable in school. But when affective education flows naturally from truly concerned, empathetic, highly skilled teachers, we seem to get quite the opposite -- children who are strong and self-confident enough to stand against the tide, to question the routines, to demand changes. To say that the teacher makes the difference is to say the obvious.[14]

One caveat in including affective education in the curriculum, and cultural pluralism, has to be awareness that the teacher does indeed make the difference.

In another, less formal approach to the question of ethnocentrism, one teacher, courageous in her innovation as related to her teaching situation, focused on the feelings aroused by prejudicial behavior. Her "program," seen on television as the "Eye of the Storm," took place in a small Iowa farming community that was 100% WASP (except for an occasional visiting American Indian). By dividing the class according to eye color and placing restrictions on the activities of first the (inferior) blue-eyed group and then the (inferior) brown-eyed group, the youngsters quickly grasped the negative self-concept held by those in minority groups. The impact of the program on these nine-year-olds was clearly visible in the tear-stained faces and drooping bodies of the "minority" and occasional gloating behavior of the "majority" group members. This role-playing activity clearly taught a lesson in a way that no textbook could. The durability of the impact is open to debate, more than its intensity, but this is the age when children are most easily influenced by what they see, hear, and read. Again, this program is only as good as its teacher. In "Eye of the Storm," the post-treatment discussion revealed a teacher with concern, empathy, and a true desire to educate her children. The learners were led to apply their experiences to the feelings of nearby Indians and other groups less familiar to them.

In 1972, the Board of Directors of the American Association of colleges for Teacher Education adopted a statement entitled "No one model America." In this statement, cultural pluralism is endorsed in clear and strong terms. Further, it stresses that "The commitment to cultural pluralism must permeate all areas of the educational experience provided for prospective teachers."[15] This means that teachers of teachers must teach, and prospective teachers must learn, to accept and understand cultural differences, and to recognize the right of such differences to exist. Teachers should explore the origins of stereotypes and question their validity as an aid to coping with and reducing their own prejudices first, and later those of their students. How we undo all the negative values that may have been acquired in their previous eighteen years of living and schooling, of course, sets the stage for a massive educational task in itself. However, "The goal of cultural pluralism can be achieved **only** if there is full recognition of cultural differences and an effective educational program that makes cultural equality real and meaningful."[16]

Banks (1976) has pointed out several erroneous assumptions about the ethnic studies curricula that emerge from such pronouncements. First, it is assumed that ethnic studies programs deal only with non-white minority groups. Second, it is assumed that only members of the minority group being studied should participate in such a course (e.g., black studies for blacks only). And the third error, ethnic studies content is assumed to be additive in nature, i.e., added **to** the course of study on occasions such as Brotherhood Week. A true ethnic studies curriculum includes none of these assumptions.[17]

In the 1960's, as interest in the Third World increased, many public school systems, aided by federal funds, designed new curriculum guides as supplements to existing programs. Whether the investment of funds and effort were worthwhile is debatable since there is a question as to whether these curricula ever reached the classroom level. Even when the new guides were presented to teachers, we can question their effectiveness with inadequately-prepared teachers.*

---

*An interview with a Philadelphia principal revealed that no one in his school or others, to his knowledge, received any of the extensive guides prepared in that district under a Title III grant.

Texts of the 1970's and 1980's

The implementation of an effective program, whether to teach cultural pluralism or some other concept, rests not only on the teachers, but also on the instructional materials they use. Most instructional materials even today, are textbooks of one kind or another, although several may be used in one classroom instead of the one of former years. Again we can ask: Are the textbooks of today still committing the sins of omission and commission? Do they present the balanced presentations needed to meet the lofty goals cited earlier? Unfortunately, we are still a long way away from meeting the needs of all students and groups.

Textbook selection committees in several states in recent years have examined a wide variety of social studies texts and readers with growing dismay. Although they have looked primarily at the treatment of blacks, they have also commented on their findings with respect to other minority groups and women. In a review of such studies, it is often noted that controversial issues and the human element are avoided.

This avoidance has its roots in part in the realities of the publishing world. Publishers obviously want to sell what they publish. Faced with conflicting demands, a large number of states (e.g., Texas, California, and several Southern states) where a limited number of texts are chosen for statewide adoption, and the fact that teachers, not students, choose texts, publishers

> . . .continue to produce materials that they hope will be all things to all people, and the inevitable result is books that offend no one -- books that may be highly colorful (and expensive) with four-color art, books that appear to be "high quality" in many respects, but books that are frequently either bland, boring, or too hard.[18]

The state adoption practice imposes conservatism and censorship prior to development and/or publication of texts, rstricting much needed innovation of ideas and content.

Textbook selection involves more than counting the number of illustrations, gauging the reading level, and checking items in the Table of Contents. We have indicated previously the criteria on our own checklist for turn-of-the-century and contemporary texts. Several states have each prepared their own guidelines for textbook selection.

Some of these are designed to assess books as a whole, with subjective judgment in response to specific criteria; other guidelines call for counting the number of non-white children or references in each text, with percentages of each to be given. The guidelines may be helpful, are sometimes vague, and are about as open to interpretation on the local level as are the statements of goals of education. One finds that, even with these attempts at direction, the available textbooks still ". . almost completely gloss over the frequent discrimination and abuse that many immigrant groups received."[19] In reports from New Jersey, California, Michigan, and other states, the majority of social science texts in particular are found to omit any discussion of the reasons for and problems of immigration, to distort history, to avoid controversy, and to exclude entirely significant minority groups from their rightful place in American history. Few of the books are found to meet state-mandated criteria for reflecting the pluralistic, multi-ethnic, and multi-racial characteristics of American society today.

Our examination of texts and teachers' manuals in use in today's public schools is discouraging. With rare exceptions, the books display the same blandness criticized earlier. The Asians are found rarely, even in illustrations. The Jews appear to not have existed between the first century and the twentieth. Those readings that include these groups frequently place them in earlier time periods or at distant locations. The lot of the immigrant child is largely ignored. There is increasing, but still insufficient attention given even now to the cultural conflict, the feeling of alienation, that the "different" child faces. The teachers' guides urge inquiry, but do relatively little to pursue an understanding of the subleties of cultural differences in values and outlooks. True multicultural education calls for more than the piñatas, Chinese dragons, exhibitions of native dress, and mock Seders suggested as supplementary enriching activities in teacher education methods texts.

It is our conclusion that cultural pluralism is a contemporary reality and that it should be an integral part of every child's education. As the older immigrant generation dies, children will have less opportunity to learn directly from those who experienced first-hand the most grueling and inspiring aspects of minority life as newcomers. It is essential, therefore, that multicultural education provide such an opportunity for each child to learn of his own heritage and that of other groups. Population mobility, too, means that even if a child lives in a homogeneous neighborhood and attends a school with a homogeneous population **now**, the situation may change rapidly, necessitating an adaptability to other groups and other outlooks on life. A valid multicultural or ethnic studies curriculum will encourage this ready adaptability. Such a program will explore social and historical events from the vantage point of many ethnic and national groups, not just one. An appropriate model has been suggested by Banks (1976), which offers every student the chance to interact effectively and knowledgeably with members of his own sub-culture and other sub-cultures. Far from being an additive factor in the curriculum, ethnic studies should be so interwoven in the course of study as to be a natural component of it.

Integration of findings

Society today, faced by constant flux, a technology that defies planning, and a community torn by conflicting emotions -- one to create total social and economic equality, another to maintain high standards of academic and technological development, and still another to maintain the status quo -- cannot define what role it wishes the school to perform. Hence, raging debates and controversy, as mentioned in the first chapter -- in West Virginia over textbooks, in New York City over decentralization, in Boston over busing, in other localities over sex education -- flourishes over curriculum in general. The same uncertainty pervades the issue of race and ethnic differences. We all accept the notion of tolerance, of accepting cultural differences, but too often give it only lip service. This is clearly reflected in the bitter harangues over neighborhood schools and busing. Both sides have valid arguments and rights. The issues are complex and emotionally charged. If the community is confused, and morally disturbed, and unsure of its attitudes, will not the schools reflect the same dilemmas?[20]

We find impressive and idealistic statements of educational goals. We detect, here and there, attempts by individual teachers to carry out the spirit of these goals. We find too many textbooks in use across the land that do little beyond include token multi-racial illustrations. In many cases, the content of the story is unchanged by the coloring of illustrations or changing of character's names. As the Coleman and Jenck's reports have amply demonstrated, the school cannot undo the influence of the home, even when that is society's stated wish and demand. Attitudes are shaped at the dinner table, the zoo, and at play as parents and neighbors respond to people and events. A close examination of the present school curricula and texts illustrates the ambivalences and misgivings and uncertainties of changing attitudes toward minorities in the United States. It is unrealistic to expect the school, as it is presently constituted, to overcome the cited preschool and extracurricular educational influences.

What we are confronted with is preaching that is unrelated to practice. It is the situation of which most clergymen complain with reference to their congregants. That which they preach in the name of "Brotherhood of Man" reaches no further than the wall of the sanctuary. In practice, lack of brotherhood prevails when the situation gets "too close to home." The idealistic, non-offensive goals of education are hung on the walls along with the immortal phrase, "All men are created equal by their Creator," and remain there to be quoted and admired, but practiced only in keeping with the constraints imposed by the community. This is as true in teacher education as it is in basic education. We have, then, to face some basic issues with respect to ideals, policies, and practices, and to answer them for ourselves. 1) Do we have a choice between the melting pot and cultural pluralism concepts in this country today? 2) In what direction are legislation and legal decisions moving us? 3) In what ways can we implement the goals of education effectively?

Multicultural education is a concept whose time has come, for the multicultural rather than the homogeneous nature of our population is apparent. We do not mean simply the addition of the study of one culture (e.g., black) to the existing curriculum of American history, for that would be insufficient. Nor do we mean the substitution of the study of one culture for another, for that would still be monocultural education. Rather, we consider multicultural education to be the study of the many different groups that have lived in this country integrated in the curriculum in appropriate contexts. For example, American history and black history are inextricably interwoven both in the centuries of slavery and in the struggles for civil rights, as well as at other points in time. The succeeding waves of immigration, resulting from a variety of problems in other countries, some of which continue to this day, have affected the course of this country's history significantly. The literature of other countries and their nationals who came here as immigrants can tell us much about national problems and styles of life that can help us understand people's behaviors in terms of their backgrounds.

If we are to implement a multicultural curriculum in the elementary classroom, our teachers have to be knowledgeable enough to tell publishers what content they want included in the elementary textbooks. The content they want should be representative of a variety of ethnic/cultural/religious groups. It should be balanced in its presentation, including positive and negative aspects of life-styles without stereotyping or preaching. It must be factually accurate and it must be realistic. "Especially in the social studies and language arts areas, every effort must be made to teach understanding of both the contributions and the differences of ethnic groups."[21] Some texts examined have already arrived at this level of quality; efforts on the part of informed teachers will prod authors and publishers to move in this direction for the remaining books and those yet to come.

We are not alone in the need for multicultural education. At the 1976 World Educators Conference of Multicultural Education in Honolulu, we heard the same need expressed by speakers concerned with the State of Hawaii whose situation differs from that on the mainland in several ways; from Micronesia, New Guinea, South Africa, India, Samoa, Korea, Norway, (French) Canada, and Australia. Not only were these speakers interested in, and in some cases already implementing, a multicultural curriculum in the grades, but they stressed repeatedly the importance of educating pre-service and in-service teachers in the historical, sociological, psychological, aesthetic, and anthropological aspects of various cultures. This is our own aim as well. Essential as the cognitive learning is, however, for a successful multicultural program, there is also a need to recognize affective learning experience in this area. We may not always be able to alter bigoted attitudes, but the teaching of content should at least lead to a new respect for other cultures where none existed previously.

Current attitudes

We have seen through the examination of contemporary texts some continuation of the conflicts of the first quarter of the century. One example is the use of shame at foreignness that persists even to this day. Although respect for other cultures is widely preached, such respect in practice apparently does not extend even to the dignity of retaining one's given name in some instances. During the period when acculturation was most strongly urged, it was the immigrant or his descendant who chose a non-ethnic name for the child. Today, it is the American culture that forces such a name upon him. There is a world of difference between voluntary decisions, even when they stem from misshapen motives, and involuntary ones. This single practice, by itself, damages the minority group member's self-concept.

In other areas, too, we perceive that the preachings of equality, personal worth, and respect for all groups is skin-deep. Whenever there is a political and/or economic crisis, scapegoating and racism occur. In the oil crisis of 1974, anti-semitism rose unmasked. Bumper stickers that read "We need oil, not Jews" were seen. Synagogues were vandalized. Some Jewish leaders spoke openly of their fears that an American pogrom would follow an Arab victory over Israel if that unhappy event occurred. As anxiety increased, Jews drew together and recognized that their Americanization, even for the native-born of the second and third generations, and their acceptance by other Americans, were only surface behaviors. Questions were raised about the allegiance of Jews in case of international disputes, although in most cases their political loyalty was clearly to the United States, even if their spiritual ties were to Israel. They were even accused of being racists, as Zionists if not as Jews, in the United Nations resolution of November 10, 1975. A black columnist wrote, following that vote, that "The vote indicated, no, says in no uncertain terms, that the ravenous jaws of anti-semitism are still very much in working order."[22]

After centuries of discrimination and persecution, Jews continue to display the effects of prolonged conditioning. The almost automatic response of many Jews to any crisis or important event is, "Is it good for the Jews or is it bad for the Jews?" There is even controversy in the Jewish community about the wisdom of including the story of Nazi persecution in the course of study. After all, it may give some heretofore passive anti-semites new ideas. The appearance of swastikas, often drawn by youths with only the vaguest notion of the significance of that symbol, is upsetting even to fourth-generation American Jews who were born after Hitler's death. To the unknowing and/or insensitive non-Jew, these reactions may seem incredible and hypersensitive. To the Jew, these are the responses natural to a people who have experienced scapegoating as an integral part of their heritage.

In some respects, the Asian Americans have fared little better.

> Perceptions of the majority groups toward Asian Americans have been a peculiar blend of naive simplicity, a dualism of favorability/unfavorability, and vicarious stereotypes. American perceptions of Chinese and Japanese have flip-flopped back and forth over time, mainly because the basic image has been a superficial one and has been perpetuated by inadequate information and prejudice.[23]

Many Americans still expect all Asians to speak "pidgin English," even if they are third or fourth generation Americans and highly educated.

With the arrival of Vietnamese refugees in 1975, there were public questions of why Americans had to care for them. They were so "different," so unadaptable to American ways. Even housing these refugees in Army camps was offensive to Asian Americans who recalled the painful experience of the World War II internment. Those who were not soon sponsored by American families faced a conflict -- to return to their devastated and Communized homeland or to face the rejection of the American public in this country. Although many of the refugees have found homes here, the rejection of the Asian contrasts sharply with the reception accorded Hungarian refugees in 1956, Cuban refugees in the 1960's, and other Westerners. (The even more recent arrival of thousands of Korean and Caribbean families has reawakened some of the old anxieties, hostilities, and concerns. Among adults, these tend to be tied, as they were earlier, to economic threats. Among teachers, anxiety is aroused by their lack of information concerning the home countries of the youngsters and their inability to communicate with them effectively.) Earlier, the Japanese-Americans were interned during World War II, as noted above, although their allies, the German-Americans, were not.

Sins of omission continue to be observed in the public press. One example among many is an editorial in which comments were made on a study of annual family income, by ethnic and religious backgrounds, that had been conducted by the National Opinion Research Center. Several ethnic, religious, and national origins groups were mentioned, but it was then stated that "Data on Latins and blacks were not included in the study."[24] Nowhere are Asian Americans mentioned, **not even** as having been omitted from the study.

A further source of ambivalence and conflict is seen in what to do about observing, or even acknowledging, the "special days" of ethnic, religious, and national groups in the public schools. In the pre-Civil Rights era, much fuss was made over Christmas and Easter in the elementary schools, despite rulings in the Everson (1947) and McCollum (1948) cases. It is not recognized that this creates a problem in terms of separation of church and state under the First Amendment, as well as being offensive to the rights and sensibilities of non-Christians. A solution has often been to stand the Chrismas tree and the Chanukah menorah side by side, and to try to equate the two holidays in some way. Apart from the commericalization of the two, the truth is that they have little in common. Similarly, Easter and Passover have quite different bases, except for the fact that the Last Supper was a Passover seder (often overlooked or deliberately not mentioned). With the arrival of many Buddhists in our schools, will we not give equal time to Tet? Should there be a social studies unit on "Appreciation of different concepts of the New Year" including such information as: the tumult of blowing horns and cocktail parties is at odds with the renewal concept of the Jewish New Year, the national observance of the New Year in Japan with poetry and courtesy calls, and the ritual and pageantry of a Chinese New Year? Such an academic inquiry into cultural differences is constitutional, in no way in conflict with the church-state separation dictum. It is the observance of one group of holidays, with its implication of superiority as the "right" or "only" way, that infringes on the sensibilities of minority group Americans.

The practice carries through in elementary textbooks as well as in classroom practice. Harris cites the existence of passages ". . .about the Christmas season that appear to be directed at a purely Christian audience. One example is: 'Christmas in the Hawaiian Islands is very much like your Christmas. . .'"[25] Pointed out is the fact that this would be less offensive it it read, ". . much like Christmas on the mainland."

Beginning with black demands for "black studies" courses, there has been a growing movement for courses, units of study, that focus on specific groups. TIME magazine (December 8, 1975) reported that many communities had acceded to such demands with the result that Portuguese language and heritage were taught in some New England schools, Spanish was required second language in the Miami area as well as California, and segments of the City University of New York offered a major in Puerto Rican studies (Lehman College) as well as a totally bilingual education (Hostos Community College).[26] The anti-Zionism resolution in the United Nations evoked similar calls for units on the Nazi holocaust and Jewish heritage, units that are now being developed.

The demands in some instances were so strident and had such potential for violent action, that courses were quickly thrown together to demonstrate how accommodating school boards could be. Action rather than planning dominated the scene. Experience in the past five to ten years, however, had led to improved programming, more moderate demands, and reduced offerings. although the courses continue to exist more because of a fear of the most activist minority leaders than because of a genuine concern for intercultural understanding. As was true for many of the elementary textbooks we examined, "only the faces have been painted." There has been little meaningful impact of ethnic studies on the curriculum as a whole, particularly at the elementary level.

Whether one is a lone female on a board of directors, a black television announcer, an Asian instructor, or the only Jew elected to an honorary position, there is always the question of "Is this tokenism?" "Is he here because of his ability or his minority background?" The voiced reassurance always points to talent, of course, yet the minority member can never feel certain of what is truth in the situation. There are oblique statements, slurs on his group or some other, to which he is in conflict about responding. He is sensitive to all such indirect remarks and only too aware that what comes before the hyphen as a " -American" still counts with come others for more than what comes after. The sensitivity seems to have been sharpened, rather than dulled, by the popular pre-occupation with "rights" and "ethnicity."

One of the difficulties we still face is that few people are aware of how the same event or action is perceived by members of different groups. Consider a perfectly neutral behavior that has no racial or ethnic undertones. An individual, Person A, perceives a principle involved in a situation. He fights for that principle over an extended period of time. He is, in a word, persistent. Person B, who does not accept that a principle is involved, calls Person A stubborn, not persistent. A difference in viewpoint is in evidence. If we turn instead to male-female behaviors, what is socially acceptable in males as "driving ambition" is perceived negatively in females as "aggressiveness." This principle holds, too, for different ethnic or racial groups. What is perceived by one American as "clever" strategy by another American becomes "sneaky" if an Asian does the same thing, or "crafty" if a Jew does it. Similarly, the Asian and the Jew often do not perceive majority behaviors from the same perspective as a majority group member. There is an urgent need to increase sensitivity overall on all sides if the current movement toward a culturally pluralistic society is to become viable.

In chapter two, we indicated that attitudes toward other groups become firmer as children progress through the elementary school grades. A recent cross-sectional study of the attitudes of American public school children toward other nations and peoples confirms that these attitudes tend to stabilize by grade eight.[27] This finding underscores the urgency of integrating multicultural studies into the curriculum in the **elementary**, not the secondary, school years.

Legislation and judicial decisions

In examining the current national position that espouses cultural pluralism rather than assimilation, one realizes that there are two strains of legislation and judicial decisions, the public attitudes, that have converged in this position. One strain has its origins in the First Amendment to the Constitution; the other, in the Civil Rights Act of 1866, closely followed by the Fourteenth Amendment.

The First Amendment, in prohibiting the establishment of a state religion, upset a century and a half of education oriented toward literacy in the service of religion. It created a pattern of church-state separation that truly came to fruition more than another century and a half later. In the interim, it was the Protestant Bible that was read in the schools, the Protestant version of the Lord's Prayer that was recited at morning exercises, and the Protestant values and beliefs that were transmitted through McGuffey's READERS and other texts. Not until 1943 did the Supreme Court acknowledge that these and other educational practices impinged on the individual's freedom to worship as he chose, even if his choice differed from the "norm." It was then that the Court ruled, in **West Virginia State Board of Education v. Barnette**, that the educational practice of requiring a flag salute was in conflict with the religious freedom of Jehovah's Witnesses who did not recognize any "graven image" or similar symbol. This was the first in a series of cases that ultimately outlawed required religious exercises from the public school classroom.

In **Engel v. Vitale** (1962), the required reading of New York's non-denominational "Regents' Prayer" was found unconstitutional. Despite its nondenominational character, the Prayer did establish a state-approved religious doctrine that violated the principle of church-state separation. A year later, the Court went even further in **School District of Abington Township (Pa.) v. Schempp** and **Murray v. Curlett**. In both cases, it was found that the classroom religious exercises, which included required Bible reading in **Schempp** and recitation of the Lord's Prayer in **Murray**, ". . .went against the petitioners' freedom of religion, and constituted State support of religion."[28] Although it **was** possible for the children involved to be excused from these religious exercises, their parents sued successfully for abolition of the exercises on the grounds that being excused drew attention to their children's difference from the majority. (The Schempp children were Unitarians and the Murrays were atheists.) Ultimately the decisions in the two cases also relieved other non-Protestants from practices contrary to their religious views.

Partly as a result of the Court's decisions, and partly as a result of civil rights activities, observances of religious holidays such as Christmas have now been largely banned in the public schools. (Individual school districts continue to try to re-introduce prayers and/or Christmas exercises into the schools, but rarely succeed in their defiance of Supreme Court rulings.) Even religious content in textbooks had rarely been as blatant in opposition to non-Christian beliefs, in this century, as were the ritual of lighting the school's Christmas tree, the Christmas concert and learning of carols, and similar events.

The second strain of influence on contemporary educational practice has a briefer, though more complex, history. The civil rights extended to blacks in 1866, and the "equal protection of the laws" guaranteed them in 1868 under the Fourteenth Amendment were the bases for the Civil Rights Act of 1964 and subsequent related legislation. The "general welfare" clause in the Preamble to the Constitution has also been used as an hypostasis for the extension of individual rights in the classroom. It was almost a century before these principles were moved from the arena of accommodations and travel to effective application in public education.

Civil rights activities by blacks in the early 1960's led to the Civil Rights Act of 1964, the Equal Educational Opportunity Act of 1964, and other legislation designed to implement the concepts of "equal protection" and equal rights guaranteed earlier. With the successful passage of these acts, other cultural groups began to speak up for their rights. The Office of Civil Rights issued regulations for compliance with the acts and enforced them, in all areas of public activity. Again, other groups saw the effectiveness of non-violent but potent and militant political protest, and sought parity for their beliefs and mores instead of inequity. The rise in ethnic pride and activity of non-black groups, however, had a milder impact on the schools.

A specific problem existed for non-English-speaking children. Although the Voting Rights Act of 1972 prohibited using English-language proficiency as a qualification for voting, children did not enjoy an extension of the same privilege in the classroom for learning.

Language minority children in this country have had no choice in most instances, but have had to attend schools which ignore their langauge and culture. School is another reminder of the discrimination and limited opportunities facing these children as members of minority groups.[29]

Whether Spanish- or Chinese-speakers, they sat through one lesson after another without comprehension of their contents. The problem is not new. Theodore Roosevelt is quoted as saying, in 1919, "We have failed to produce literacy in bilingual children; we failed to produce bilingualism in literate adults."[30] A few states passed legislation in the early 1970's mandating bilingual education for these children where there were twenty or more of them speaking a common foreign language in a single school district. Yet the hour or two a day of being taught English as a second language was inadequate. The children did not have an equal opportunity to achieve academically. As adults they would, as a result, be likely to suffer economic, political, and social handicaps as well. The United States Commission on Civil Rights pointed out that "Unlike earlier non-English-speaking children in this country, these children face an increasingly technical, skills-oriented society. There has been a shift in jobs from manual labor to skilled occupation."[31]

This situation has been especially true in the case of Asian children. Since the repeal of restrictive immigration laws in 1965, almost one million Asians have entered the United States. "Of the 519,661 Asian school-aged children (K-12) in 1973, over 50 percent were foreign-born. It is assumed that nearly all the foreign-born children have little or no English language skills."[32] Their frustration in the classroom led to a suit against the San Francisco school district, alleging that they were not receiving equal protection under the school laws. In ruling on the suit, the Supreme Court declared that

Under these state-imposed standards there is no equality of treatment merely by providing students with the same facilities, textbooks, teachers, and curriculum; for students who do not understand English are effectively foreclosed from any meaningful education.

Basic English skills are at the very core of what these public schools teach. Imposition of a requirement that, before a child can effectively participate in the educational program, he must already have adquired those basic skills is to make a mockery of public education.

214

We know that those who do not understand English are certain to find their classroom experiences wholly incomprehensible and in no way meaningful.[33]

Further,

It seems obvious that the Chinese-speaking minority receives less benefits than the English-speaking majority from respondents' school system which denies them a meaningful opportunity to participate in the educational program. . .[34]

The **Lau v. Nichols** decision was based on provisions of Title VI of the 1964 Civil Rights Act. Although initially aimed at relieving Chinese-speaking students, one reviewer of the decision has averred that

. . .the **Lau** decision portends some significant changes including but not limited to increased federal intervention in local governmental affairs and new efforts on the part of school systems to educate children from non-English-speaking homes. In addition, it foreshadows some important doctrinal changes in constitutional law that could have an even more widespread impact on the operation of public schools.[35]

The Supreme Court did not order specific remedial measures, but did require that the children be given the opportunity to learn subject matter content concurrently with learning English language skills. Indeed, what the children and their parents sought ". . .was an educational program that, given adequate motivation, they could make effective use of. They did not seek to eliminate the risk that students might not make effective use of the schools."[36] In a sense this is reminiscent of the dreams of golden **opportunities** brought to this country by the earlier masses of immigrants.

There had been scattered programs for non-English-speaking pupils even prior to the **Lau** decision. Most of these approached the problem through teaching English as a second language (TESL). Such instruction was usually on a part-time basis, varying from one hour of instruction per week to one or two hours per day. A total immersion technique, in which the child heard only English all day, was less frequently used, perhaps because its effectiveness was minimal with respect to overall educational achievement. A third approach offered the child subject matter instruction in the native language as well as

215

English language instruction, as ordered by the Court in **Lau**. The most affirmative program, however, in the sense of recognizing and demonstrating respect for cultural as well as language diversity, is one that is bilingual and bicultural.

A major aspect of bilingual bicultural education is inclusion in the curriculum of the child's historical, literary, and cultural traditions for purposes of strengthening identity and sense of belonging and for making the instructional program easier to grasp.[37]

In the programs most devoted to this principle of mutual respect and ethnic identification, all children in the school, regardless of language background, share in studying the traditions and language of both cultures. At the Potter-Thomas School in Philadelphia, for example, where there is a large proportion of students who speak Spanish as a native language, the Spanish-speakers initially receive 90 percent of their instruction in Spanish and 10 percent in English. At the same time, the English-speaking children start out with 10 percent of their classwork in Spanish and 90 percent in English. By sixth grade, both groups spend an equal amount of time learning in English and Spanish, having become effectively bilingual. The Chinese community in San Francisco has moved in a similar direction since the **Lau** decision. In these and other communities, native speakers are creating instructional materials that will enhance the teaching of the culture, history, and language of the minority group. It is increasingly recognized that such bilingual bicultural education enriches the lives of all learners involved and does not merely remediate the "disadvantage" of the culturally and linguistically different. Thus it is apparent that the legislative and judicial efforts to provide equal protection for all is beginning to have significant impact on classroom practices.

Whether bilingual bicultural education is sufficient to meet the needs of a truly pluralistic society is another question. Such programs are beneficial within local communities to resolve or reduce local problems. However, they are too limited to ameliorate effectively the learned distrust of or hostility toward the many "different" groups with whom an individual is likely to come into contact as he matures and moves into the larger society.

Although the emphasis of both the disestablishment of religion and the civil rights strains of influence have been made relevant to educational policy and practice primarily, there has been little spillover to the realm of the textbook. As noted elsewhere, investigations of textbooks were first concerned with their treatment of blacks, under the Civil Rights Act of 1964, and then with the treatment of Chicanos and Puerto Ricans. The enactment of stricter regulations for textbook selection in the various states followed an analogous path. Today, in some school districts, the criteria have been expanded to concern for inclusion of appropriate Asian content and exclusion of content offensive to any religious or ethnic group. Though by no means yet ideal in practice, there is cause for cautious optimism that legislatively- and judicially-supported respect for cultural pluralism will one day replace the enforced assimilation practices of the "melting pot" ideal of earlier years. The recommendations that follow indicate techniques that can move us toward that goal.

NOTES

1. c.f. for legislation, Harry Rider, "Legislative Notes and Reviews, Americanization," AMERICAN POLITICAL SCIENCE REVIEW, 14 (1920), 110-15.

2. Benjamin E. Andrews, THE UNITED STATES IN OUR OWN TIME (New York: Charles Scribner and Sons, 1903), pp. 298-99.

3. Andrew C. McLaughlin, A HISTORY OF THE AMERICAN NATION (New York: Appleton and Co., 1899), pp. 538-39.

4. John Higham, STRANGERS IN THE LAND (New Brunswick: Rutgers Univ. Press, 1955), p. 247.

5. Nathan Glazer, "Ethnicity and the Schools," COMMENTARY, 58, No. 3 (1974), 55-59.

6. Horace Kallen, "Democracy Versus the Melting Pot," NATION, 100 (May, 1915), 219-20.

7. Harris S. Broudy, "Cultural Pluralism," EDUCATIONAL LEADER-SHIP, 33 (1975), 173-75.

8. James A. Banks, "Ethnic Studies as a Process of Curriculum Reform," SOCIAL EDUCATION, 40 (1976), 76-80.

9. Richard M. Merelman, "Public Education and Social Structure: Three Modes of Adjustment," JOURNAL OF POLITICS, 4 (November, 1973), 798-829.

10. Erik Erikson, GANDHI'S TRUTH (New York: W. W. Norton, 1969), p. 432.

11. **Ibid.**, p. 433.

12. David S. Martin, "Ethnocentrism Toward Foreign Culture in Elementary School Studies," ELEMENTARY SCHOOL JOURNAL, 75 (1975), 382.

13. **Ibid,** pp. 386-87.

14. Diane Divocky, "Affective Education: Are We Going To Far?" LEARNING, 2, No. 2 (1975), 27.

15. "No One Model American," JOURNAL OF TEACHER EDUCATION, 24 (1973), 264.

16. **Ibid.,** p. 265.

17. Banks, "Ethnic Studies," pp. 76-80.

18. Eric Broudy, "The Trouble with Textbooks," TEACHERS COLLEGE RECORD, 77 (1975), 28-29.

19. "Roots of America," New Jersey Education Association, 1975.

20. "Americans Debate Role of Schools," NEW YORK TIMES, November 16, 1975; "Schools Won't Change Society," Pennsylvania State Education Association VOICE, November 17, 1975.

21. Todd Clark, "Why We Need Better Multiethnic Education," SOCIAL EDUCATION, 42 (1978), 164.

22. Claude Lewis, "The U.N. Vote on Zionism," PHILADELPHIA BULLETIN, November 14, 1975.

23. Albert Yee, "Asian Americans in Educational Research," EDUCATIONAL RESEARCHER, 5, No. 2 (1976), 7-8.

24. PHILADELPHIA INQUIRER, November 1, 1975.

25. J. J. Harris, THE TREATMENT OF RELIGION IN ELEMENTARY SCHOOL SOCIAL STUDIES TEXTBOOKS (New York: Anti-Defamation League, 1963).

26. "Ethnics All" TIME, December 8, 1975, p. 57.

27. Thomas S. Barrows and Anne Jungeblut, "Children's Attitudes Toward and Perception of Other Nations and Other Peoples," Annual Meeting of the American Educational Research Association, San Francisco, 1976.

28. Lita L. Schwartz, AMERICAN EDUCATION: A PROBLEM-CENTERED APPROACH, 3rd ed. (Washington: University Press of America, 1978), p. 238.

29. U.S. Commisison on Civil Rights, A BETTER CHANCE TO LEARN: BILINGUAL-BICULTURAL EDUCATION (Washington: Clearinghouse Publications 51, 1975), p. 138.

30. Vivian M. Horner, "Bilingual Literacy," In John B. Carroll and Jeanne S. Chall, eds., TOWARD A LITERATE SOCIETY (New York: McGraw-Hill, 1975), p. 191.

31. U.S. Commission on Civil Rights, p. 14.

32. **Ibid.**, p. 13, n.45.

33. Lau v. Nichols, 414 U.S. 563, 1974, p. 566.

34. **Ibid.**, p. 568.

35. Tyll van Geel, "Law, Politics, and the Right to be Taught," SCHOOL REVIEW, 83 (1975), 248; c.f. Roger Rice, "Recent Legal Developments in Bilingual/Bicultural Education," INEQUALITY IN EDUCATION, 19 (1975), 51-53.

36. U.S. Commission on Civil Rights, p. 265.

37. **Ibid.**, p. 29.

CHAPTER EIGHT

RECOMMENDATIONS

In answer to the questions posed, it is obvious that the "melting pot" concept has never worked in the ways anticipated three generations ago. We are a nation of many peoples, rarely unanimous in agreement on anything -- even a definition of what is "an American." cultural pluralism **is** a fact of life in America today, as it has always been. Desegregation rulings, civil rights and equal opportunity legislation, and related official pronouncements merely confirm this fact. It is therefore society's responsibility to create mutual respect for our differences and diversity, to reduce the antagonisms that stem from ignorance.

The school an an agency of society has another function and duty: besides teaching the children the majesty of diversity and individualism of human society, it must provide the one learning site where all groups can mingle and communicate with each other. If the progressives and their educational theories over-emphasized the "melting pot" to the detriment of minority cultures, many liberals and their supporting theorists have stressed diversity and ethnicity excessively, devaluing the mastery of common cultural traditions. Hence, "Black English" should be taught in neighborhood schools where appropriate because of its rich colloquial imagery and oral tradition. It is imaginative and has a rich verbal artistry, but few outside the black community understand it. Spanish children in bilingual schools should be encouraged to remain fluent in their language and heritage while learning to master English. Children should not be deprived of their cultural heritage, but in order for them to exist in our work world and in order for them to communicate effectively in the larger society, to observe and maintain the rich diversity of our intellectual resources, we must help them to learn and preserve our national **shared** history as Americans. Therefore, all of our children must master English; they must all learn to read and write. They must all observe in both school and society certain codes of behavior, observances, and traditions that are common to the national scene, and that transcend our peculiar differences -- civility, **respect** for authority (not fear), civic responsibility, honesty, moral probity, and respect for others' rights. These are the qualities necessary, by consensus, for all people, if we are to preserve a civilized and sane society.

Throughout this book, wherever appropriate, recommendations and suggestions were offered that would enrich education for all children. In this chapter, we are bringing together the varied ideas so that rationale and practice can be viewed as a coherent whole.

It would be impossible for the curriculum, the textbooks, and supplementary materials to include enough pertinent and positive information about each and every immigrant group and its contributions to the American culture. Black history is distinct and should be incorporated into American history all through the grades as an intrinsic part of the American experience. What should be emphasized continually in the schools are intergroup relationships, frequently interdependent in nature, and a pride in each person's heritage to enhance each child's self-esteem. Our children at very young ages, can be taught to appreciate the value of group differences and ethnic characteristics, to be sensitive to others' feelings, and to improve their relations with members of different groups.

We have already noted that the attention, or lack of it, paid to the immigrants in the schools and textbooks of the early twentieth century is no surprise in view of the public attitudes of the time. Today, however, there is no such justification. The official public attitude, as expressed in abundant legislation and court decisions of the past two decades, is concerned with equality for everyone. Civil rights activities have caused increased sensitivities, sometimes oversensitivity, to the feelings of individuals and groups. In private, of course, and sometimes on an unofficial public level, hatred and bigotry still exist. In the schools, curriculum guides and administrative directives point out the need to be aware of and sensitive to cultural differences, to avoid negative impact on students' self-esteem, and to stress tolerance and respect for all. Neither the official nor the administrative rulings, however, can themselves change personal attitudes and consequent behaviors. Nor have these rulings resulted in meaningful substantive changes in instructional materials regarding the role and problems of migration, or the existence of Asians, Jews, and other groups in our multi-cultural society.

The schools have acknowledged this new approach and even on occasion have attempted to cope with it. There has been some improvement in the textbooks, and school administrators now even take into account the problems of minorities in the evaluation of school materials. In an earlier chapter, we indicated the varied directions that educational goals have taken. We agree with some of the progressive educators' goals, and concur with the idealistic and humanistic desires of the avant-garde attempts to achieve equality and dignity for each individual student. Neither of these achievements can be undertaken by contemporary educators, however, unless there is a compelling purpose to instill skills in reading and writing as a foundation for these goals. The texts, even if improved substantially, cannot influence the students if the students cannot read them with comprehension.

The task of the educator is made far more difficult in the present environment because the mass media -- television, telephone, and radio -- have reduced the significance of both reading and writing in the overall acquisition of knowledge and experience. The media have made our students passive, apathetic receivers of canned information that is often meaningless to them. Constant television viewing has created an audience with limited attention span, an inability to concentrate or to **listen** for a prolonged time period to complicated or semi-abstract concepts. We need to restore to our students the ability to think critically, to analyze, to synthesize, and to evaluate. These attributes are polished and cultivated only through reading and writing when the students have to make choices, judgments, and reason intelligently. Unless all of our children develop a high level of skills in these basic aptitudes, they cannot hope to achieve academically so that they can participate fully in the fruits of our technological society. They will be unable to acquire or profit from the desired opportunities for economic and social equality that are offered.

How then are the schools to accomplish effectively these tasks, to achieve the multiple assignments and goals demanded by our modern society? In every phase of teaching, emphasis must once again be placed on skills, and this emphasis must recur in all courses and through all curricula. This does not mean an end to current educational innovations. Many, if used properly, would add immeasurably to our children's abilities, but in too many schools, in too many programs, innovation has become so important and so involved that the projects, role-playing, simulation games, audio-visual aids, television modeling, drawing, and other techniques have become the end of the educational process rather than the supplemental means to teaching the basic tools of reading, writing, and critical thinking. The present obsession with innovative techniques is not entirely the case, but in an environment where children gain most of their knowledge through **watching** (educational and commercial television programs), where they learn to communicate rapidly and effectively on the telephone, the **written** word commands less and less attention or interest. Magazines, newspapers, and books are still a vital part of middle-class culture, but are of far less significance in the pre-school life of the small child, particularly if this child is both poor and culturally different.

In any program developed to help our children appreciate cultural diversity and to develop understanding for those who differ culturally, therefore, cognizance must be taken of the importance of utilizing every opportunity to integrate reading and writing. With this aim firmly anchored at the core of our program, we can suggest a series of recommendations for the improvement of teaching a multicultural curriculum. Skills in reading and writing can be taught, but for the child and the adult to remain fluent and articulate, he has to practice them continually. Vocabulary, sentence structure, and composition ability can only be learned and strengthened through constant and continual practice. Compositions and research papers must be assigned frequently, and the supplemental activities must include reading assignments.

Innovations begun in many school systems lend themselves very well to an emphasis on skills. The disappearance of marks and grades are no hindrance to the child's achievement, provided the teacher insists that each pupil gain a proficiency and mastery of his material before he can move to the next level of learning. In fact, the ungraded system can be used effectively to enable the youngster to move at a slower or a more rapid pace, stressing his individual needs, without hurting his self-esteem. The open classroom, too, used with proper skill and discipline, as it was intended, can accomplish the same task as the approach in the traditional schoolroom.

We must remember that in the present educational system, the teacher has assumed great importance. The teacher is the pivot of the learning process, especially in the transference of attitudes. She or he can direct the class and subject with more independence than years ago, and chooses the text material that continues to be important in the classroom. The text is still the basis for lesson plans, and provides the factual framework upon which the more innovative, stimulating, and action-oriented materials rest. The teacher's prejudices, feelings, and unspoken gestures convey her or his feelings concerning intergroup relations and ethnicity, in the classroom or in the text materials. Thus it is crucial that the teacher be well-educated, knowledgeable, and very sensitive in order to communicate the value of cultural diversity effectively.

Teacher education must then be strengthened in this area of content. Although often mentioned, most schools do not **stress** the significance and problems of cultural diversity. In the period of the 1960's, ethnic studies courses flourished in the university curricula. Now, in a period of financial retrenchment and student concern with more "practical" courses, these programs are diminishing. We recommend that the new courses **not** be abandoned. Indeed, they should be strengthened, with their function more fully developed as adjuncts to the requirements in schools of education or inservice programs. Teachers should be apprised in their preparation of the importance of cultural diversity, although because of the complexity and cultural wealth of innumerable groups, no one can master all the varieties of experience extant in American life. However, teachers, counselors, and other professionals in contact with culturally different groups must become empathetic, knowledgeable, and able to work with the people in such groups. A productive way for professionals to serve their communities and schools is to be trained in programs stressing cultural pluralism that are conducted by local colleges and universities. We feel that in-service courses, educating teachers in techniques of learning about and working with Chinese, Estonian, Ukranian, black, or Jewish heritages are equally, if not more, important than additional credits in other methods courses. Understanding language, gestures, customs, and history of these groups leads to the development of empathy and might ease the tremendous schism that now exists between public institutions, including the schools, and individuals in the local communities.

Whether coursework is taken as part of an in-service program or in the traditional pre-service college curriculum, the concepts of cultural pluralism can enhance both the usual methods course for teaching elementary social studies and those specifically oriented to teaching ethnic studies programs. In the traditional methods course, it is desirable to have a text supportive of integrating our concern with different groups into the total social studies curriculum. Greater familiarity with several disciplines in the social sciences (e.g., anthropology, geography, history, and psychology) and in the humanities (art, music, literature) will strengthen the teacher's presentations in the classroom. An intensive research study of the life-style, values, attitudes toward education, child-rearing techniques, and community participation of one or more cultural groups, perhaps of the teacher's own group and one or two others, will contribute a depth of understanding to such presentations.[1]

To mount a significant multicultural curriculum, several approaches can be employed concurrently. Without disturbing the major areas of the social studies curriculum, for example, the primary grades can continue to focus on family and local community relationships, but in a more comparative way. It can easily be shown that every cultural or ethnic group structure has some unique features and some that are common to most groups. At the intermediate level, more emphasis could be placed on cultural diversity and similarity in other fields, and at the secondary level (with which we are not primarily concerned in this book), Federal policy over the years with regard to immigration could be studied.[2] In conjunction with these emphases, related materials could be introduced into the studies of literature, music, art appreciation, drama, and language arts. To do this effectively, the teachers themselves must be knowledgeable and flexible.

Following the scheme of Bruner's spiral curriculum, concepts from the several disciplines within the social studies can be presented in simple form in the early grades, and re-introduced in gradually more complex ways in higher grades. The concepts of cultural diversity and universality, for example, can begin with pre-schoolers describing themselves and then finding the ways in which they are similar to and different from their classmates. It can be pointed out that a single child may be like several other children in one characteristic (e.g., hair color), part of another group in another characteristic (e.g., eye color), and part of still a third group in a third characteristic (e.g., preferred games), but that all the children can and do take part in a variety of activities together. As a slightly higher grade level, diversity and similarity may focus on ways in which birthdays or holidays are celebrated, always emphasizing that difference does not imply "better" or "worse."

By the middle and upper elementary grades, the themes of multicultural education will be well established and can be demonstrated in variations among ethnic/racial groups in this country, both in terms of immigrants and the current scene, here and abroad. A similar pattern of development can be followed with respect to concepts in economics, geography, history, political science, psychology, and sociology, with several disciplines often integrated into one activity or text.

As we have stated previously, the textbook has remained important as a teaching tool. Whatever their limitations, texts in history, and even readers, provide a background of information and learning. Readers and literature collections introduce ideas and vocabulary study; histories provide rudimentary facts that students must learn before they can engage in projects, games, and other stimulating experiences. The variety and richness of the ethnic contributions to American culture and the quality of our lives, however, is so extensive that no textbook or program can include every such cultural contribution. Even if it were possible to include all groups, many volumes would be required to describe, explain, and assess the role of all the minority groups that play such a marvelous and important part in the creation of our unique American style. Although neither the classroom teacher nor the text may be able to treat **all** minorities adequately, the necessity of treating the history of immigration as a whole remains, and is still a significant issue that has, in most areas, not been taught in proper perspective.

The story of immigration, its influence on contemporary American history, the people and the cultures who have been part of the story, **do** need to be included in the learning experiences of the young. Similarly, the theme of persecution of minorities as well as their triumphs over adversity needs to be included in the learning experience. These cannot be taught in isolation, however. They are part of mankind's common heritage and are part of our contemporary problems. Indeed, much American history of the past two centuries cannot be taught apart from world history. We recommend, therefore:

1. that the story of immigration to the United States be taught in the context of world events, whether it be with reference to the Irish potato famine, Russian pogroms, victims of war, Nazi persecution, or dreams of a better life;

2. that selections reflecting immigrant history, prejudice, and culture conflicts be incorporated into reading texts along with stories of inventions, poems, and other content. Further, that teachers' editions as well as student texts ask pertinent questions, appropriate for the grade level, about the feelings of people in the selections, demonstrations of prejudice, biased writing, and similar matters;

3. that supplementary materials relevant to minority groups of the local community be integrated into the curriculum to enrich learning in various subjects: In California, for example, this would mean the Chinese, Italians, Japanese, Mexicans, and Spanish immigrants; in Minnesota, the Scandinavians; in Louisiana, and parts of New England, the French Canadians; in Michigan and New York, the Dutch; and so on.

It is a fact that some groups especially in urban areas, may be especially predominant in a single school's population. Recognition of the cultural mores, unique and universal beliefs, heritage, problems, and contributions to the international and national scene of such a group should be part of the curriculum in that school. Specific techniques to be used might include:

invitations to leaders of the ethnic group in that community to serve as resource persons for all the children in the school, to speak to the teachers and staff as well as the pupils in order to increase understanding and appreciation of the group's culture;

2. assignment of projects in language arts and social studies courses that focus on the group's history, language, and values, possibly resulting in custom-made instructional materials where commercially published materials are sparce or non-existent. (This might be especially true, for example, for Bolivians, modern Greeks, Vietnamese, Iranians, and Zambians, among other groups.) The reports of each student could be duplicated and distributed to all members of the class so that everyone has a "text" on the group.

3. Integration of the disciplines should be encouraged and utilized more fully. Literature, history, geography, and even anthropology, can illustrate and expand cultural studies. The maps (both physical and pictorial) show the areas from which the immigrants came, and where they settled in the United States. History lessons state the story of a nation, for example, China. Poetry and literature selections stress the stories and myths of that culture, examine family life and structure showing their relationship to the geography and economy (e.g., the rice culture), and other aspects of Chinese civilization. In the United States, instruction could describe the transmission of Chinese culture to a new setting, the adversities and biases, the new immigration, the conflicts between "old" Chinese and "new," the Chinese culture here today. Eleven elementary-junior high grade activities using bamboo have been suggested

as a vehicle, also, for studying Asian culture. This multi-disciplinary approach would involve reading, geography, botany, customs, music, art, home economics, and arts and crafts projects.[3] In other words, basic skills and all the disciplines can be interwoven and utilized effectively to teach any group culture that the school or teacher wishes to emphasize.

4. Wherever possible, children should visit community groups in action. Some examples are a trip to an Italian market, a Greek Orthodox bazaar, a Ukranian folk festival, Chinatown Cultural Center, or whatever community activity is available. Discussion of the source of particular customs and other cultural aspects should both precede and follow such field trips.

5. Simulations should always be used **in conjunction with** interdisciplinary studies. For instance, a teacher might, if possible, conduct an hour or two of a class entirely in a foreign language, using both speech and writing, so that the children might develop a sense of what it must be like for an immigrant child who does (or did) not speak English to attend school here. If the teacher cannot do this, a local resident who can might be recruited.

6. If foreign students attend a local college or university, they might be brought to visit and speak with the children. Recent immigrants to the community might also serve as learning resources in the classroom.

7. Development of a multilingual vocabulary in terms of greetings and words used commonly in the school and home can be used to enrich the study of language arts and prepare for foreign language study at the secondary level. Discovering the common roots of these words can serve as a basis for studying the different national groups subsumed under a great language umbrella. An example of such a study is the research into the question of why Finnish resembles medieval Hungarian when the countries are so far apart geographically. Further, the study of "foreign" words that have become part of the American vocabulary should underline the contributions of various cultural groups to this country.

8. An ancillary means of studying about other countries can be the use of stamp collections, since stamps portray principal figures and events in a nation's history. Different coinage and monetary systems can be used as well, for mathematics and other subjects.

These are examples of how innovative techniques can be integrated with basic skills into the teaching program. To implement such integration, appropriate teacher education is imperative. If teachers are to present multi-cultural studies in a meaningful way, they must have the requisite knowledge about and respect for the peoples about whom they are teaching. In addition to the continuation of their education through the in-service programs we have already suggested, we further recommend that teacher education include:

1. development of research skills that will enable the teacher to utilize published and community resources effectively;

2. preparation of sample supplementary units that explore topics untouched in textbooks, such as immigration, cultural diversity, varied cultural contributions to the larger society, genocide, and the damaging effects of war rather than its glorious battles;

3. opportunities to work with people from different cultures on an informal basis to provide for relationships built on personal involvement rather than academic knowledge alone. This can be done in social service activities, musical groups, recreation activities, home visits, intercultural events on school and university campuses, etc.;

4. training in critical reading skills so that the teacher can detect (and overcome) bias in instructional materials; and

5. education in sensitivity to the feelings of others, and how to minimize individual affronts and inter-group tensions.

We agree with the thesis that

Ethnic studies programs should aim to build a cultural pluralism that is genuinely creative, rather than a pluralism of isolated groups, ignorant of and callous towards others. Above all, ethnic studies should adhere strictly to the highest standards of scholarship in research for truth that are absolute requirements for true education, in the best sense of the word.[4]

This is true for teacher and student alike, even at the elementary and junior high school levels.

The recommendations we have made are in no way the absolute and solely correct responses to the present educational dilemma.

What we are trying to accomplish is to bring to the present educational scene a sense of what is possible. We hope that perhaps a lessening of ideological struggle will begin, and once more teachers will devote themselves to a more pragmatic approach to achieving desirable goals. These goals in themselves, however, should be realistic. Remaking society, destroying class lines, eradicating poverty, and educational equality cannot be achieved by the schools alone. What **can** be realized is that our children be taught the skills necessary for them to use as a basis for reaching toward such goals, and a broader and more meaningful concept of inter-group relations so that they can see and move toward such goals. The rest of our social ideals -- upward mobility, and a more humane, decent society -- must be sought, accomplished, and sustained by the society itself.

We believe that innovative, enrichment, and multi-media programs can contribute substantially to multicultural education. If the child cannot read and comprehend what he is assigned to read, or cannot express his feelings clearly in speech and writing, however, such activities have diminished effectiveness. We urge most strongly that mastery of the basic skills of language and communication -- reading, writing, and speaking -- be restored to their position of prime priority in education and be incorporated into all instructional units. Possession of these abilities will contribute to the child's positive self-concept as a person with capabilities worthy of respect by the society at large. In making this recommendation, we seek to assure the children of all groups that they will have the skills needed to walk any avenue in our society, although each may ultimately choose which one to tread.

We stress the need for realistic multicultural education that creates respect for each cultural heritage within the child and his peers, that promotes respect for differences while recognizing similarities, and that maintains the integrity and self-respect of every child. Such a program places a heavy responsibility on textbook authors and publishers and on teacher educators, as well as on the teachers who select and use instructional materials.

With mastery of basic skills, with unbiased and broad-based texts, and with a greater understanding of the values of cultural diversity, the child and the teacher will be able to view more critically and thoughtfully those issues and events, the behaviors and beliefs, that make up America today. That is the least to which we as educators should aspire; it may be the most that we can realistically attain.

NOTES

1. c.f. Ronald Gallimore and Alan Howard, eds., "Studies in a Hawaiian Community: Na Makamaka o Nanakuli." Honolulu: PACIFIC ANTHROPOLOGICAL RECORDS NO. 1, (1968).

2. James A. Banks, TEACHING STRATEGIES FOR ETHNIC STUDIES (Boston: Allyn and Bacon, 1975).

3. Brother Raymond Antolik, "Bamboo: Strategies for Teaching about Aspects of Asian Cultures," SOCIAL EDUCATION, 42 (1978), 144-46.

4. Richard Gambino, A GUIDE TO ETHNIC STUDIES PROGRAMS IN AMERICAN COLLEGES, UNIVERSITIES, AND SCHOOLS (New York: The Rockefeller Foundation, 1975), p. 14.

APPENDIX A

Immigration Data

Table 1.

Immigration from China, India, and Japan, by decades, 1820-1974.
(Adapted from 1974 Annual Report:
Immigration and Naturalization Service, pp. 56-58)

Decade	China	India	Japan
1820	1	1	-
1821-1830	2	8	-
1831-1840	8	39	-
1841-1850	35	36	-
1851-1860	41,397	43	-
1861-1870	64,301	69	186
1871-1880	123,201	163	149
1881-1890	61,711[a]	269	2,270
1891-1900	14,799	68	25,942
1901-1910	20,605	4,713	129,797
1911-1920	21,278	2,082	83,837
1921-1930[b]	29,907	1,886	33,462
1931-1940	4,928	496	1,948
1941-1950[c]	16,709	1,761	1,555
1951-1960	9,657	1,973	46,250
1961-1965	8,156	2,602	19,759
1966-1970[d]	26,608	24,587	20,229
1971-1974	35,299	52,314	21,198
Total 1820-1974	478,602	93,110	386,582

[a]1882: Chinese Exclusion Law passed
[b]1924: restrictive immigration law passed
[c]1941-45: United States, India, and China at war with Japan
[d]1965: Immigration Act of 1965 reopened immigration from
Eastern Hemisphere

Table 2.
Immigrants admitted from China, India, Japan, and Southeast Asia, 1965-74. (Adapted from 1974 Annual Report: Immigration and Naturalization Service, pp. 3 and 59)

Country/Region of Birth	1965	1974	%Change	1965-1974
China & Taiwan	4,057	18,056	+ 345.1	146,914
Hong Kong	712	4,629	+ 550.1	39,535
India	582	12,779	+ 2095.7	85,580
Japan	3,180	4,860	+ 52.8	42,110
Korea	2,165	28,028	+ 1194.6	111,914
Philippines	3,130	32,857	+ 949.7	210,269
Thailand	214	4,956	+ 2215.9	21,488
Viet Nam	226	3,192	+ 1312.4	17,225

TABLE 3.

Median years of school completed and percent High School Graduates of Japanese, Chinese, Filipino, Hawaiian, and Korean populations (aged 25 years and older), by Urban and Rural Residence: 1970. (Adapted from U.S. Bureau of the Census, 1970 Census, Subject Report: JAPANESE, CHINESE, AND FILIPINOS IN THE UNITED STATES. Final Report PC (2) - IG. Washington: U.S. Government Printing Office, 1973, pp. 9,68,127,178,180.)

	Japanese	Chinese	Filipino	Hawaiian[a]	Korean[a]
TOTAL					
MED.Yrs.C.	12.5	12.4	12.2	12.1	12.9
% HS Grad.	68.8	57.8	54.7	53.2	71.1
URBAN					
Med.Yrs.C.	12.5	12.4	12.4	--	--
% HS Grad.	70.7	57.6	58.9	--	--
RURAL NonFarm					
Med.Yrs.C.	12.1	12.7	8.0	--	--
% HS Grad.	52.8	64.9	31.9		
RURAL Farm					
Med.Yrs.C.	12.2	12.1	6.0		
% HS Grad.	58.5	52.2	17.0		

[a]Data for Hawaiians and Koreans available only as total and for selected cities.

236

REFERENCES

We have consulted the following archives and collections:

American Jewish Committee, New York City

Rare Book Collection, New York Public Library, New York City

Witz Collection of Historical Textbooks, University of Hawaii, Honolulu

YIVO Institute of Jewish Research, New York City.

Abbott, Edith. HISTORICAL ASPECTS OF THE IMMIGRATION PROBLEM: SELECT DOCUMENTS. Chicago: University of Chicago Press, 1926.

Abdian, G. N. "The Future Americans -- the Ultimate Man." IMMIGRATION, 1 (Nov. 1909), 20-22.

Abelson, Paul. "The education of the immigrant by the Educational Alliance." JOURNAL OF SOCIAL SCIENCE, 44 (1906), 163-72.

Abrahams, Rober D. "Cultural differences and the melting pot ideology." EDUCATIONAL LEADERSHIP, 29, No. 2 (1971), 118-21.

Abrahams, Roger D., and Troike, R.C., eds. LANGUAGE AND CULTURAL DIVERSITY IN AMERICAN EDUCATION, Englewood Cliffs, N.J.: Prentice-Hall, 1972.

Addams, Jane. "Foreign-born Children in the Primary Grades." JOURNAL OF PROCEEDINGS AND ADDRESSES OF THE THIRTY-SIXTH ANNUAL MEETING. Washington: National Education Association, 1897, 104-12.

Addams, Jane. "Immigrants." SURVEY, 26 (1909), 453-54.

Addams, Jane. "The Public School and the Immigrant Child." JOURNAL OF PROCEEDINGS AND ADDRESSES. Washington: National Education Association, 1908, 99-102.

Allemann, Albert. "Immigration and the Future American Race." POPULAR SCIENCE MONTHLY, 75 (Dec. 1909), 586-96.

Allen, William C. "Americanization in Some of Our Public Schools." SCHOOL AND SOCIETY, 22 (5 Oct. 1925), 422-25.

"The Americanization Movement." SCHOOL AND SOCIETY, 9 (11 Jan. 1919), 52-53.

"Americans Debate the Role of Schools." THE NEW YORK TIMES, 16 Nov. 1975.

Andrew, E. Benjamin. HISTORY OF THE UNITED STATES, 2 vols. New York: Scribner's, 1894.

Andrews, E. Benjamin. THE UNITED STATES IN OUR TIME: A HISTORY FROM RECONSTRUCTION TO EXPANSION. New York: Charles Scribner's Sons, 1895, 1896,1903.

Antin, Mary. THE PROMISED LAND. Boston: Houghton Mifflin, 1912; 2nd ed., 1969.

Antolik, Brother Raymond. "Bamboo: Strategies for teaching about Aspects of Asian Cultures." SOCIAL EDUCATION, 42 (1978), 144-46.

Appel, John. J. "Hansen's Third-Generation 'Law' and the Origins of the American Jewish Historical Society." JEWISH SOCIAL STUDIES, 23 (Jan. 1961), 3-20.

Archer, Marguerite P. "Minorities in easy reading through Third Grade." ELEMENTARY ENGLISH, 49, No. 5 (1972), 746-49.

Arkoff, Abe, Meredith, Gerald, and Iwahara, Shinkuro. "Male-dominant and Equalitarian Attitudes in Japanese, Japanese-American, and Caucasian-American Students." JOURNAL OF SOCIAL PSYCHOLOGY, 64 (1964), 225-29.

ASIANS IN AMERICAN TEXTBOOKS. New York: Asia Society, 1976.

Ayres, Leonard. SURVEY OF SCHOOL SURVEYS. New York: Russell Sage Foundation, 1918.

Baca, Leonard, and Kane, Karen. "A Dialogue on Cultural Implications for Learning." EXCEPTIONAL CHILDREN, 40 (1974), 552-63.

Bagley, W.C. "The Textbook and Methods of Teaching." THIRTIETH YEARBOOK OF THE NATIONAL SOCIETY FOR THE STUDY OF EDUCATION, Part II. Bloomington, Ill.: Public School Publishing Co., 1931.

Bailyn, B. EDUCATION IN THE FORMING OF AMERICAN SOCIETY. New York: Vintage Books, 1960.

Bainbridge, Oliver. "The Chinese Jews." NATIONAL GEOGRAPHIC MAGAZINE, 18, No. 10 (Oct. 1907), 621-33.

Baker, G.C. "Multicultural Education: A Priority for the Future." THE INNOVATOR, 7, No. 9 (4 July 1976), 14-16.

Baker, Roscoe. THE AMERICAN LEGION AND AMERICAN FOREIGN POLICY. New York: Book Associates, 1954.

Banks, James A. "'Americanizing' the Curriculum." TEACHER, 93. No.3 (1975), 19-27.

Banks, James A. "Imperatives in Ethnic Minority Education." PHI DELTA KAPPAN, 53 (1972), 266-69.

Banks, James A. "Teaching for Ethnic Literacy: A Comparative Approach." SOCIAL EDUCATION, 37. No. 8 (1973), 738-50.

Banks, James A. "Ethnic Studies as a Process of Curriculum Reform." SOCIAL EDUCATION, 40 (1976), 76-80.

Barron, M., ed. MINORITIES IN A CHANGING WORLD. New York: Knopf, 1967.

Barrows, Thomas S., and Jungeblut, Ann. "Children's Attitudes Toward and Perceptions of Other Nations and Other Peoples." Paper presented at the Annual Meeting of the American Educational Reseaarch Association (San Francisco), 1976.

Barth, Gunther. BITTER STRENGTH: A HISTORY OF THE CHINESE IN THE UNITED STATES, 1850-1870. Cambridge, Mass.: Harvard University Press, 1964.

Bass, Herbert, ed. THE STATE OF AMERICAN HISTORY. Chicago: Quadrangle Books, 1970.

Bassett, B.B. "The Historical Information Necessary for the Intelligent Understanding of Civic Problems. SEVENTEENTH YEARBOOK OF THE NATIONAL SOCIETY FOR THE STUDY OF EDUCATION, Part I. Chicago: University of Chicago Press, 1918, 81-89.

Beard, Annie E.S. OUR FOREIGN-BORN CITIZENS, 6th ed. New York: Thomas Y. Crowell, (1968 rpt. of 1922 ed.).

Bell, Reginald. "Public School Education of Second-Generation Japanese in California." EDUCATION AND PSYCHOLOGY, 1, No. 3 (1935).

Bender, E.I., and Kagiwada, G. "Hansen's law of Third Generation Return and the Study of American Religious Ethnic Groups." PHYLON, 29 (1968), 360-70.

Bennett, J.E. "Chinese Tong War in San Francisco." HARPERS WEEK-LY, 44 (1900), 947-48.

Bennett, John W., ed. THE NEW ETHNICITY: PERSPECTIVES FORM ETHNOLOGY. St. Paul and New York: West Publishing, 1975.

Bennett, Marion T. AMERICAN IMMIGRATION POLICIES, A HISTORY. Washington: Publich Affairs Press, 1963.

Berger, H., Abel, T., and Page, C.H., eds. FREEDOM AND CONTROL IN MODERN SOCIETY. New York: Octagon Books, 1964.

Berkson, Isaac B. THEORIES OF AMERICANIZATION, A CRITICAL STUDY. New York: Teachers College, Columbia University, 1920.

Bernheimer, Charles S. "Prejudice Against Jews in U.S." INDEPENDENT, 60 (12 Nov. 1908), 1105-08.

Bernheimer, Charles S. THE RUSSIAN JEW IN THE UNITED STATES. Philadelphia: John C. Winston, 1905.

Bernstein, J.E. "Minority Group Representation in Contemporary Fiction for American Children Between the Ages of 3 and 5." URBAN REVIEW, 5, No. 5 (1972) 42-44.

Berrol, Selma Cantor. IMMIGRANTS AT SCHOOL: NEW YORK CITY, 1898-1914. City University of New York: Unpublished Doctoral Dissertation, 1967.

Berrol, Selma. "The Schools of New York in Transition, 1898-1914." URBAN REVIEW, 1 (Dec. 1966), 15-20.

Black, Hillel. THE AMERICAN SCHOOLBOOK. New York: William Morow, 1967.

Blaustein, Miriam, ed. MEMOIRS OF DAVID BLAUSTEIN, EDUCATOR AND COMMUNAL WORKER. New York: McBride, Nast, and Co., 1913.

Blaylock, Enid. V. "Article 3.3: California's Answer to Cultural Diversity in the Classroom." PHI DELTA KAPPAN, 57 (1975), 203.

Blom, G.E., Waite, R.R., and Zimet, S.G. "A Motivational Content Analysis of Children's Primers." USOE Cooperative Research Project No. 3004. In P.H. Mussen, J.J. Conger, and J. Kagan, eds. READINGS IN CHILD DEVELOPMENT AND PERSONALITY, 2nd ed. New York: Harper & Row, 1970.

Bond, Leo. "Is It Good for the Jews? Some Observations on the Rise of Ethnic Studies in Public Schools." THE PEDAGOGIC REPORTER, (June 1972), 5-7.

Blum, John M. "Nativism, Anti-radicalism and the Foreign Scaare 1917-1920." MIDWEST JOURNAL, 8 (Winter 1950-51), 46-53.

Boas, Franz. "Race Problems in America." SCIENCE, (1909), 839-49.

Bogardus, Emory S. "Cultural Pluralism and Acculturation." SOCIOLOGY AND SOCIAL RESEARCH, 34 (Nov.-Dec. 1949), 125-29.

Bogardus, Emory S. IMMIGRATION AND RACE ATTITUDES. Boston: D.C. Heath, 1928.

Bogen, Boris D. BORN A JEW. New York: Macmillan, 1930.

BOOKS FOR SCHOOLS AND THE TREATMENT OF MINORITIES. Hearings before the Ad Hoc Subcommittee on De Facto Segregation of the Committee on Education and Labor, U.S. House of Representatives, 89th Congress. Washington, (23 Aug.- 1 Sept. 1966).

Booth, Clare. "Ever Hear of Homer Lea?" SATURDAY EVENING POST, 214 (7 March 1942), 12-13, 69-72; (14 March 1942), 27, 39-42.

Boyer, William H. "Education For Survival." PHI DELTA KAPPAN, 52 (1971), 258-62.

Boze, Nancy S. "Ethnic Literature: Replacing Old Stereotypes with Positive Concepts." CLEARING HOUSE, 44, No. 9 (1970), 527-30.

Brameld, Theodore. MINORITY PROBLEMS IN THE PUBLIC SCHOOLS: A STUDY OF ADMINISTRATIVE POLICIES AND PRACTICES IN SEVEN SCHOOL SYSTEMS. New York: Harper & Row, 1946.

Brigham, John C. "Ethnic Stereotypes." PSYCHOLOGICAL BULLETIN, 76, No. 1 (1971), 15-38.

Broudy, Eric. "The Trouble with Textbooks." TEACHERS COLLEGE RECORD, 77 (1975), 13-34.

Broudy, Harry S. "Cultural Pluralism." EDUCATIONAL LEADERSHIP, 33 (1975), 173-75.

Brown, Francis J., and Roucek, Joseph S. ONE AMERICA, 3rd ed. New York: Prentice-Hall, 1952.

Brown, Lawrence Guy. IMMIGRATION: CULTURAL CONFLICT AND SOCIAL ADJUSTMENTS. New York: Longmans, Green, 1933.

Brown, Marion. "Is There A Nationality Problem in Our Schools?" IN Clarence J. Karier, ed. MAN, SOCIETY, AND EDUCATION. Chicago: Scott, Foresman, 1967.

Bruce, J. Campbell. THE GOLDEN DOOR: THE IRONY OF OUR IMMIGRATION POLICY. New York: Random House, 1954.

Bryant, William Cullen, Gay, Sideny Howard, and Brooks, Noah. SCRIBNER'S POPULAR HISTORY OF THE UNITED STATES. 3 vols. New York: Scribner's, 1876, 1881, and 1896.

Buchanan, John T. "How to Assimilate the Foreign Element in Our Population." FORUM, 32 (1902), 686-94.

Buell, Raymond Leslie. "The Development of the Anti-Japanese Agitation in the United States." POLITICAL SCIENCE QUARTERLY, 37 (Dec. 1922), 605-38; 38 (Mar. 1923), 57-81.

Burgess, Charles. "Two Tendencies of Educational Thought in the New Nation." PAEDOGOGICA HISTORIES, 4 (1964), 326-42.

Butler, Nicholas Murray. BUILDING THE AMERICAN NATION. New York: Scribner's, 1923.

Calhoun, Daniel. "The City as Teacher: Historical Problem" HISTORY OF EDUCATION QUARTERLY, 9 (Fall 1969), 312-25.

Carlson, Robert A. THE QUEST FOR CONFORMITY: AMERICANIZATION THROUGH EDUCATION. New York: John Wiley, 1975.

Carpenter, Charles. HISTORY OF AMERICAN SCHOOLBOOKS. Philadelphia: University of Pennsylvania Press, 1963.

Carpenter, John A., and Torney, Judith V. "Beyond the Melting Pot to Cultural Pluralism." CHILDREN AND INTERCULTURAL EDUCATION, Part II. Washington: Association for Childhood Education International, 1974, 14-24.

Caudill, W.A. "Japanese-American Personality and Acculturation." GENETIC PSYCHOLOGY MONOGRAPHS, 45 (1952), 3-102.

Chang, Francis. "An Accomodation Program for Second Generation Chinese." SOCIOLOGY AND SOCIAL RESEARCH, 24 (July-Aug. 1934), 541-53.

Chapin, F. Stuart. "Education and the Mores." STUDIES IN HISTORY, ECONOMICS, AND PUBLIC LAW. New York: Columbia University, 1911.

Charnofsky, S. EDUCATING THE POWERLESS. Belmont, Calif.: Wadsworth, 1971.

Chesterton, Cecil. A HISTORY OF THE UNITED STATES. New York: George H. Doran Co., 1919.

Chilcott, John H. "A Proposal for the Unification of Secondary School Courses through Anthropology." In Joan I. Roberts and Sherrie K. Akinsaya, eds. EDUCATIONAL PATTERNS AND CULTURAL CONFIGURATIONS. New York: David McKay, 1976.

Chinese-Americans: School and Community Problems. Chicago: Integrated Education Associates, 1972.

"Christ in the Public Schools." BOOKMAN, 26 (Jan. 1908), 476-68.

"Christmas without Christ." CURRENT LITERATURE, 44, No. 1 (Jan. 1908), 62-63.

Chun-Hoon, L. "Jade Snow Wong and the Fate of Chinese-American Identity." AMERASIA JOURNAL, 1 (1971), 52-63.

Ciancolo, Patricia Jean. "A Recommended Reading Diet for Children and Youth of Different Cultures." ELEMENTARY ENGLISH, 48 (1971), 779-87.

REPORT OF THE CITIZENS COMMISSION ON BASIC EDUCATION. Harrisburg: Commonwealth of Pennsylvania, 1973.

Claghorn, Kat H. "Immigration 1908-1909." SURVEY, (9 Apr. 1910), 91-93.

Clark, Todd. "Why We Need Better Multi-ethnic Education." SOCIAL EDUCATION, 42 (1978), 163-64.

Cogan, John, and Litcher, John H. "Social Studies after Curriculum Reform: Some Unfinished Business." ELEMENTARY SCHOOL JOURNAL, 75 (1974), 55-61.

Cohen, D.K. "Immigrants and the Schools." REVIEW OF EDUCATIONAL RESEARCH, 40 (1970), 13-27.

Cohen, Sol. "The Industrial Education Movement, 1906-17." AMERICAN QUARTERLY, 20 (Spring 1968), 95-110.

Cole, Cheryl L. A HISTORY OF THE JAPANESE COMMUNITY IN SACRAMENTO, 1883-1972: ORGANIZATIONS, BUSINESSES, AND GENERATIONAL RESPONSE TO MAJORITY DOMINATION AND STEREOTYPES. San Francisco: R and E Research Associates, 1974.

Cole, M., and Bruner, J.S. "Cultural Differences and Inferences about Psychological Processes." AMERICAN PSYCHOLOGIST, 26 (1971), 867-76.

Collier, M. "An Evaluation of Multi-ethnic Basal Readers." ELEMENTARY ENGLISH, 44, No.2 (1967), 152-57.

Committee of Seven, THE STUDY OF HISTORY IN SCHOOLS: REPORT TO THE AMERICAN HISTORICAL ASSOCIATION. New York: Macmillan, 1899.

Commons, John R. "Amalgamation and Assimilation." CHAUTAU-QUAN, 39 (May 1904), 217-27.

Cook, Jane Perry. "Primary Aims in Geography Teaching." JOURNAL OF GEOGRAPHY, 9 (1911), 203.

Coolidge, Archibald Cary. THE UNITED STATES AS A WORLD POWER. New York: Macmillan, 1908.

Coolidge, Mary Roberts. CHINESE IMMIGRATION. New York: Henry Holt, 1909 (rpt. Arno Press, 1969).

Cooper, C.E. "A Method for Judging and Scoring Textbooks in Grade School Geography." JOURNAL OF EDUCATIONAL METHOD, 4 (1925), 325-33.

Coopersmith, S. THE ANTECEDENTS OF SELF-ESTEEM. San Francisco: W.H. Freeman, 1967.

Corbally, John. "Orientals in Seattle Schools." SOCIOLOGY AND SOCIAL RESEARCH, 16 (Sept.-Oct. 1931), 61-67.

Cordova, Fred. "The Filipino-American, There's Always an Identity Crisis." In S. Sue and N. N. Wagner, eds. ASIAN-AMERICANS: PSYCHOLOGICAL PERSPECTIVES. Palo Alto: Science and Behavior Books, 1973, 136-39.

Cottle, Thomas J. THE VOICES OF SCHOOL: EDUCATIONAL ISSUES THROUGH PERSONAL ACCOUNTS. Boston: Little, Brown, 1973.

Counts, George S. THE SOCIAL FOUNDATIONS OF EDUCATION. New York: Scribner's, 1934.

Cremin, Lawrence. THE AMERICAN COMMON SCHOOL: AN HISTORIC CONCEPTION. New York: Bureau of Publications, Teachers College, Columbia University, 1951.

Cremin, Lawrence A. THE GENIUS OF AMERICAN EDUCATION. New York: Vintage Books, 1966.

Cremin, Lawrence A. THE TRANSFORMATION OF THE SCHOOL. New York: Knopf, 1961.

Cremin, Lawrence A. THE WONDERFUL WORLD OF ELLWOOD PATTERSON CUBBERLEY. New York: Teachers College, Columbia University, 1965.

"Cruelty of Immigration Rules." INDEPENDENT, (22 July 1909), 204-05.

Cubberley, Ellwood P. PUBLIC EDUCATION IN THE UNITED STATES. Boston: Houghton Mifflin, 1919.

Curti, Merle. THE SOCIAL IDEAS OF AMERICAN EDUCATION. New York: Scribner's 1935.

Dale, J. "Teaching Literature by and about Minorities." EDUCATIONAL LEADERSHIP, 28 (1970), 289-91.

Daniels, Roger. THE POLITICS OF PREJUDICE. Berkeley: University of California Press, 1962 (rpt. 1968).

Daniels, R., and Kitano, H.H. AMERICAN RACISM. Englewood Cliffs, N.J.: Prentice-Hall, 1970.

Davis, Alexander Vincent. THE LITERATURE OF ADVANCED SCHOOL READERS IN THE UNITED STATES, 1785-1900. University of Chicago: Unpublished Doctoral Dissertation, 1934.

Davis, Allen F., and Haller, Mark H., eds. THE PEOPLES OF PHILADELPHIA (A HISTORY OF ETHNIC GROUPS AND LOWER-CLASS LIFE, 1790-1940). Philadelphia: Temple University Press, 1973.

Davis, Phillip. "The Story of an Immigrant's Experience." CHAUTAUQUA, 48 (Sept. 1907), 100-09.

DeMotte, M. "California. . .White or Yellow?" THE ANNALS, 93 (1921), 18-23.

Derr, Richard L. A TAXONOMY OF SOCIAL PURPOSES OF PUBLIC SCHOOLS: A HANDBOOK, New York: David McKay, 1973.

Devine, Edward T. "Immigration as a Relief Problem (Charities)." SURVEY, 12 (6 Feb. 1904), 129-33.

DeWitt, Mallory R. "Racial Characteristics and Environment." IMMIGRATION, 2 (Jan. 1910), 15-17.

Diab, Lutfy N. "Factors Affecting Studies of National Stereotypes." JOURNAL OF SOCIAL PSYCHOLOGY, 59 (1963), 29-40.

Dinnerstein, Leonard, and Reimers, David M. ETHNIC AMERICANS: A HISTORY OF IMMIGRATION AND ASSIMILATION. New York: Dodd, Mead, 1975.

Divocky, Diane. "Affective Education: Are We Going Too Far?" LEARNING, 4, No.2 (1975), 20-27.

245

Dobie, Charles Caldwell. SAN FRANCISCO'S CHINATOWN. New York: Appleton-Century-Crofts, 1936.

Donovan, H.L. "How to Select Textbooks." PEABODY JOURNAL OF EDUCATION, 2 (July 1924), 1-11.

Doob, L. PUBLIC OPINION AND PROPAGANDA. Handen, Conn., 1966.

Douglas, J.H. "Mental Health Aspects of the Effects of Discrimination upon Children." YOUNG CHILDREN, 22 (1967), 298-305.

Dreeben, Robert. ON WHAT IS LEARNED IN SCHOOL. Reading, Mass.: Addison-Wesley, 1968.

Dresslar, F.R. "Chinese Pedagogics in Practice." EDUCATION, 20 (1899), 136-42.

Driencourt, Jacques. LA PROPAGANDE NOUVELLE FORCE POLITIQUE. Paris: Libraire Armand Colin, 1900.

Drotman, Gilda. "Take the Crisis out of Christmas." LEARNING, 2, No.3 (1973), 62-63.

Duff, Donald F., and Arthur, Ransom J. "Between Two Worlds: Filipinos in the U.S. Navy." In S. Sue and N.N. Wagner, eds. ASIAN-AMERICANS: PSYCHOLOGICAL PERSPECTIVES. Palo Alto: Science and Behavior Books. 1973.

Dugmore, A.R. "New Citizens for the Republic." THE WORLD'S WORK, (April 1903), 3323-26.

Duncan, W.L. "Parent Child Isolations." THE FAMILY, 10 (1929), 115-18.

Dunn, Lynn P. ASIAN AMERICANS: A STUDY GUIDE AND SOURCE-BOOK. San Francisco: R. and E Research Associates, 1975.

Ehrlich, H.J., and Rinehart, J.W. "A Brief Report on the Methodology of Stereotypes Research," SOCIAL FORCES, 43 (1965), 564-75.

Elliott, Michael J., and Kennedy, Kerry J. "Australian Impressions of Social Studies Theory and Practice in Secondary Schools in the United States." SOCIAL EDUCATION, 43 (1979), 291-296.

Ellul, Jacques. PROPAGANDA, THE FORMATION OF MEN'S ATTITUDES. Konrad Keller and Jean Lerner, trans. New York, 1966.

Elson, R.M. "American Schoolbooks and Culture in the Nineteenth Century." MISSISSIPPI VALLEY HISTORICAL REVIEW, 46 (Dec. 1959).

Elson, R.M. GUARDIANS OF TRADITION. Lincoln: University of Nebraska Press, 1964.

Elson, R.M. "Immigrants and Schoolbooks in the Nineteenth Century." Paper presented at the History of Education Society Eastern Regional Meeting, April 1971.

Erikson, Erik H. GANDHI'S TRUTH. New York: Norton, 1969.

Eschenbacher, Herman F. "Social Studies, Social Science, and School Reform." INTELLECT, 102 (1974), 507-09.

Estensen, E.V. "McGuffey - A Statistical Analysis." JOURNAL OF EDUCATIONAL RESEARCH, 39 (Feb. 1946), 445-57.

Ether, J.A. "Cultural Pluralism and Self-Identity." EDUCATIONAL LEADERSHIP, 27 (1969), 232-34.

"Ethnics All." TIME, (8 Dec. 1975), 57.

"Ethnic Groups in American Life." DAEDALUS, (Spring 1961).

Ettinger, William L. "Americanization." SCHOOL AND SOCIETY, 9 (1919), 129-33.

Evans, Eli N. THE PROVINCIALS. New York: Atheneum, 1973.

Faderman, Lillian, and Bradshaw, Barbara, eds. SPEAKING FOR OURSELVES: AMERICAN ETHNIC WRITING. Glenview, Ill.: Scott, Foresman, 1969.

Fairchild, Henry Pratt. IMMIGRATION, A WORLD MOVEMENT AND ITS AMERICAN SIGNIFICANCE. New York: Macmillan, 1913.

Fairchild, Henry Pratt. IMMIGRATION, A WORLD MOVEMENT AND ITS AMERICAN SIGNIFICANCE, rev. ed. New York: Macmillan, 1930.

Fairchild, Henry Pratt. "Immigration Differences." YALE REVIEW, (May 1910), 79-97.

Fairchild, Henry Pratt. THE MELTING POT MISTAKE. Boston: Little, Brown, 1926.

Fairchild, Henry Pratt. "The Restoration of Immigration." AMERICAN JOURNAL OF SOCIOLOGY, 17 (Mar. 1912), 637-46.

Fausey, J.R. "Evening School for Foreigners." IMMIGRATION, 1 (Sept. 1909)., 5-6.

Fein, Isaac M. THE MAKING OF AN AMERICAN JEWISH COMMUNITY. Philadelphia: Jewish Publication Society, 1971.

Fell, S. Marie-Louise. THE FOUNDATIONS OF NATIVISM IN AMERI-CAN TEXTBOOKS, 1783-1860. Washington: Catholic University of America, 1941.

Fellows, Donald Keith. A MOSAIC OF AMERICA'S ETHNIC MINORI-TIES. New York: John Wiley, 1972.

Fenton, Ronald. "Asian History through Western Glasses." UNESCO COURIER, (May 1956).

Ferrier, W.W. NINETY YEARS OF EDUCATION IN CALIFORNIA, 1846-1936. Oakland: West Coast Printing Co., 1937.

Fersh, Seymour. "Orientals and Orientation." PHI DELTA KAPPAN, 53 (1972), 315-18.

Finney, Ross. A SOCIOLOGICAL PHILOSOPHY OF EDUCATION. New York: Macmillan, 1929.

Flanders, Jesse Knowlton. LEGISLATIVE CONTROL OF THE ELEMENTARY CURRICULUM. New York: Bureau of Publications, Teachers college, Columbia University, 1925.

Fong, S.L.M. "Assimilation and Changing Social Roles of Chinese Americans." JOURNAL OF SOCIAL ISSUES, 29 (1973), 115-27.

Fong. S.L.M. "Assimilation of Chinese in America: Changes in Orienta-tion and Social Perception." AMERICAN JOURNAL OF SOCIOLOGY, 71 (1965), 265-73.

Franzen, R.H., and Knight, F.B. TEXTBOOK SELECTION. Baltimore: Warwick & York, 1922.

Freedman, Theodore. "Introduction: Why Teach about the Holocaust?" SOCIAL EDUCATION, 42 (1978), 263.

Friedman, Isaac K. WORLD'S WORK, (Sept. 1904), 5287-90.

Frost, J.L., and Hawkes, G.R., eds. THE DISADVANTAGED CHILD; ISSUES AND INNOVATIONS, 2nd ed. Boston: Houghton Mifflin, 1970.

Fryer, J. COMMUNITY INTEREST AND PUBLIC SPIRIT. Boston, 1919.

Gallimore, Ronald, and Howard, Alan, eds. STUDIES IN A HAWAIIAN COMMUNITY: NA MAKAMAKA A NANAKULI. Honolulu: Pacific Anthropological Records No.1, 1968.

Gambino, Richard. A GUIDE TO ETHNIC STUDIES PROGRAMS IN AMERICAN COLLEGES, UNIVERSITIES, AND SCHOOLS. New York: Rockefeller Foundation, 1975.

248

Gast, D.K. "Minority groups in Children's Literature." ELEMENTARY ENGLISH, 44, No. 1 (1967), 12-23.

Gates, A.I. "The Psychological vs. the Chronological Order in the Teaching of History." THE HISTORICAL OUTLOOK, 11 (1920), 227-230.

Gay, G. "Needed: Ethnic Studies in Schools." EDUCATIONAL LEADERSHIP, 28 (1970), 292-95.

Gibbons, Herbert Adams. "The Jewish Problem." CENTURY MAGAZINE, 102 (Sept. 1921), 783-92.

Gittler, Joseph B. UNDERSTANDING MINORITY GROUPS. New York: John Wiley, 1956.

Glancy, Barbara. "The Beautiful People in Children's Books." CHILDHOOD EDUCATION, 46 (1970), 365-70.

Glazer, Nathan. "Ethnicity and the Schools." COMMENTARY, 58, No. 3 (Sept. 1974), 55-59.

Glazer, Nathan, and Moynihan, Daniel P. BEYOND THE MELTING POT. Cambridge: The M.I.T. Press, 1963.

Glick, Carl. SHAKE HANDS WITH THE DRAGON. New York: McGraw Hill, 1941.

Gold, Michael. JEWS WITHOUT MONEY. New York: Liveright Publishing, 1930. (rpt. 1935).

Goldstein, S., and Goldscheider, C. JEWISH-AMERICANS: THREE GENERATIONS IN A JEWISH COMMUNITY. Englewood Cliffs, N.J.: Prentice-Hall, 1968.

Gomez, R., ed. ETHNIC MINORITIES. Lexington: Mass.: D.C. Heath, 1972.

Gonzalez, Josue. "Coming of age in Bilingual/Bicultural Education: A Historical Perspective." INEQUALITY IN EDUCATION, 19 (1975), 5-17.

Goodman, Leroy V. "Tending the 'Melting Pot'." AMERICAN EDUCATION, 10, No. 10 (1974), 20-23.

Goodwin, E.J. "Exclusion of Religious Instruction from the Public School." EDUCATIONAL REVIEW, (Feb. 1909), 129-38.

Gordon, M.M. ASSIMILATION IN AMERICAN LIFE. New York: Oxford University Press, 1964.

Gordon, Samuel. STRANGERS AT THE GATE, TALES OF RUSSIAN JEWRY. Philadelphia: Jewish Publication Society, 1902.

Graham, Patricia Albjerg. COMMUNITY AND CLASS IN AMERICAN EDUCATION, 1865-1918. New York: John Wiley, 1974.

Grant, Madison. THE PASSING OF THE GREAT RACE OR THE RACIAL BASIS OF EUROPEAN HISTORY. New York: Scribner's, 1916.

Greeley, Andrew M. ETHNICITY IN THE UNITED STATES. New York: John Wiley, 1974.

Greenbaum, William. "America in Search of a New Ideal: An Essay on the Rise of Pluralism." HARVARD EDUCATIONAL REVIEW, 44 (1974), 411-40.

Greene, Maxine. THE PUBLIC SCHOOL AND THE PRIVATE VISION: A SEARCH FOR AMERICA IN EDUCATION AND LITERATURE. New York: Random House, 1965.

Greenfield, Meg. "Lest We Forget." NEWSWEEK, (Feb 2, 1976).

Greer, Colin, "Immigrants, Negroes, and the Public Schools." URBAN REVIEW, 3 (Jan. 1969), 9-12.

Greer, Colin, ed. THE DIVIDED SOCIETY. New York: Basic Books, 1974.

Greer, Colin. THE GREAT SCHOOL LEGEND: A REVISIONIST INTER-PRETATION OF AMERICAN PUBLIC EDUCATION. New York: Basic Books, 1972.

GUIDELINES FOR TEXTBOOK SELECTION: THE TREATMENT OF MINORITIES. Harrisburg: Pennsylvania Dept. of Public Instruction, 1969.

Gulick, Sidney L. THE AMERICAN JAPANESE PROBLEM. New York: Scribner's, 1914.

Guttman, Allen. THE JEWISH WRITER IN AMERICA: ASSIMILATION AND THE CRISIS OF IDENTITY. New York: Oxford University Press, 1971.

Hahn, Melanie, and Dobb, Frederick. "Lost in the System; Korean School Children in San Francisco." INTEGRATED EDUCATION, 13, No.4 (1975), 14-16.

Hall, Prescott F. IMMIGRATION AND ITS EFFECTS UPON THE UNITED STATES. New York: Henry Holt, 1906.

Hall, Prescott F. "New Problems of Immigration." FORUM, 30 (Jan. 1901), 555-67.

Hall, Prescott F. "Selection of Immigration." ANNALS OF THE AMERICAN ACADEMY OF POLITICAL AND SOCIAL SCIENCE, 24 (1904), 169-84.

Hall, Prescott F. "The Future of American Ideals." NORTH AMERICAN REVIEW, 195 (Jan. 1912), 94-102.

Hall-Quest, Alfred Lawrence. THE TEXTBOOK. New York: Macmillan, 1920.

Haller, H.S. "Minority History: What? Why? How?" Harrisburg: Pennsylvania Dept. of Education, 1970.

Handlin, Oscar. ADVENTURE IN FREEDOM: THREE HUNDRED YEARS OF JEWISH LIFE IN AMERICA. New York: McGraw Hill, 1954.

Handlin, Oscar. "American Views of the Jew at the Opening of the Twentieth Century." PUBLICATIONS OF AMERICAN JEWISH HISTORICAL SOCIETY, 40 (1951), 325-26.

Handlin, Oscar, ed. CHILDREN OF THE UPROOTED. New York: GEORGE BRAZILLER, 1966.

Handlin, Oscar, ed. IMMIGRATION AS A FACTOR IN AMERICAN HISTORY. Englewood Cliffs, N.J.: Prentice-Hall, 1959.

Handlin, Oscar. "The Goals of Integration." DAEDALUS, 95 (Winter 1966).

Handlin, Oscar. THE UPROOTED, 2nd ed. Boston: Little, Brown, 1951, 1973.

Handlin, Oscar and Mary. DANGER IN DISCORD. New York: Anti-Defamation League, 1948.

Handlin, Oscar and Mary. "Historical Perspectives on the American Ethnic Group." DAEDALUS. 90 (Spring 1961), 220-32.

Hansen, M.L. THE PROBLEM OF THE THIRD GENERATION IMMIGRANT. Rock Island, Ill.: Augustana Historical Society Publications, 1938.

Hansen, Marcus Lee. "The Third Generation in America." COMMENTARY, 14 (Nov. 1952), 492-500.

Hanus, Paul H. "School Instruction in Religion." EDUCATION, 27, No.1 (Sept. 1906), 10-17; 27, No.2 (Oct. 1906), 73-84.

Hapgood, Hutchins. THE SPIRIT OF THE GHETTO. 1902. (rpt. Belknap Press of Harvard University Press, 1967).

Harris, J.J. THE TREATMENT OF RELIGION IN ELEMENTARY SCHOOL SOCIAL STUDIES TEXTBOOKS. New York: Anti-Defamation League, 1963.

Hart, Jerome A. "The Japanese in California." WORLD'S WORK, (Mar. 1907), 8689-93.

Hartley, E.L., Rosenbaum, M., and Schwartz, S. "Children's Perceptions of Ethnic Group Membership." JOURNAL OF PSYCHOLOGY, 26 (1948), 387-98.

Hartmann, Edward George. THE MOVEMENT TO AMERICANIZE THE IMMIGRANT. New York: Columbia University Press, 1948.

Hauser, C.A. LATENT RELIGIOUS RESOURCES IN PUBLIC SCHOOL EDUCATION. Philadelphia, 1924.

Havighurst, Robert J. and Neugarten, Bernice L. SOCIETY AND EDUCATION. Boston: Allyn and Bacon, 1967.

Hedzer, Caroline. "The Kindergarten as a Factor in Americanization." NEA JOURNAL OF ADDRESSES AND PROCEEDINGS, 56 (1918), 169-71.

Henderson, Bertha. "Cultural and Training Values of Geography." JOURNAL OF GEOGRAPHY, 14 (1915), 100-01.

Hendrick, Burton J. "The Great Jewish Invasion." McCLURE'S. (Jan. 1907), 307-21.

Hendrick, Burton L. "The Jewish Invasion of America." McCLURE'S (Mar. 1913), 123-65.

Hendrick, Burton J. "The Skulls of Our Immigrants." McCLURE'S. (May 1910), 36-51.

Herberg, Will. "Religion and Education in America." in RELIGIOUS PERSPECTIVES IN AMERICAN CULTURE. Princeton: Princeton University Press, Vol.2, 11-51.

Herman, Judith, ed. THE SCHOOLS AND GROUP IDENTITY: EDUCATING FOR A NEW PLURALISM. New York: American Jewish Committee, 1974.

Hewett, Edgar L. "Ethnic Factors in Education." In J.I. Roberts and S.K. Akinsanya, eds. EDUCATIONAL PATTERNS AND CULTURAL CONFIGURATIONS. New York: David McKay, 1976, 27-36.

Higham, John. "Another Look At Nativism." CATHOLIC HISTORICAL REVIEW, 44 (July 1958), 147-58.

Higham, John. "Integration vs. Pluralism: Another American Dilemma." CENTER MAGAZINE, 7, No.4 (July-Aug. 1974), 67-73.

Higham, John. STRANGERS IN THE LAND. New Brunswick: Rutgers University Press, 1955.

Hogg, T.C., and McComb, M.R. "Cultural Pluralism: Its Implications for Education." EDUCATIONAL LEADERSHIP, 27 (1969), 245-38.

Horner, Vivian M. "Bilingual Literacy." In John B. Carroll and Jeanne S. Chall, eds. TOWARD A LITERATE SOCIETY. New York: McGraw-Hill, 1975.

Hosokawa, B. NISEI -- THE QUIET AMERICAN. New York: William Morrow, 1969.

Howe, Irving, WORLD OF OUR FATHERS. New York: Harcourt, Brace, Jovanovich, 1976.

Hsu, Francis L.K. AMERICANS AND CHINESE: PURPOSE AND FULFILLMENT IN GREAT CIVILIZATIONS. Garden City, N.Y.: Natural History Press, 1953, 1970.

Hsu, Francis L.K. AMERICANS AND CHINESE: TWO WAYS OF LIFE. New York: Henry Schuman, 1953.

Hsu, Francis L.K. THE CHALLENGE OF THE AMERICAN DREAM: THE CHINESE IN THE UNITED STATES. Belmont, Calif.: Wadsworth Publishing, 1971.

Ichihashi, Yamamoto. JAPANESE IN THE UNITED STATES. Stanford: Stanford Univeristy Press, 1932. (rpt. ARNO PRESS and THE NEW YORK TIMES)

"Immigration." PUBLIC OPINION, 14 (10 Dec. 1892), 221-22. INTERGROUP RELATIONS IN TEACHING MATERIALS: A SURVEY AND APPRAISAL. Washington: American Council on Education, 1949.

Irwin, Wallace. SEED OF THE SUN. New York: George H. Brown, 1921.

Irwin, Will. PROPAGANDA AND THE NEWS, 1936.

Isaacs, Abram S. "The Jew in America." NORTH AMERICAN REVIEW. (Nov. 1905), 676-84.

Isaacs, Harold R. SCRATCHES ON OUR MINDS. New York: John Day, 1958.

Jarolimek, John. "Born Again Ethnics: Pluralism in Modern America." SOCIAL EDUCATION, 43 (1979), 204-09.

Jaworski, Irene D. BECOMING AMERICAN, THE PROBLEMS OF IMMIGRANTS AND THEIR CHILDREN. New York: Harper, 1950.

Jenkins, Esther C. "Multi-ethnic Literature: Promise and Problems." ELEMENTARY ENGLISH, 50, No.5 (1973), 693-99.

Jones, Dorothy B. THE PORTRAYAL OF CHINA AND INDIA ON THE AMERICAN SCENE, 1896-1955. Cambridge: M.I.T. Center, 1955.

Jones, Maldwyn A. AMERICAN IMMIGRATION. Chicago: University of Chicago Press, 1960.

Jordan, David Starr. "Closed Doors or the Melting Pot." In C.J. Karier, ed. SHAPING THE AMERICAN EDUCATIONAL STATE. New York: Free Press, 1975, 215-19.

Joseph, Samuel, JEWISH IMMIGRATION TO THE UNITED STATES, FROM 1881-1910. New York, 1914. (rpt. Arno Press, 1969).

Jovanovich, William. "The American Textbook: An Unscientific Phenomenon - Quality without Control." THE AMERICAN SCHOLAR, 38 (1969), 227-39.

Joyce, W.W. "Minorities in Primary-Grade Social Studies Textbooks: A Progress Report." SOCIAL EDUCATION, 37 (1973), 218-33.

Kaestle, Carl F. THE EVOLUTION OF AN URBAN SCHOOL SYSTEM, NEW YORK CITY, 1750-1850. Cambridge: Harvard University Press, 1973.

Kallen, Horace M. CULTURAL PLURALISM AND THE AMERICAN IDEA. AN ESSAY IN SOCIAL PHILOSOPHY. Philadelphia: University of Pennsylvania Press, 1956.

Kallen, Horace M. "Democracy versus the Melting Pot." THE NATION, 100 (May 1915), 219-20.

Kane, Michael B. MINORITIES IN TEXTBOOKS: A STUDY OF THEIR TREATMENT IN SOCIAL STUDIES TEXTS. Chicago: Quadrangle Books, 1970.

Karier, C.J., Violas, P.C. and Spring, J. Roots of Crisis: AMERICAN EDUCATION IN THE TWENTIETH CENTURY. Chicago: Rand, McNally, 1973.

Katz, Daniel, et al., eds. PUBLIC OPINION AND PROPAGANDA. New York, 1954.

Katz, D., and Braly, K.W. "Racial Prejudice and Racial Stereotypes." JOURNAL OF ABNORMAL AND SOCIAL PSYCHOLOGY, 28, (1933), 175-93.

Katz, M.B. THE IRONY OF EARLY SCHOOL REFORM. Cambridge: Harvard University Press, 1968.

Katz, M.B., ed. SCHOOL REFORM: PAST AND PRESENT. Boston: Little, Brown, 1971.

Kepner, Tyler. "The Influences of Textbooks upon Method." YEAR-BOOK OF NATIONAL COUNCIL FOR THE SOCIAL STUDIES, 5th Yearbook, Philadelphia, 1935, 143-72.

King, Edmund J. SOCIETY, SCHOOLS, AND PROGRESS IN THE U.S.A., Oxford, England: Pergamon Press, 1965.

Kitano, H.H.L. JAPANESE-AMERICANS: THE EVOLUTION OF A SUBCULTURE. Englewood Cliffs, N.J.: Prentice-Hall, 1969.

Kitano, Harry H.L., and Sue, Stanley. "The Model Minorities." JOURNAL OF SOCIAL ISSUES, 29 (1973), 1-10.

Klapper, Paul. THE TEACHING OF HISTORY. New York: Appleton, 1926.

Knight, Edgar W. PUBLIC EDUCATION IN THE SOUTH. Boston: Ginn and Company, 1922.

Kohler, M.J. "UnAmerican Character of Race Legislation." ANNALS OF AMERICAN ACADEMY OF POLITICAL AND SOCIAL SCIENCE, 29)Sept. 1909), 55-73.

Kolm, Richard. "The Role of Ethnic Studies in Educational Equality." ERIC: ED 079 188.

Kreger, Sara Finn, and Kroes, William H. "Child-rearing Attitudes of Chinese, Jewish, and Protestant Mothers." JOURNAL OF SOCIAL PSYCHOLOGY, 86 (1972), 205-10.

Kung, S.W. THE CHINESE IN AMERICAN LIFE: SOME ASPECTS OF THEIR HISTORY, STATUS, PROBLEMS, AND CONTRIBUTIONS. Seattle: University of Washington Press, 1962.

Lambert, Wallace E., and Klineberg, Otto. CHILDREN'S VIEW OF FOREIGN PEOPLES. New York: Appleton-Century-Crofts, 1967.

Lange, Richard A., and Kelley, William T. "The Problem of Bias in the Writing of Elementary History Textbooks." JOURNAL OF GENERAL EDUCATION, 22 (1971), 257-67.

"Language as an Asset for Our Foreign-born Citizens." SURVEY, (14 Aug. 1909), 677-78.

Lasker, Bruno, RACE ATTITUDES IN CHILDREN. New York: Henry Holt, 1929 (rpt. Greenwood Printing, 1968).

Lau v. Nichols, 414 U.S. 563, 1974.

Lawler, Thomas Bonaventure. SEVENTY YEARS OF TEXTBOOK PUBLISHING, 1867-1937: A HISTORY OF GINN AND COMPANY. Boston: Ginn and Co., 1938.

Lazerwitz, Bernard, and Rawitz, Louis. "The Three-Generation Hypothesis." AMERICAN JOURNAL OF SOCIOLOGY, 69 (Mar. 1964), 529-38.

Lea Homer. THE VALOR OF IGNORANCE. New York: Harper & Brothers, 1909.

Lea, Homer. THE DAY OF THE SAXON. New York: Harper & Brothers, 1942.

Lee, Rose Hum. THE CHINESE IN THE UNITED STATES OF AMERICA. Hong Kong: Hong Kong University Press, 1960, and Cambridge: Oxford University Press, 1960.

Levine, Gene N., and Montero, Darrel M. "Socioeconomic Mobility among Three Generations of Japanese Americans." JOURNAL OF SOCIAL ISSUES, 29, No.2 (1973), 33-47.

Levy, Sydelle Brooks. "Shifting Patterns of Ethnic Identification among the Hassidim." In John W. Bennett, ed. THE NEW ETHNICITY: PERSPECTIVES FROM ETHNOLOGY. St. Paul and New York: West Publishing, 1975.

Lew, Chew. "The Biography of a Chinaman." INDEPENDENT, 55 (1903), 417-23.

Lewis, Claude. "The U.N. Vote on Zionism." PHILADELPHIA BULLETIN, 14 Nov. 1975.

Lin, Adet, and Lin, Anor. OUR FAMILY. New York: John Day, 1939.

Lindberg, Stanley. THE ANNOTATED MCGUFFEY: SELECTIONS FROM THE MCGUFFEY ECLECTIC READERS, 1836-1920. New York: Van Nostrand Reinhold, 1976.

Lodge, Henry Cabot. "Efforts to Restrict Undesirable Immigration." CENTURY MAGAZINE, 67 (Jan. 1904), 466-69.

Louis, K.K. "Program for Second Generation Chinese." SOCIOLOGY AND SOCIAL RESEARCH, 16 (1932), 455-62.

Lowe, Pardee. FATHER AND GLORIOUS DESCENDANT. Boston: Little, Brown, 1943.

Lui, Ching. "Chinese versus American Ideas Concerning the Family." JOURNAL OF APPLIED SOCIOLOGY, 10 (1925-26), 243-48.

Lui, Kwang-Ching. AMERICANS AND CHINESE. Cambridge: Harvard University Press, 1963.

Lung, C.F. "A Chinese Student and Western Culture." SOCIOLOGY AND SOCIAL RESEARCH, 16 (Nov. 1931), 23-38.

Lyman, Stanford. THE ASIANS IN THE WEST. Reno: University of Nevada, Desert Research Institute, 1970.

Lynn, Robert W. PROTESTANT STRATEGIES IN EDUCATION. New York: Association Press, 1964.

MAKERS OF AMERICA: HYPHENATED AMERICANS. 8 vols. Chicago: Field Publishing, 1971.

Makielski, S.J., Jr. BELEAGUERED MINORITIES: CULTURAL POLITICS IN AMERICA. San Francisco: W.H. Freeman, 1973.

Marden, Charles F., and Meyer, Gladys. MINORITIES IN AMERICAN SOCIETY, 3rd ed. New York: American Book, 1968.

Martin, David S. "Ethnocentrism toward Foreign Culture in Elementary School Studies." ELEMENTARY SCHOOL JOURNAL, 75 (1975), 380-88.

Masaoka, Naoichi. JAPAN TO AMERICA. New York: Putnam, 1915.

Mason, Gregory. "An Americanization Factory." In Clarence J. Karier, ed. MAN, SOCIETY, AND EDUCATION. Chicago: Scott, Foresman, 1967.

Masuda, M., Matsumoto, G.H., and Meredith, G.M. "Ethnic identity in Three Generations of Japanese Americans." JOURNAL OF SOCIAL PSYCHOLOGY, 81 (1970), 199-207.

Masuoka, J., and Johnson, C.S. ORIENTALS AND THEIR CULTURAL BACKGROUND. Nashville: Fisk University, Social Science Institute (Social Science Source Departments, No.4), 1946.

Maxwell, C.R. "The Selection of Textbooks." SCHOOL AND SOCIETY, 9 (11 Jan. 1919), 44-52.

Maykovich, Minako Kurokawa. "Reciprocity in Racial Stereotypes: White, Black, and Yellow." AMERICAN JOURNAL OF SOCIOLOGY, 77 (1972), 876-97.

Maykovich, Minako Kurokawa. "White-Yellow Stereotypes, An Empirical Study." PACIFIC SOCIOLOGICAL REVIEW, 14 (1971), 447-67.

McAulay, J.D. "An Evaluation of 120 Recent Elementary School Social Studies Programs." EDUCATIONAL HORIZONS, 53 (1975), 171-75.

McClatchy, V. "Japanese in the Melting Pot: Can They Assimilate and Make Good Citizens?" THE ANNALS, 93 (1921), 29-34.

McKenzie, R.D. ORIENTAL EXCLUSION. Chicago: University of Chicago Press, 1927.

McLaughlin, Andrew C. A HISTORY OF THE AMERICAN NATION. New York, 1899.

McMaster, John Bach. WITH THE FATHERS: STUDIES IN THE HISTORY OF THE UNITED STATES. New York: Appleton, 1896.

McMurray, Frank M. "A Critical Appraisement of Proposed Reorganizations." TWENTY-SECOND YEARBOOK OF THE NATIONAL SOCIETY FOR THE STUDY OF EDUCATION. Bloomington, ILL,: Public School Publishing Co., 1923.

McWilliams, Carey. BROTHERS UNDER THE SKIN. Boston: Little, Brown, 1943.

Mead, Margaret. "Uniqueness and Universality." CHILDHOOD EDUCATION, 51 (1974), 58-63.

Mears, Eliot Grinnell. RESIDENT ORIENTALS ON THE AMERICAN PACIFIC COAST. Chicago: University of Chicago Press, 1928.

Melendy, H.B. THE ORIENTAL AMERICANS. New York: Hippocrene Books, 1972.

Meltzer, Hyman. CHILDREN'S SOCIAL CONCEPTS: A STUDY OF THEIR NATURE AND DEVELOPMENT. New York: Bureau of Publications, Teachers College, Columbia University, 1925.

Meltzer, Milton. REMEMBER THE DAYS. New York: Zenith Books, 1974.

Merelman, Richard M. "Public Education and Social Structure: Three Modes of Adjustment." THE JOURNAL OF POLITICS, 4 (Nov. 1973), 798-829.

Metzker, Isaac, ed. A BINTEL BRIEF ("A BUNDLE OF LETTERS" TO THE JEWISH DAILY FORWARD). New York: Ballantine Books, 1971.

Meyerson, A. "The Conflict Between New and Old Generations." THE FAMILY, 3 (1922), 163-65.

Miel, Alice, and Kiester, Edwin, Jr. THE SHORTCHANGED CHILDREN OF SUBURBIA. New York: American Jewish Committee, 1967.

Miller, L.P. "Materials for Multi-ethnic Learners." EDUCATIONAL LEADERSHIP, 28, No.2 (1970), 129-32.

Miller, S.C. THE UNWELCOME IMMIGRANT. Berkeley: University of California Press, 1969.

Miller, Zane L. THE URBANIZATION OF MODERN AMERICA. New York: Harcourt, Brace, Jovanovich. 1973.

Mills, Nicolaus. "Community Schools: Irish, Italians, and Jews." SOCIETY, 11, No.3 (1974), 76-84.

Minckley, Loren Stiles. AMERICANIZATION THROUGH EDUCATION. No Publisher, 1917.

Minnich, Harvey C. WILLIAM HOLMES MCGUFFEY AND HIS READERS. New York: American Book Co., 1936.

Mitchell, John. ANNALS OF THE AMERICAN ACADEMY OF POLITICAL AND SOCIAL SCIENCE, (July 1909), 125-29.

Mock, R.S. "Racial and Religious Prejudice in American Literature Textbooks." INDIANA SOCIAL STUDIES QUARTERLY, 22 (Autumn, 1969), 15-18.

Morais, Nina. "Jewish Ostracism in America." NORTH AMERICAN REVIEW, 133 (1881), 369-70.

Mosier, Richard D. Making the American Mind: SOCIAL AND MORAL IDEAS IN THE MCGUFFEY READERS. New York: Russell and Russell, 1965.

Murphy, Paul L. "Sources and Nature of Intolerance in the 1920's." JOURNAL OF AMERICAN HISTORY, 54 (June 1964), 60-76.

Nahirny, Vladimir, and Fishman, Joshua A. "American Immigrant

Groups: Ethnic Identification and the Problem of Generations." THE SOCIOLOGICAL REVIEW, 13 (Nov. 1965), 311-26.

Nee, Victor G., and Nee, Brett DeBary. LONGTIME CALIFORN': A DOCUMENTARY STUDY OF AN AMERICAN CHINATOWN. New York: Pantheon books, 1973.

Newman, William M. AMERICAN PLURALISM: A STUDY OF MINORITY GROUPS AND SOCIAL THEORY. New York: Harper & Row, 1973.

Nieto, S. Children's literature on Puerto Rican themes -- Part I: The messages of fiction. INTERRACIAL BOOKS FOR CHILDREN BULLETIN, 1983, 14 (1 & 2), 6-9.

Nietz, John A. OLD TEXTBOOKS. Pittsburgh: University of Pittsburgh Press, 1961.

"No One Model American." JOURNAL OF TEACHER EDUCATION, 24 (1973), 264.

North, Hart H. "Chinese and Japanese Immigration to the Pacific Coast." CALIFORNIA HISTORICAL SOCIETY QUARTERLY, 28 (Dec. 1949), 343-50.

Norton, Eliot. "The Diffusion of Immigration." ANNALS OF AMERICAN ACADEMY OF POLITICAL AND SOCIAL SCIENCE, 24 (1904), 161-65.

"Notable Children's Trade Books in the Field of Social Studies." SOCIAL EDUCATION, 40 (1976), 238-44.

Ogawa, Dennis M. FROM JAPS TO JAPANESE: AN EVOLUTION OF JAPANESE-AMERICAN STEREOTYPES. Berkeley: McCutchan Publishing, 1971.

Ogawa, Dennis. "The Jap Image." In Stanley Sue and Nathaniel N. Wagner, eds. ASIAN-AMERICANS: PSYCHOLOGICAL PERSPECTIVES. Palo Alto: Science and Behavior Books, 1973, 3-12.

Ogg, Frederic Austin. "American Immigration at High Tide." WORLD'S WORK, 14 (May 1907), 8879-86.

Olmsted, Roger, and Wollenberg, Charles, eds. NEITHER SEPARATE NOR EQUAL: RACE AND RACISM IN CALIFORNIA. California Historical Society, 1971.

Otis, E.M. "A Textbook Scorecard." JOURNAL OF EDUCATIONAL RESEARCH, 7 (Feb. 1923), 132-36.

"Our Responsibility for Immigrants after Landing." SURVEY, (9 April 1910), 74-77.

Park, No-Yong. AN ORIENTAL VIEW OF AMERICAN CIVILIZATION. Boston: Hale, Cushman, and Flint, 1934.

Park, No-Yong. CHINAMAN'S CHANCE. Boston: Meador Publishing, 1940.

Park, R.E. THE IMMIGRANT PRESS AND ITS CONTROL. New York: Harper, 1922.

Patton, J.H. FOUR HUNDRED YEARS OF AMERICAN HISTORY. 2 vols. New York: Fords, Howard, and Hubert, 1882, 1891, 1892.

Penrose, Boies. "Chinese Exclusion and the Problems of Immigration." INDEPENDENT, 54 (2 Jan. 1902), 12-15.

Perkinson, H.J. THE IMPERFECT PANACEA: AMERICAN FAITH IN EDUCATION, 1865-1915. New York: Random House, 1968.

Perlmutter, Philip. "Ethnic Education: Can It be Relevant?" THE MASSACHUSETTS TEACHER (Feb. 1974).

Phelan, J. "Why California Objects to the Japanese Invasion." THE ANNALS, 93 (1921), 16-17.

Pierce, Bessie Louis. CIVIC ATTITUDES IN AMERICAN SCHOOL TEXTBOOKS. Chicago: University of Chicago Press, 1930.

Polak, M. "Interview: I.I. Chang." PHILADELPHIA INQUIRER, 28 Mar. 1976.

Pollard, Diane S. "Educational Achievement and Ethnic Group Membership." COMPARATIVE EDUCATION REVIEW. (oct. 1973), 362-74.

Polos, N.C. "A Yankee Patriot: John Swett, the Horace Mann of the Pacific." HISTORY OF EDUCATION QUARTERLY, 4 (1964), 17-31.

Potter, David M. PEOPLE OF PLENTY, ECONOMIC ABUNDANCE, AND THE AMERICAN CHARACTER. Chicago: University of Chicago Press, 1954.

Prattle, Richard. THE PUBLIC SCHOOL MOVEMENT. New York: David McKay, 1973.

Price, Robert D. "Textbook Dilemma in the Social Studies." THE SOCIAL STUDIES, 57 (Jan. 1966), 21-27.

Quinn, Larry D. "'Chink, Chink, Chinaman,' Beginning of Nativism in Montana." PACIFIC NORTHWEST QUARTERLY, 57, No. 2 (Apr. 1967), 82-89.

"Race Prejudice Against Jews." INDEPENDENT, (17 Dec. 1908), 1451-57.

Radke, M., Trager, H.G., and Davis, H. "Social Perceptions and Attitudes of Children." GENETIC PSYCHOLOGY MONOGRAPHS, 40 (1949), 327-447.

Radzinski, J.M. "The American Melting Pot: Its Meaning to Us." AMERICAN JOURNAL OF PSYCHIATRY, 115 (1959), 873-86.

Ravage, M.E. AN AMERICAN IN THE MAKING: THE LIFE STORY OF AN IMMIGRANT. New York: Harper & Brothers, 1917.

Ravitch, Diane. THE GREAT SCHOOL WARS. New York: Basic Books, 1974.

Reeder, Rudolph R. THE HISTORICAL DEVELOPMENT OF SCHOOL READERS AND METHOD IN TEACHING READING. New York: Columbia University, Unpublished Doctoral Dissertation, 1900.

Reid, Virginia M., et al. REPORT of the Committee on Reading Ladders for Human Relations of the National Council of Teachers of English, 5th ed., 1972.

Reisner, Edward H. THE EVOLUTION OF THE COMMON SCHOOL. New York: Macmillan, 1930.

Reisner, Edward H. NATIONALISM AND EDUCATION SINCE 1789. New York: Macmillan, 1922.

Resnick, Lauren, and Robinson, Betty H. "Motivational Aspects of the Literacy Problem." In John B. Carroll and Jeanne S. Chall, eds. TOWARD A LITERATE SOCIETY. New York: MCGraw-Hill, 1975.

Rice, Joseph Mayer. THE PUBLIC SCHOOL SYSTEM OF THE UNITED STATES. New York: Century, 1893.

Rice, Roger. "Recent Legal Developments in Bilingual/Bicultural Education." INEQUALITY IN EDUCATION, 19 (1975), 51-53.

Rider, Harry. "Legislative Notes and Reviews, Americanization." AMERICAN POLITICAL SCIENCE REVIEW, 14 (1920), 110-15.

Riis, Jacob. HOW THE OTHER HALF LIVES. New York, 1912, (rpt. Dover, 1967).

Ringer, Benjamin B. THE EDGE OF FRIENDLINESS: A STUDY OF JEWISH-GENTILE RELATIONS. New York: Basic Books, 1967.

Ripley, W.Z. "Race Progress and Immigration." ANNALS OF ACADEMY OF POLITICAL AND SOCIAL SCIENCE, (July 1909), 130-38.

Rischin, M. THE PROMISED CITY: NEW YORK'S JEWS, 1870-1914. Cambridge: Harvard University Press, 1962.

Robinson, R.R. TWO CENTURIES OF CHANGE IN THE CONTENT OF SCHOOL READERS. Nashville: George Peabody College for Teachers, 1930.

Rosenau, William. "Cardinal Gibbons and his Attitudes toward Jewish Problems." PUBLICATIONS OF THE AMERICAN JEWISH HISTORICAL SOCIETY, 31 (1928), 219-24.

Rosenberg, Stuart E. THE SEARCH FOR JEWISH IDENTITY IN AMERICA. New York: Anchor, 1965.

Rosenstock, Morton. LOUIS MARSHALL, DEFENDER OF JEWISH RIGHTS. Detroit: Wayne State University Press, 1965.

Roskolenko, Harry. "America, the Thief." In Thomas C. Wheeier, ed. THE IMMIGRANT EXPERIENCE. Baltimore: Penguin Books, 1971, 151-78.

Ross, Edward A. "The Causes of Race Superiority." ANNALS OF ACADEMY OF POLITICAL AND SOCIAL SCIENCE, 18 (1901).

Rossiter, W.S. "Common Sense View of Immigration Problem." NORTH AMERICAN REVIEW, (Sept. 1908), 360-71.

Rosten, Leo. THE JOYS OF YIDDISH. New York: McGraw-Hill, 1968.

Ruesch, J. "Social Technique, Social Status, and Social Change in Illness." In C. Kluchkohn and H.A. Murray, eds. PERSONALITY IN NATURE, SOCIETY AND CULTURE. New York: Knopf, 1948.

Rugg, Earle. "How the Current courses in History, Geography, and Civics Came to be What They Are." TWENTY-SECOND YEARBOOK OF THE NATIONAL SOCIETY FOR THE STUDY OF EDUCATION. Bloomington, Ill.: Public School Publishing Co., 1923, 48-75.

Rugg, H.O. "Problems of Contemporary Life as the Basis for Curriculum-Making in the Social Studies." TWENTY-SECOND YEARBOOK OF THE NATIONAL SOCIETY FOR THE STUDY OF EDUCATION. Bloomington, Ill.: Public School Publishing Co., 1923, 260 ff.

Ruggles, Alice McGuffey. THE STORY OF THE MCGUFFEYS. New York: American Book Co., 1950.

Russell, Francis. "The Coming of the Jews." ANTIOCH REVIEW, 15 (Mar. 1955), 19-38.

Sanborn, Alvan F. "The New Immigration to America." INDEPENDENT, 54 (13 Nov. 1902), 2696-98.

Sandmeyer, Elmer C. THE ANTI-CHINESE MOVEMENT IN CALI-
FORNIA. Urbana: University of Illinois Press, 1939.

Sargent, Frank P. "Problems of Immigration." ANNALS OF AMERI-
CAN ACADEMY OF POLITICAL AND SOCIAL SCIENCE. 24 (1904),
153-58.

Schroeder, H.H. "Religious Element in Public Schools." EDUCATION-
AL REVIEW, (Apr. 1909), 375-89.

Schwartz, Audrey James. "The Culturally Advantaged: A Study
of Japanese-American Pupils." SOCIOLOGY AND SOCIAL
RESEARCH, 55 (1971), 341-53.

Schwartz, Lita Linzer. AMERICAN EDUCATION: A PROBLEM-
CENTERED APPROACH, 3rd ed. Washington: University Press of
America. 1978.

Schwartz, Lita Linzer. EDUCATIONAL PSYCHOLOGY: FOCUS
ON THE LEARNER, 2nd ed. Boston: Holbrook Press, 1977.

"Sexism and Racism in Popular Basal readers, 1964-76." New York:
Racism and Sexism Resource Center for Educators, 1976.

Shankland, Rebecca H. "The McGuffey Readers and Moral Education."
HARVARD EDUCATIONAL REVIEW, 21 (Winter 1961), 60-72.

Shankman, Arnold. "Atlanta Jewry, 1900-1930." AMERICAN JEWISH
ARCHIVES, 25 (Nov. 1973), 131-55.

Sherman, C. Bezalel. THE JEW WITHIN AMERICAN SOCIETY.
Detroit: Wayne State University Press, 1961.

Sherman, Philip Edward. "Immigration from Abroad into Massachusetts." NEW ENGLAND MAGAZINE, 29 (Feb. 1904), 671-81.

Sherry, Nora. "Social Attitudes of Chinese Immigrants." JOURNAL
OF APPLIED SOCIOLOGY, 7 (July-Aug. 1923), 325-33.

Simms, Richard L. "Bias in Textbooks: Not Yet Corrected." PHI
DELTA KAPPAN, 57 (1975), 201-02.

Simons, A.M. SOCIAL FORCES IN AMERICAN HISTORY. New
York: Macmillan, 1911. Simpson, George Eaton, and Yinger, J. Milton.
RACIAL AND CULTURAL MINORITIES. New York: Harper &
Row, 1953.

Sims. R. "What has happened to the 'all-white' world of children's
books?" PHI DELTA KAPPAN, 1983, 64, 650-653.

Sizer, Theodore, ed. RELIGION AND PUBLIC EDUCATION. Boston:
Houghton Mifflin, 1967.

Sizer, Theodore R. SECONDARY SCHOOLS AT THE TURN OF THE CENTURY. New Haven: Yale University Press, 1964.

Sklare, Marshall, ed. THE JEWS: SOCIAL PATTERNS OF AN AMERICAN GROUP. Glencoe, Ill.: The Free Press, 1958.

Smith, Bradford, AMERICANS FROM JAPAN. New York: J.B. Lippincott, 1948.

Smith, Mayo-Richmond. EMIGRATION AND IMMIGRATION: A STUDY IN SOCIAL SCIENCE. New York: Scribner's, 1890.

Smith, Timothy. "Immigrant Social Aspirations and American Education, 1880-1930." AMERICAN QUARTERLY, 21 (Fall 1964), 523-34.

Smith, Timothy. "New Approaches to the History of Immigration." AMERICAN HISTORICAL REVIEW, 71 (July 1966), 1265-79.

Smith, Timothy. "Progressivism in American Education, 1880-1900." HARVARD EDUCATIONAL REVIEW, 31 (Spring 1961), 168-92.

Smith, William C. "The Second Generation Oriental American." JOURNAL OF APPLIED SOCIOLOGY, 10 (Nov-Dec. 1925), 16-68.

Smith, William C. THE SECOND GENERATON ORIENTAL IN AMERICA. Honolulu: R and E Research Associates, 1927.

Sollenberger, R.T. "Chinese-American Child-rearing Practices and Juvenile Delinquency." JOURNAL OF SOCIAL PSYCHOLOGY, 74 (1968), 13-23.

Sommers, V.S. "Identity Conflict and Acculturation Problems in Oriental-Americans." AMERICAN JOURNAL OF ORTHOPSYCHIATRY, 30 (1960), 637-44.

Sone, M. NISEI DAUGHTER. Boston: Atlantic Monthly Press, 1953.

Spears, Harold. "Kappans Ponder the Goals of Education." PHI DELTA KAPPAN, 55 (1973).

Spitzer, Richard C. "Discovering America." AMERICAN EDUCATION, 11, No. 7 (1975), 24-27.

"Springfield, Ohio: A Battle for Multicultural Texts." Interracial Books for Children BULLETIN, 6, No. 1 (1975), 1, 6-7.

Starr, K. AMERICANS AND THE CALIFORNIA DREAM 1850-1915. New York: Oxford University Press, 1973.

State of Delaware. ANNUAL REPORT OF THE DEPARTMENT OF PUBLIC INSTRUCTION FOR THE YEAR ENDING JUNE 30, 1922. Wilmington, 1922.

Stein, H.F. "Ethnicity, Identity, and Ideology." SCHOOL REVIEW, 83 (1975), 273-300.

Stein, Leon, Conan, Abraham P., and Davis, Lynn, trans. THE EDUCATION OF ABRAHAM CAHAN. Philadelphia: Jewish Publication Society, 1969.

Steinberg, Stephen. THE ACADEMIC MELTING POT. New York: McGraw-Hill, 1974.

Stent, M.D., Hazard, W.R., and Rivlin, H.N. CULTURAL PLURALISM IN EDUCATION: A MANDATE FOR CHANGE. New York: Appleton-Century-Crofts, 1973.

Stern, E.G. MY MOTHER AND I. New York: Macmillan, 1917.

Stewart, Ida Santos. "Cultural Differences between Anglos and Chicanos." INTEGRATED EDUCATION, 13, No.6 (1975), 21-23.

Stockwell, A.W. "Immigrants' Bill of Rights." AMERICAN JOURNAL OF SOCIOLOGY, (July 1909), 21-31.

Strong, Edward K., Jr. and Bell, Reginald. "Vocational Aptitudes of Second-Generation Japanese in the United States." EDUCATION-PSYCHOLOGY, ! (1933).

Sue, David. "A Silent-Minority Member Speaks Out." TODAY'S EDUCATION, 63, No. 2 (1974), 84-86.

Sue. D.W. "Ethnic Identity: The Impact of Two Cultures on the Psychological Development of Asians in America." In Stanley Sue and Nathaniel N. Wagner, eds. ASIAN-AMERICANS: PSYCHOLOGICAL PERSEPCTIVES. Palo Alto: Science and Behavior Books, 1973, 140-49.

Sue, D., and Frank, Austin C. "A Typological Approach to the Psychological Study of Chinese and Japanese American College Males." JOURNAL OF SOCIAL ISSUES, 29, no.2 (1973), 129-48.

Sue, Stanley, and Kitano, Harry H.L. "Stereotypes as a Measure of Success." JOURNAL OF SOCIAL ISSUES, 29, No.2 (1973), 83-93.

Sue, Stanley, and Sue, D.W. "Chinese-American Personality and Mental Health." AMERASIA JOURNAL, 1 (1971), 36-49.

Sue, Stanley, Sue, Derald W., and Sue, David W. "Asian Americans as a Minority Group." AMERICAN PSYCHOLOGIST, 30 (1975), 901-10.

Sue, Stanley, and Wagner, Nathaniel. N. ASIAN-AMERICANS: PSYCHOLOGICAL PERSPECTIVES. Palo Alto: Science and Behavior Books, 1973.

Sugimoto, E.I. A DAUGHTER OF THE SAMURAI. New York: Doubleday Doran, 1928.

Sung, Betty Lee. MOUNTAIN OF GOLD. THE STORY OF THE CHINESE IN AMERICA. New York: Macmillan, 1967.

Swett, John. PUBLIC EDUCATION IN CALIFORNIA. 1911 (rpt. Arno Press, 1969).

Tesconi, Charles A., Jr. SCHOOLING IN AMERICA: A SOCIAL PHILO-SOPHICAL PERSPECTIVE. Boston: Houghton Mifflin, 1975.

Thernstrom, Stephan. THE OTHER BOSTONIANS: POVERTY AND PROGRESS IN THE AMERICAN METROPOLIS, 1880-1970. Cambridge, Mass., 1973.

Toffler, Alvin, ed. THE SCHOOLHOUSE IN THE CITY. New York: Praeger, 1968.

Tom, S. "Mental Health in the Chinese Community of San Francisco." Cited in Sue, Stanley, and Nathaniel N. Wagner, eds. ASIAN-AMERI-CANS: PSYCHOLOGICAL PERSPECTIVES. Palo Alto: Science and Behavior Books, 1973, p. 124. n. 16.

Trager, Helen G., and Yarrow, Marian Radke. THEY LEARN WHAT THEY LIVE. New York: Harper & Brothers, 1952.

TREATMENT OF ASIA IN TEXTBOOKS. Washington: American Council on Education, 1946.

Tresize, Robert L. "Developing Performance Objectives in Social Studies in Michigan." SOCIAL EDUCATION, 38, No.1 (1974), 24-29.

Tsukamoto, Mary. "An American with a Japanese Face." In CHIL-DREN AND INTERCULTURAL EDUCATION, Part I. Washington: Association for Childhood Education International, 1974.

Turner, Thomas N. "Making the Social Studies Textbook a More Effective Tool for Less Able Readers." SOCIAL EDUCATION, 40 (Jan. 1976), 38-41.

Tyack, D.B. "Forming the National Character: Paradox in Educational Thought of the Revolutionary Generation." HARVARD EDUCATION-AL REVIEW, 36 (Winter 1966).

Tyack, David B. THE ONE BEST SYSTEM. Cambridge: Harvard University Press, 1974.

Tyack, David B., ed. TURNING POINTS IN AMERICAN EDUCATION-AL HISTORY. Waltham, Mass.: Blaisdell Publishing, 1967.

U.S. Bureau of the Census. CENSUS OF POPULATION: 1970. SUBJECT REPORTS. Final Report PC (2) - 1G: Japanese, Chinees, and Filipinos in the United States. Washington: U.S. Government Printing Office, 1973.

U.S. Commission on Civil Rights. A BETTER CHANCE TO LEARN: BILINGUAL-BICULTURAL EDUCATION. Washington: Clearinghouse Publication 51, 1975.

U.S. Immigration and Naturalization Service. 1974 ANNUAL REPORT. Washington: U.S. Government Printing Office, 1975.

Vail, Henry H. A HISTORY OF THE MCGUFFEY READERS. Cleveland, 1910.

Van Denburg, Joseph King. CAUSES OF THE ELIMINATION OF STUDENTS IN PUBLIC SECONDARY SCHOOLS IN NEW YORK CITY. New York: Teachers College, Columbia University, 1911.

Van Geel, Tyll. "Law, Politics, and the Right to be Taught English." SCHOOL REVIEW, 83 (1975), 245-72.

Weaver, Gary R. "American Identity Movements: A Cross-Cultural Confrontation." INTELLECT, 103 (1975), 376-80.

Weiss, M.S. "Division and Unity: Social Process in a Chinese-American Community." In Stanley Sue & Nathaniel Wagner, Eds., ASIAN AMERICANS: PSYCHOLOGICAL PERSPECTIVES. Palo Alto: Science and Behavior Books, 1973.

Weitzman, L.J., and Rizzo, D. "Images of Males and Females in Elementary School Textbooks in Five Subject Areas." BIASED TEXTBOOKS. Washington: National Foundation for the Improvement of Education, 1974.

Wells, H.G. THE FUTURE IN AMERICA: A SEARCH AFTER REALITIES. New York: Harper & Brothers, 1906.

Wesley, Edgar B. NEA: THE FIRST HUNDRED YEARS. New York: Harper & Row, 1957.

Whiteman, Maxwell. "Philadelphia's Jewish Neighborhoods." In Allen F. Davis and Mark H. Haller, eds. THE PEOPLES OF PHILADELPHIA. Philadelphia: Temple University Press, 1973.

Wiggins, Gladys A. EDUCATION AND NATIONALISM. New York: McGraw-Hill, 1962.

Willey, D.A. "Americans in the Making." PUTNAM, (Jan. 1909), 450-63.

Willis, Rudy. SCHOOLS IN AN AGE OF MASS CULTURE. Englewood Cliffs, N.J.: Prentice-Hall, 1963.

Wilson, H.B. "The Minimum Essentials in Elementary-School Subjects." FOURTEENTH YEARBOOK OF THE NATIONAL SOCIETY FOR THE STUDY OF EDUCATION, Part I. Chicago: University of Chicago Press, 1915, 9-20.

Wischnitzer, Mark. TO DWELL IN SAFETY, THE STORY OF JEWISH MIGRATION SINCE 1800. Philadelphia: Jewish Publication Society, 1948.

Wittke, Carl. WE WHO BUILT AMERICA. Cleveland: Press of Western Reserve University, 1939.

Wong, Jade Snow. FIFTH CHINESE DAUGHTER. New York: Harper & Brothers, 1945.

Wood, Irving E. "Immigration and American Ideals." IMMIGRATION, 2 (June 1910), 57-60.

Woofter, T.J., Jr. RACES AND ETHNIC GROUPS IN AMERICAN LIFE. New York: McGraw-Hill, 1933.

Wright, Kathleen. THE OTHER AMERICANS: MINORITIES IN AMERICAN HISTORY. Greenwich, Conn.: Fawcett, 1969.

Yee, Albert H. "Asian Americans in Educational Research." EDUCATIONAL RESEARCHER, 5, No.2 (1975), 5-8.

Yee, Albert H. "Myopic Perceptions and Textbooks: Chinese Americans' Search for Identity." JOURNAL OF SOCIAL ISSUES, 29, No.2 (1973), 99-113.

Young, Lauren S. "Multicultural Education: A Myth into Reality?" JOURNAL OF TEACHER EDUCATION, 26 (1975), 127.

Ysung, Kwok Tsuen, "The Intelligence of Chinese Children." JOURNAL OF APPLIED PSYCHOLOGY, 5 (1922), 267-74.

ABOUT THE AUTHORS

Natalie Isser received her Ph.D. in European history from the University of Pennsylvania in 1962 and is presently Associate Professor of History at The Pennsylvania State University, Ogontz Campus. She has written numerous articles dealing with minority problems in a majority culture. She is also the author of a book, THE FRENCH SECOND EMPIRE AND THE PRESS.

Lita Linzer Schwartz (Ph.D., Bryn Mawr) is Professor of Educational Psychology at The Pennsylvania State University, Ogontz Campus. In addition to her work with Dr. Isser in the field of ethnic studies, she is the author, co-author, or editor of several books in the fields of educational psychology, exceptional children, and American education, and of forty articles on college teaching, gifted children, psychology of women, modern-day cults, religious conversion, child custody, and divorce. A licensed psychologist, Dr. Schwartz also hold a Diplomate from the American Board of Forensic Psychology.

Drs. Isser and Schwartz have developed and taught together two courses in the field of ethnic studies, one on Cultural Pluralism that was a direct outgrowth of the research in this book, and one on ethnicity in the American experience. They continue to collaborate in research on the cults, religious conversion and commitment in the 19th and 20th centuries, and on the education of women.